MAA

D1577650

WITHDRAWN

ON AND OFF THE FLIGHT DECK

ON AND OFF

THE FLIGHT DECK

Reflections of a naval fighter pilot in
World War II

AN AUTOBIOGRAPHY

HANK ADLAM

BOOK 1: THE YEARS 1941 – 1948

Pen & Sword
AVIATION

940.54494

First published in Great Britain in 2007 by
Pen & Sword Aviation
an imprint of
Pen & Sword Books Ltd
47 Church Street
Barnsley
South Yorkshire
S70 2AS

Copyright©Henry Amyas Adlam 2007

Maps on pages 149 and 167 copyright©Aza Adlam 2007

ISBN 978 1 84415 6290

The right of Henry Amyas Adlam to be identified as Author
of this work has been asserted by him in accordance with the
Copyright, Designs and Patents Act 1988.

A CIP catalogue record for this book is
available from the British Library.

Illustrations scanned by 4Word, Bristol
Typeset in 10 on 12 point Palatino by
Victoria Arrowsmith-Brown, Bristol

Printed and bound in
England by CPI UK

Pen & Sword Books Ltd incorporates the imprints of Pen & Sword Aviation,
Pen & Sword Maritime, Pen & Sword Military, Wharncliffe Local History,
Pen & Sword Select, Pen & Sword Military Classics and Leo Cooper.

For a complete list of Pen & Sword titles please contact
PEN & SWORD BOOKS LIMITED
47 Church Street, Barnsley, South Yorkshire, S70 2AS, England
E-mail: enquiries@pen-and-sword.co.uk
Website: www.pen-and-sword.co.uk

Dedication

This book is dedicated to my much loved wife and companion, Saccie, with whom I shared fifty-three happy years, and to my dear son, Jeremy, whose great pleasure was to read a book.

Would that they were both here to read this one.

This story is about my war and the worst of it was the loss of so many friends with whom I flew, and who did not have my luck to have survived. Also, therefore, this book is dedicated to them.

Acknowledgments

Mary James, who encouraged me to start writing and taught me how to write short stories good enough to be published.

Aza, my daughter, who encouraged me to keep writing, and turned out to be such a very good editor.

David Reed, who had to work hard in correcting my grammatical errors and who thought of the title for this book.

Victoria Arrowsmith-Brown, who advised me and led me by the hand through the strange world of publishers and literary agents.

Contents

List of illustrations and maps

Author's Note

My memories of the events and happenings described in this story are strong and clear, albeit that they occurred over sixty years ago now. But, although squadron diaries and log books are a help, I have to acknowledge that on the sequence of these events, their precise dates, and on some names, my memory sometimes may be at fault.

CHAPTER ONE

Fledgling Flight

T his is my first solo at night and I am tense and nervous, as I line the aircraft up along the side of the flare path. Set the gyro compass, turn the cockpit lights right down, check the trim, select propeller at fine pitch, flaps up, plenty of fuel – then slowly now, I open the throttle fully while concentrating on keeping straight alongside the flare path. Flare path indeed … nothing but a line of paraffin flares set twenty yards apart and across nothing more than a large meadow at Shrewton, the satellite airfield to our aerodrome at Netheravon. Airborne now and eyes straight onto the instruments, never mind the absolute blackness outside. At eight hundred feet turn to port ninety degrees and there sure enough I see the flare path over my left shoulder. I feel more at ease in the black night now. All that remains, I tell myself, is to follow the well-known circuit procedure and to line up carefully on the final approach to land. 'Come on Henry, stop sweating. It's not really a problem.'

On the final approach, the flare path is beginning to slide away under me to my right. Bank right and quickly left again to line up … that's it. Start throttling back now, get the nose up a bit more and some right rudder … the sudden stall. And I am much too high and she drops like a brick – the port wing hits first – full throttle and full right rudder – all too late – an almighty crashing and grinding sound as the aircraft scrapes over the ground with bits coming off it in all directions. Sudden silence – except for a tinkling noise from the smashed engine and I am sitting strapped into the cockpit still holding the control column. Lights and figures coming towards me and shouting. I must get out … quickly! I undo straps and parachute harness, scramble out on to the ground because the port wing isn't there, and stumble into the arms of friends. Except for a bruise on the right side of my head, I am in apparent good order. This is more than can be said for the Miles Master which, constructed of wood, has broken its back and left bits of itself, including the wings, all along the scraped path of its passage along the ground. There go my wings too, I thought as I had most probably just failed the flying course.

Four months earlier on 3 January 1941, I had arrived at St Vincent's barracks in Gosport to join a total of one hundred and sixteen young men, some of them boys really of age eighteen or nineteen, on the 23rd Pilots' course of the Fleet Air Arm, which included an unusually high colonial intake of thirty-five New Zealanders and fourteen Canadians. The course consisted of classroom work on navigation, theory of flight, signals, information on warships and their operation but the emphasis was on square bashing and parades. It was intended obviously as a short, sharp introduction to naval life and discipline to mould a bunch of civilian boys into young men with sufficient gumption for wartime aviation. It needed to generate too, in a period of two months, an enthusiasm for the Royal Navy and a feeling of belonging to it. Sunday 'Divisions', when the entire barracks of four hundred men paraded in their No. 1 uniforms for inspection by the Captain and Officers with the Marine band playing, was a part of it.

It was not difficult for grammar and public schoolboys to learn new classroom subjects but, for those from grammar school accustomed to life at home, it must have been particularly difficult to adapt to the bad food, myriads of cockroaches and uncomfortable conditions. The Royal Navy appeared to be convinced too that doors to lavatories were tantamount to unsafe sex and that those grossly overloaded and filthy lavatories, as they were in the main building, would in time un-clog themselves without the aid of plumbers. Except for those unpleasant lavatories outside, I could cope with the accommodation conditions in the barracks itself since in some respects they were much better than they had been at Harrow. For example, at the end of the passage on each dormitory floor of the barracks there were two lavatories, two urinals, two showers and twelve wash-basins with hot water. Whereas, at Harrow, the nearest lavatory to the study-bedrooms had been down in the basement, four floors below, while washing facilities had consisted of a basin and jug of water with cold showers downstairs.

Learning how to integrate and get on with the other young men from commonwealth countries with such different backgrounds was an education in itself for us Brits as indeed, vice versa, it was for them. It was surprising how well we all got on together, although the very occasional fist fight did occur. I became involved in one against a Rhodesian boy, over where we sat in the classroom. He swept my books, which I had left to mark my place, on to the floor. No one could be less of an aggressive fighter than me, but I took a swing at him and knocked him so that he tripped backwards on to the floor. He came flying off the floor at me and we bashed at each other until the others, thank heavens, held us both back while I made feeble struggles to get at him again. He, on the contrary, appeared only too anxious to continue the fight and really did have to be restrained. The officer who was to teach us then appeared, whereupon the bloodthirsty New Zealanders implored the officer to declare a formal fight in the Gym. This was the Navy way of settling scores between quarrelling sailors, a bloody battle in the ring until one or the other was knocked senseless in front of a yelling crowd of sailors. The officer, very angry, told us that we were supposed to be officer material and not to act like slum children and refused any such nonsense. What a relief!

This Rhodesian lad and I, some time later, found ourselves alone by chance in a street bomb shelter, which we had been detailed to clean up after part of it had been demolished by a direct hit. After we had finished clearing up, while waiting for transport to take us back to barracks, we started to talk. He told me how strange and out of place he felt in our English cities and, being obviously of mixed race, he had met prejudice and felt unwelcome here. How awful it was that this young man had volunteered to come to our land to fight for us and was made to feel rejected. We made friends and I tried hard to bring him in amongst my group, but he was so very prickly that it didn't work. I learned two years later that he had been killed flying a Swordfish at night from an Escort Carrier.

All this could have been difficult enough but this course coincided with the heavy bombing almost every night of Portsmouth and Gosport resulting in little sleep at nights when guard duties on storage depots to deal with looters and fire-bombs were regular tasks. There was also the selection at early morning parade each day of men for the 'Pick and Shovel Party' which had the grim task of clearing bombed buildings after the previous night's air raids. We all shuffled around falling in for that early parade trying to dodge this loathsome and sometimes gruesome job. There was never any let up on the work and activities of the course, which remained intensive regardless of the bombing. With so little sleep at night, I was nearly always very tired, hungry and dirty, as no doubt were the others, but there was a strong sense of comradeship among us. We went out to the pubs at any opportunity and played two games of rugby, Brits against the New Zealanders. They won both times.

After five weeks, unexpectedly, we were granted a long week-end leave and I took the cross-country trains to arrive at Taplow desperate for some longed for sleep and good food at home. I had not been able to warn mother on the telephone that I was coming and I was shattered, when I arrived, to find she was away visiting friends. Our neighbours, Howard and Philippa, took me in and put me to bed where I slept for sixteen hours until midday on the Saturday when, after a heavenly hot bath, they provided me with a huge meal using their precious rations to do so. I slept almost continuously again until a bath and another good meal with them on Sunday. What true Samaritans they were. Then back to the barracks again on Sunday evening, refreshed and ready to enjoy life once more. The truth is that in spite of the bloody bombs, life was fun.

At Luton for *ab initio* flying training we were accommodated some twelve miles away from the airfield in a large house, right in the country with not even a village nearby, owned I seem to remember by people called Cassels. It didn't matter who they were because we never caught sight of them anyway and they certainly never came near us. The living quarters were their three big ground floor rooms filled with double bunks, one on top of the other, and nothing else except the ground floor lavatory. Buses were provided to take us to the airfield where we had breakfast, midday meal and supper and then to return us to our stark and dreary habitation. Sometimes we would miss supper to share a taxi to and from the airfield to a pub in Luton. Not often, we couldn't afford it.

The only thing was to get on with learning to fly Magisters, small monoplanes, and to concentrate on the ground instruction both of which demanded our maximum effort. Despite the miserable living arrangements for us, I don't recall that we minded very much as we were so intent on the excitement of flying. The instructors were all regular members of the Royal Air Force, men who were nearly all anxious to complete their stint of instructing and to join operational squadrons. But they were good at their job, most of them, even though they wanted to be elsewhere.

My instructor was a small, elderly and grizzled sergeant pilot, who though rather gruff and morose on the ground, was a good enough instructor in the air for me to go solo safely after just under four hours of flying with him; a bit better than the average time. Going solo was the first rung of the ladder. To be airborne alone and in charge of the Magister was enormously exciting and what a wonderful feeling it was to taxi in after landing, knowing that I had done it. The snag with my little old sergeant was that he evidently did not like aerobatics. As the course continued, all the others were doing aerobatics all over the sky, or so they said, and I longed to be shown how to do them. I even tried by myself but succeeded only in scaring myself. Eventually, one fine morning, he demonstrated a rather wobbly loop to me and a ropey slow roll which became a barrel roll. He allowed me a couple of goes at them myself but just that and no more before we landed. That lack of instruction stayed with me all my flying life. Eventually, I became able to put an aircraft where I wanted usually in whatever position I wanted, but I never had that particular and precise control of the aircraft so essential for good aerobatics.

There was an examination on ground subjects and a flying test at the end of this *ab initio* part of the flying course, which had lasted four weeks. Seven failed the test and were sent away for normal duty aboard ships. The rest of us at Luton understood that the next stage of the flying would be at Netheravon near Salisbury, but apparently there was a delay and we were sent to the Fleet Air Arm barracks at Lee-on-Solent instead.

Once again we were back into naval procedures and discipline, which meant early parade in the morning where we would be detailed off to do various cleaning jobs or armament and ship instruction if not square bashing. But I was in luck because I was with a group of twelve in one dormitory and amongst us was Jack Cole. Jack was in our terms elderly, about twenty-five years old and a natural streetwise character. He had sussed out the naval procedures and realised that, provided we never attended the morning parade, the Petty Officers would not know who we were or what we were supposed to be doing. Consequently, when the wakey wakey bugle call was made on the Tannoy for us to get up out of our bunks, dress and go to the parade, Jack called out 'Stop, nobody move!' It was a risk; we would be up before the Commander and serious trouble for the lot of us if found there.

Jack was absolutely right. No one came to check and at 10 am, the mid morning time for break, he said it was now safe to go to the canteen for our breakfast. After breakfast, Jack assembled us outside the dormitory block, told us to carry our rolled towels and then marched us smartly and correctly to the gates, called us to attention and reported to the Chief Petty Officer, 'Bathing Party from Collingwood all correct, Chief, permission to proceed to the baths please.' 'Carry on,' replied the Chief Petty Officer and we marched smartly through the gates down to the pubs. Because of Jack, our seven days in barracks became a holiday rest period. The other members of our flying course were furiously jealous.

Later on I accompanied Jack on weekend escapades to such places as Torquay. I felt that there was so much I could learn from him, particularly about women, who seemed ready to fall over backwards for him at anytime. I could not understand it.

He was really quite gross in appearance with a rubicund round face and thick cherry red lips with a head of smooth but sparse black hair and yet he had a sexual magnetism, some magic that made women want him. There was I, slim and rather good looking I thought but, with Jack, I had to accept being a girl's second choice. Perhaps I was not sexy enough but the more likely truth was that I was too young, gauche and even rather prudish still. Whatever the reason, I was having a conspicuous lack of success with women. I was learning that younger women and girls were more interested in older men – or should I say – more interested in men rather than boys? My problem was how to acquire the experience to become the former rather than the latter. I lost touch with Jack and I am not sure what happened to him. But I have the feeling that he gave up the flying course after a few weeks at Netheravon.

From Lee-on-Solent we were taken by bus to Netheravon for the Advanced Flying course. And what a cracking good and welcome surprise Netheravon was for all of us. The expectation of us all was to suffer the austerity of yet another naval barracks. It was nothing of the sort. Although we were still dressed as sailors and regarded officially as such, we found ourselves accommodated in what had been double cabins for officers and we were to use the Officers' Mess, which included the dining hall, comfortable lounge with leather armchairs and a bar. Our flying Instructors were RAF again but a new and separate Mess had been built for them leaving us with the exclusive use of their old accommodation. The cooks and stewards who looked after us were all WAAFs and our control and discipline was in the hands of Sergeants instead of Petty Officers.

At Netheravon we were selected as budding Fighter pilots or as Torpedo/Bomber pilots. I have no knowledge on what basis the selection was made or who made it. Thank heavens someone, somewhere and for whatever reason had considered me as suitable to be a Fighter pilot. As such I was appointed to a dispersal where I would fly the very latest training aircraft, the Miles Master. What luck; for it was a low-wing monoplane with a powerful radial engine, and the nearest thing to a modern fighter as it was possible to be. It was a powerful looking monster of an aircraft and very daunting. Both cockpits were enclosed in separate glass canopies with the Instructor in the rear. Communication with each other and with the ground was via one of the new Radio/Telephone sets.

My Instructor was Flying Officer Michael Helm, a tall gangly, dark young man who was my second bit of luck because he was a superb instructor as well as a good pilot. In the air he was quietly spoken and very competent in his demonstrations and instructions. When he first showed me the cockpit of the Miles Master, I felt dazed by the mass of instruments but he patiently explained them all and their place in the scheme of things so that, before we flew, I understood them and had compartmented them in my mind. The acceleration as we took off on our first flight remains in my memory but more memorable, some three flying hours later, was my first solo in this powerful aircraft which I found even more exciting than the earlier first solo in the Magister. I felt that I really was on the way to becoming a fighter pilot but, as the flying training progressed and I made so many mistakes, came the sobering realisation that I had a long way to go and much to learn before I could hope to gain my Wings.

The advanced flying training, as it was called, was divided into two parts: the first forty hours or so on learning to fly the Miles Master competently and with assurance and then another twenty or more doing more difficult exercises such as formation flying, cross-country flights, low flying and night flying. There was a flying test with a Squadron Leader at the end of the first part. I nearly failed this when I all but put us into a hedge on the final approach of a practice forced landing but it turned out to be not entirely my fault as the engine had hiccupped when I opened the throttle wide to get clear. The engineers found a fault with the petrol pump after we landed back at Netheravon so the Squadron leader, somewhat reluctantly, I thought, passed me fit for the next stage.

Low flying was great fun but had its penalties for those who flew too low or without sufficient concentration. Two chaps on our course were killed flying in formation too low down when one took a sudden turn to miss a tree and they collided. We were to complete two cross-country flights in the second part of the course. I managed one of them all right but on the second, in deteriorating weather, would have become completely lost on the way back if I had not seen a small grass airfield below. I wasn't going to mess about in that weather; the airfield seemed empty so I steep turned round, selected wheels down and landed there. An RAF sergeant came up to the cockpit and I shouted for directions to Netheravon. He didn't appear surprised, obviously I wasn't the first sprog pilot to land there, so he pointed to the direction for me and with his hands and fingers indicated twenty miles. Before I opened the throttle to taxi away, I put my finger to my mouth in a hush gesture obviously asking him not to report me to Netheravon. He laughed, nodded in agreement and gave me the thumbs up.

The next big hurdle was night flying. This took place at Shrewton, no more than a very large field near the village of that name about five miles from Netheravon. The procedure was for two senior instructors to drive there as an advance party with a van from which the aircraft would be controlled and a bus to act as a rest room for the pupil pilots. The Instructors would decide the wind direction and then supervise the laying down of a line of 'goose flares' along the take-off path. These flares were just pots of burning paraffin when lit. We pupils, about eight of us for each night, flew to Shrewton with our Instructors in the late afternoon. I was extremely nervous at the prospect of night flying and I could sense that Michael Helm, my Instructor, was at least uneasy about it too. One of the pupils on our course had been killed the night before on his solo flight and, not unnaturally, we were all of us a bit uptight. Presumably he had lost contact with the flare path and his smashed aircraft and body had been found several miles away.

All we were expected to do was a take-off, fly a circuit of the airfield area and a landing. There would be no more than two aircraft in the circuit at one time and the first two before us had already started up their engines and were preparing to taxi out. It was an absolutely black night and all that could be seen of the aircraft were their wing and tail lights and the exhaust flames from their engines until the amber Aldis light from the control van stabbed through the darkness to give them clearance to taxi on to the line of the flare path. My instructor and I were in our aircraft, with engine not yet started, watching carefully.

The first aircraft moved forward and lined up about ten yards on the right hand side of the flares It stayed there with engine running fast against the brakes and Helm reminded me that the pilots were meticulously setting the correct reading for the gyro compass which, after three ninety-degree turns in the circuit, would help them to line up on the final approach to land. As the aircraft gathered speed down the flare-path and became airborne I could see its lights clearly. The second followed the same procedure and was given clearance to take off only when the first aircraft could be seen by its lights to have turned on to the downwind leg.

The plan for this night was that the instructor would do the first circuit and landing from the back cockpit, from which incidentally the visibility was very poor, then each student pilot would complete two circuits and landings overlooked by his instructor from the back cockpit. On the subsequent night the student would do one more landing with his Instructor and then he must complete two night landings solo. We started our engine, already warmed and tested earlier, and when we received the amber light Helm taxied to the take-off position and lined the aircraft up alongside the flare path. As he opened up the throttle, I surreptitiously set my gyro compass on '0' instead of on the correct compass reading. I had decided that this would help me to keep close to the airfield when the time came for me to go solo; it would simplify checking the exact ninety-degree turns in the circuit. So I did it now to see how it would work; Helm need never know. On the other hand, as I was aware, this same idea might have killed the student on the previous night because, if he had lost sight of the flares, he could have become completely lost in the blackness without a correct compass setting and flown into the hillside.

Once airborne, it was absolutely black outside and I could see nothing other than our cockpit instruments. Helm spoke on the R/T, 'Don't begin looking for the flare path until after the first ninety-degree turn, just concentrate on instrument flying, correct airspeed and height.' He carried on talking quietly all the way round the circuit, explaining what he was doing. Lucky me to have such a good instructor just when I was feeling really frightened. He did a good landing, although I could see little of it, because I could not quite orientate myself with the ground during the final approach.

Came my turn to fly the circuit and land. I did not do well. My scheme with the gyro compass helped me to keep the flares in sight as I flew the downwind and crosswind legs, but on the final approach for some reason I kept losing sight of the flare path. Helm talked me down safely for the two landings with him and he did so without touching the dual controls. It was a cold night but I had sweated all the way round the circuit. There was a van ready to take us back to Netheravon, leaving the aircraft there ready to fly on the next night. The local pub was still open and, in company with fellow students, I sank two large and much needed whiskies. And so to bed.

I had something else very much on my mind as well as the awful prospect of the solo flight on the following night. As if that wasn't enough to worry about, my other problem was that Philippa, our neighbour at Taplow, had telegraphed to confirm that she would arrive the next evening to stay at a local hotel for two nights. Ever since the weekend when she and her husband, Howard, had looked after me so kindly, there had been correspondence between us. I cannot explain how this situation had arisen except perhaps that, as a gormless boy, I had liked the idea of being chased by a mature, married woman who had appeared to be interested in me. I didn't want to be involved in an affair with her so how had it developed to this stage? There were so many factors against it. She was much older (albeit with a nice firm body) and really I preferred young girls. And overall I was preoccupied with the worries and intensity of flying and earning my wings. But letters from her had continued and I had failed to signal a firm 'no' so now here I was with the prospect of a real affair on my hands.

I was due to drive to the George Hotel in Amesbury to join her there at around 9 or 10 pm depending on what time I finished my night flying. I had arranged that I would drive to Shrewton in Emma, my little old Austin Seven, since the aircraft would already be dispersed there. I had been reconciled to the prospect of sleeping with 'Booful' as I unkindly called her and thought that, under her mature guidance, I would lose my virginity at last. This would be an essential step forward, I considered, enabling me perhaps to make better progress next time I was attracted by a pretty young girl.

It didn't happen like that at all. None of it – because that was my first solo at night and was the night that I crashed and completely wrote off an aircraft.

Immediately after the crash, my Instructor, Michael Helm, was kind and encouraging. I told him that I had weekend leave and an immediate date with a girl in Amesbury and please could I go? I felt a bit shaky and I wanted desperately to get away and to relax. There was a young RAF doctor who looked me over and agreed I could go. But I would have to report, with my instructor, to the Wing Commander in charge of training at 10 am on the following morning. So off I went in Emma.

Amesbury was only a few miles away and I stopped at a pub on the way for a large whisky and felt slightly less shaky. Arriving at the George Hotel I asked for 'Mrs Smith' and was told she had left a message to go straight up to her room. I knocked on the door and went in to find Philippa sitting up in bed, wearing a flimsy little nightie, and looking as attractive as she could. But to me at that moment the most attractive thing in the room was the bed. Perhaps it was a delayed form of shock or something, I don't know, but I was trembling and I longed for sleep. I told her briefly as I undressed that I had written an aircraft off but was unhurt except for a bang on the head. Normally I would have been modest about undressing but now I just took my shoes, socks and uniform off as fast as I could then without hesitation vest and pants and climbed naked into bed with her. If she hoped my trembling was with passion then it must have been all the more disappointing for Philippa because I fell into her arms, put my head on the pillow, and went fast asleep without so much as a single bounce.

She was an absolute sweetie that Philippa: I was hardly aware of it but she cuddled me in her arms all that night and made no demands on me. I woke up in daylight to see an elderly maid come in with the breakfast which Philippa had ordered and leave us, with a kindly smile on her face, as we sat up in bed and enjoyed the hot coffee and breakfast. I said how sorry I was to have been so useless but she replied that I shouldn't worry, it was just bad luck and anyway, it had given her pleasure to hold the body of a young naked boy in her arms all night. Oh dear, back to being a boy, I groaned to myself, when I had hoped to rise proudly as a full-blooded man. We talked it over and both decided that what had happened, or not happened to be more accurate, was a good thing as neither of us wished to hurt Howard, her husband. I would have to go to learn my fate from the Wing Commander and so we had a sibling style farewell kiss and I left her to report back to Netheravon.

I got off lightly but Michael Helm, my Instructor, was reprimanded and so was the young Doctor, both of them for allowing me to leave instead of reporting to sick bay after the accident as I should have done. I was to remain under medical observation until Monday night when, if I was passed as fit, I must carry out my two solo night flights. It was made clear that if I failed these, then I would also have failed the course.

Monday night was not quite so dark and there was even a glimmer of moon. I had become much calmer and worked out in my mind that I needed to overshoot slightly on the crosswind leg and so turn in later towards the final approach. Also I must aim at the last line of flares rather than peering down and side-slipping towards the nearer flares below the aircraft. It worked and I made two good landings.

Early next morning, eight of us had to fly the aircraft from Shrewton back to Netheravon. The engine on mine failed to start at first and I took off about ten minutes after the other six who were led by a young instructor. After a few minutes, at a thousand feet, I flew into a bank of thick low misty cloud. A bit frightening at that level on instruments but I was sensible enough not to let down through the low cloud. Instead I started a careful turn through one eighty degrees, came out of the cloud, saw Shrewton airfield and landed. The mist cleared about an hour later and then I could fly to Netheravon. I arrived to find a disaster had occurred. Apparently there had been a dangerous muddle near the airfield as six pilots and their Instructor had tried to fly under the very low cloud level to reach the field for a landing. One student pilot had hit the ground and was killed. A sad ending to our course and the instructor was very properly court-martialled; more than the one student could have been killed. He should have flown ahead of the others, seen the weather conditions and postponed their take-off.

I remember my time at Netheravon as a period of great pleasure, good comradeship and excitement as gradually I gained the necessary flying skills. I had shared a cabin initially with Jack and, after he left, I shared with Basil Bartlett, rather a shy young man of my own age but we became good friends. He and two others, Tony and Bruce, were my best friends at that time although all of us on the course got on well together. Discipline was nothing like as severe as in a naval barracks but strong enough that we had to behave ourselves. Use of the Officers' Mess made life so much more comfortable and pleasant although sorties into Salisbury for smart dinners or booze were quite frequent. Masses of young soldiers dominated the City and consequently girls were in short supply there. Some of the more capable of us, not me, were able to find girl friends among the WAAFs at Netheravon.

Several visits were made by ENSA to entertain the whole Station and we flying students, in our classy Officers' Mess, were able to invite them to drinks (beer only) with us afterwards. I met Lalline, who danced and sang a bit on the ENSA stage, a girl of twenty-three who seemed to quite like me. I invited her to dine with me at the 'Haunch of Venison' in Salisbury and thereafter we met from time to time over the next few years whenever the war and our obligations would allow. She was responsible for the loss of my virginity at last, although I cannot remember exactly at which hotel this happened – only that I enjoyed the experience. Lalline was a sensible girl and would not permit me, just because we were in bed together, to imagine that I was having a great love affair. She told me just to get on with it and enjoy it when we could. As a romantic boy still, I had rather wanted a grand affair but I would have to be satisfied with having been successfully deprived of my virginity.

Paying for smart hotels and restaurants was no problem. I had never been so wealthy and very rarely have I been so since then. Twice a month we formed a queue at the Pusser's desk for our pay and, in accordance with naval tradition, this was placed on the top of our caps which we held out in front of us. Flying pay made the difference and the total came to £5 and 12 shillings every fortnight. Everything else, other than our booze and pleasure, was paid for already. Our accommodation, our meals and uniforms were all free. Thus we were truly rich.

I do believe that the significant factor about life at Netheravon was the delightful laid-back atmosphere of the place because, despite the seriousness of their purpose and their undoubted competence, the attitude of the instructors and senior officers was relaxed. Later FAA pilot courses were sent to America to train and I am so enormously thankful that I trained at Netheravon and Yeovilton. I much preferred the flavour of Britain at war where, for example, the airfield at Netheravon sometimes closed on Saturdays for twenty minutes and all flying stopped while the local hunt, in their pinks and on their horses with their yelping hounds, were allowed to stream across the airfield making silly noises on their hunting horns. I loved that gloriously dotty English attitude in wartime England with all its lovely pubs, as compared with drinking coke and the intense formality of flying training in America.

Examinations took place during the last three days of the course. There were few visits to Salisbury or the pubs during the week beforehand, which was taken up with revising all the ground work on navigation, theory of flight and armament, etc, which many of us had neglected to study thoroughly earlier. I was worried because I had been lazy and intent on enjoying life rather than bothering with these boring ground subjects. But many before me had failed the exams and never gained their wings as the result.

The utter relief and the joy when I was included on the list of those who were awarded their priceless 'wings.' This was followed by a formal letter from the Admiralty in lovely old-fashioned and pompous wording to inform me that their Lordships were pleased to commission me as a Midshipman in the Voluntary Reserve of the Royal Navy. They also sent me a grant of £40 to purchase my uniforms. There followed two weeks leave during which I rushed to

Gieves in London, where the same representative who had fitted me for my Harrow school uniform fitted me with my reefer jacket with the maroon tabs of an RNVR midshipman. Best of all, of course, were the gold-braided wings on the left sleeve.

CHAPTER TWO

Fighter Course

Four Midshipmen walked through the main gates of the Royal Naval Air Station at Yeovilton, Somerset in June 1941. They were self-conscious in their new uniforms which were without any gold stripes of rank, but the maroon coloured tabs on the lapels of the jackets marked them as midshipmen of the RNVR, regarded as the lowest of the low in any Officers' Mess of the Royal Navy. However, they did have on the left arm sleeve of their jackets the small gold-braided wings worn by pilots of the Fleet Air Arm. The four were Bruce Clark, Tony Harris, Basil Bartlett and myself. We were walking on naval ground not as ordinary sailors, but for the first time as officers and we were nervously uncertain how to conduct ourselves. In consequence we might have appeared too excited and loud as we walked talking down the main roadway towards the airfield and, as we passed an officer amongst other naval personnel, he stopped, turned towards us and commanded, 'Halt there. Stand to attention and salute.' We all promptly did so, our faces red with embarrassment.

He was a small Lt Commander with RN stripes of rank and sporting what in the Navy are termed 'buggery grips' being tufts of hair on each side of his purple angry face.

'Is it your normal practice as midshipmen to pass a senior officer without saluting?' he demanded angrily. 'Because if it is and you ever do it again I will have you before the Commander and confined to the Station for a month.' He harangued us at some length about how lowly we were and of the particular necessity therefore for us to show respect to higher rank. All this, while sailors and others were passing by and listening.

I noticed that he had wings on his sleeve and I would normally have accorded him willingly my respect, as would my companions, but he was so unnecessarily unpleasant and such a repellent little man

15

that we could only feel dislike for him. What an unfortunate start to our Fighter Course at Yeovilton.

The Air Station had been established some eighteen months earlier as the Fighter School for the training of Fleet Air Arm fighter pilots. All our instructors were naval officers and each one of them had seen a great deal of action during the early years of the war. Most of them were Battle of Britain pilots and I make the point here that, not only did two FAA squadrons fight that battle in Hurricanes, but also that another fifty-six FAA fighter pilots fought in RAF squadrons. I emphasize this because not many people seem to be aware that the FAA made a major contribution to the Battle of Britain.

My expectation and fear was that the awful little Lt Commander RN, who had harangued us, would be one of our flying instructors and that he might be typical of them all. In fact, our instructors were quite different in character; they were self-assured and confident men ranked as lieutenants, most of them RNVR and some of them with DSC ribbons, who took their job as flying instructors seriously but regarded it as a quiet interval before resuming the war. The next appointment for many of them would be as Commanding Officer of one of the many new FAA squadrons about to be formed.

Our relations with these naval aviation instructors was very different than those with our RAF instructors previously. The pre-flight briefings, the flying and the post flight observations were all just as deadly serious but, here at Yeovilton, we were all officers and pilots together and they were prepared to talk and drink with us as if on equal terms. As a sprog pilot and midshipman not yet twenty years old, I was fully aware how far apart I was from these men who had so much experience, but there was much to learn from talking and listening to them over a pint of beer in a pub or a glass of gin in the Mess.

The squadron offices and aircraft dispersal area were alongside the main runway and, once we had met our instructors, no time was wasted before we were examining the Hurricanes which we were to fly and studying their cockpit layout with the Pilot's Notes. The Hurricane Mk. 1, with its eight 0.3 machine guns, was a magnificent looking fighter aircraft and it seemed to me that every line of it proclaimed its aggression and robust strength. Those we were to fly were slightly old and battered having completed several months of service in operational squadrons but I think that, whilst we were all of us anxious and to some extent fearful of our first flight in such a powerful machine, we were looking forward to it.

The cockpit of the Hurricane looked to me at first sight as if someone had chucked a handful of the controls haphazardly into the bare metal interior of the cockpit and, by a bit of luck the throttle controls, for example, had landed on the left hand side where they were needed. But the weird gate arrangement for the undercarriage selector had landed low down on the right where the pilot would have to change hands on the control column, immediately he was airborne, to raise the undercarriage. There seemed to be no actual floor to the cockpit and the pilot's seat appeared from above to be floating without apparent support in the middle of it. Inside the cockpit there was a never to be forgotten strong smell of glycol and oil from the Rolls Royce engine. It was so different and much more exciting than the clean and orderly cockpit of the Miles Master. My first flight in the Hurricane would be next morning so I spent the whole afternoon in the cockpit learning the precise position of every control and the exact procedure for using them.

In the cockpit, for my first flight in a Hurricane, I watched the propeller grind slowly round under the power from the outside electric battery and then burst into life with a great puff of black smoke from the exhausts. It responded with a powerful roar as I opened the throttle against the chocks to check the magnetos. I have written earlier of the fear and excitement of my first solo in the Magister and then the thrill of that first flight in the Miles Master but this was different. This time as I taxied out to the runway, I was excited but absolutely confident of my ability to fly this famous fighter aircraft and I felt no fear of it. I knew that I was as good a pilot as others who had flown it for the first time and better than many of them. My take-off was straight and steady and no problem as I changed hands to select the undercarriage up. I must remember to put the lever back to neutral otherwise it would become difficult later to select wheels down. I am up and climbing away with exhilarating power up to eight thousand feet ready to try the Hurricane at different attitudes and stalling speeds. Even under my inexperienced hands for the first time, the Hurricane responds beautifully and I am enjoying myself putting it through steep turns, stalls and even some tentative aerobatics.

All that was fine; now back to the circuit for the landing. How nice and steady she is on final approach at low speed with wheels and flaps down, I start to hold off then – bang – I have hit the runway already – ballooning up – open the throttle wide and round again struggling to get the undercarriage and flaps up without stalling.

Second attempt and this time I am holding off too high and the Hurricane thumps down on the runway and one of the wheels is damaged. My instructor, Lt Ken Firth RNVR, is kind and puts me into another aircraft to go up again immediately. But I have the same problem landing; I cannot seem to judge my height on the final approach and I damage the undercarriage again.

At the end of the afternoon, I am called into the instructors crew room and office and told that I have failed the Fighter Course but they would recommend that I might be suitable for second-line flying as a transport pilot. I was utterly devastated with disappointment. I had been focused on becoming a fighter pilot and for the first time in my young life I had found an objective, something I desperately wanted to do. But I had flunked and it was all over.

I drove back to the Wardroom in my latest little Ford, which had replaced Emma and bumped into a wall as I parked it. 'I can't even drive a car properly,' I said to myself. That evening I kept well away from the others and sat by myself in a corner of the Mess drinking far too much whisky. I was surprised to be joined by another member of our course, a fair-haired rather pimply young chap whom I had not yet come to know well.

'I guess that you and I are in the same boat,' he said, 'since both of us are being sent to second-line non-operational flying.' I asked him how he had failed and he told me that he had found the Hurricane too difficult and had asked to be taken off the course.

I left him and returned early to my cabin to think about what had happened. How could I have made such a botch of landing the Hurricane? Then I remembered bumping my car into the wall. That was odd too; very odd in fact. Could there be something wrong with my eyes, perhaps? I went to bed early and had a long sleep of exhaustion.

First thing after an early breakfast, I presented myself at the sick bay to see the doctor as I wanted him to check my eyes. He was quite a young RNVR doctor who diagnosed that there was nothing fundamentally wrong with either eye and that in fact my eyesight was excellent. But, he told me, 'It is possible that you could have suffered a lazy eye perhaps from the unconscious anxiety and stress associated with the solo flight in a fighter aircraft.'

I had decided what I would do and at the Squadron dispersal I asked to see the senior instructor, Major Ronnie Hay, DSC, RM and with him my instructor Ken Firth. I entered their crew room and office and in front of all the instructors pleaded with them for another chance. I pointed out that the other chap had asked to be taken off the course and that this must therefore leave a space for me. I told them of the possibility that my eyes had failed temporarily but were now good and normal. They sent me out while they thought about it. Then Ken Firth came out and told me to get ready for a flight with him in the dual Miles Master, an aircraft slightly different from those I had flown at Netheravon having an in-line Rolls Royce engine. No matter, I flew it round the circuit twice and landed it with no trouble at all. We taxied back to the parking area and Ken told me to take the next available Hurricane and to do a couple of landings in it while he would watch.

I was quite calm as I took off and turned into the circuit ready to approach for a landing. But I was nervous on the final approach as I came over the aerodrome boundary. Would I be able to see well enough to judge my height? I closed the throttle, held off and ... the Hurricane sank and settled gently on to the runway. Exactly the same happened on the next landing. I couldn't stop smiling and laughing with relief as I went with Ken to see Major Hay. That wonderful fighter pilot, with many victories already to his credit, was smiling too as he confirmed that I was back on the course and he congratulated me for my perseverance.

So far my time at Yeovilton had been on the downward path. But the next weeks were interesting and great fun although sometimes frightening as we flew twice a day on a programme of dog-fights in which we tried ineffectually to shoot our instructors down using camera guns, 'Follow my Leader' in which we would have to follow in line astern every tricky manoeuvre made by the instructor, a means of showing us how to fly a fighter aircraft to its maximum ability, formation flying, either close or loose cross-over formation for combat and strafing and dive bombing targets on the ground. Some of these exercises took place at heights of 28,000 feet where the Hurricane became sloppy and difficult to manoeuvre.

Later in the course, we flew ADDLs which were dummy deck-landings to learn firstly how to make the final approach on a turn and with the aircraft 'sinking' down in the nose up landing attitude and, at the same time, following the signals from the Deck Landing Control Officer. These would be essential skills for actual deck-landings on a Carrier.

And then came the dreaded night flying which we did in Fulmars, an absurd lumbering thing of a so-called fighter aircraft of Admiralty design intended to include an observer in the back. I can only presume that we used Fulmars because it did not matter much if we wrote them off with night accidents. I found night flying at Yeovilton, with its aerodrome lights and proper runway lights, so much easier than at the Shrewton airfield. But I still didn't like it although I managed not to break anything this time.

Finally, we flew to a piece of rough earth, I cannot describe it as an airfield, somewhere at the back of Teignmouth for the purpose of air-firing over the sea at a drogue towed by an elderly aircraft. This patch of earth was so rough and so small that we had to use the ADDLs approach, as for a ship's deck, to land on it. The bullets in our machine guns were dipped in different colours so that, when the drogue was recovered, it was possible to identify which of us had hit it – if indeed any of us had.

We were accommodated in a very good hotel in Teignmouth and life was pleasant. One evening, Brian, a friend and fellow pilot on the course, spotted two nice looking young Wrens having dinner by themselves in the Hotel. He was much better at chatting up girls than me and so I gladly accepted his suggestion that we go over and try to join the two girls. They appeared pleased at this and we learned that they were living in a WAAF hostel. During the conversation they disclosed that they were involved in collecting and repairing the very drogues we fired upon, which were dropped on their local field, and it was they who counted the coloured bullet holes and phoned in the results. We had struck gold! There were only four more days of air firing before we were due to return to Yeovilton but, in that remaining period, the firing results of Sub Lt Brian Prentice and Midshipman Henry Adlam showed a considerable and significant improvement which much impressed the instructors.

We had struck gold in another way too because the Wrens were both attractive girls who, after very little persuasion, agreed during the course of the next evening with us to sneak up to our hotel bedrooms after dinner. Jennifer, my girl, had short wavy auburn hair over a cheeky little face and, like me, was not quite twenty years old. We were no sooner in the room before she was undressing fast and urging me to get my shoes, trousers and pants off quickly. There was no time calmly and gently to admire and touch her pretty figure with its upturned breasts and protruding little bottom, as I would have liked so much to do. Her urgency was such that what followed could only be compared, in my experience, to a ding-dong hard-hitting tennis rally from the baseline ending with my final rush to the net to put the ball away with a final volley. The whole encounter left me breathless and exhausted. It should have been a perfect match. Jennifer was just the girl I had been hoping to meet being the same age and attractive with the sort of slim figure I liked. And yet somehow I felt dissatisfied with the experience. I was such an amateur lover that I had not realised how girls could be every bit as randy and sexy as men were expected to be. Maybe I was still a bit of a prude and had hoped for rather more than just sex, although I could not have explained exactly what I was seeking. I did not see Jennifer again. In the words of the song current at the time, I didn't think she was 'my kind of gel'.

Our fighter course at Yeovilton had been completed. At the start of it there had been thirty-three students including six Canadians, four New Zealanders and six Midshipmen, the latter still in their teens. Only seven of us out of the original thirty-three would survive the next four years until the end of the war. One of the thirty-three would earn a VC, four would earn DSCs and two would be 'Mentioned'. This little Midshipman was happy just to have survived.

One of us had been killed during the course. He had been a quiet young man, well liked, and twenty of us had piled into a lorry to attend the funeral at a small village church. It was the custom to have a party on these occasions and I remember thinking what unfeeling, inhuman creatures we must appear to be as, through the window of the village pub, I watched the grieving parents walk past to their car. We were singing our Fleet Air Arm songs and they were bound to hear the noise of our singing as they looked towards the pub in disbelief. They could not know that this was our way of expressing the sadness we felt at the loss of a friend and fellow pilot.

After finishing the course at Yeovilton, and now qualified as fighter pilots, we all expected to be sent to operational Squadrons. But not enough combat aircraft were available and only very few of the luckier ones were appointed immediately to existing Fighter Squadrons. My three best friends and I were appointed to a second line squadron at a Naval Air Station in Cornwall at St Merryn. We would have to wait there, carrying out all sorts of second-line flying duties, until new Fighter Squadrons were formed. How naïve and young we were as we desperately hoped that the wait would not be for long.

CHAPTER THREE

A Pause

S t Merryn was rather like a museum featuring all the disastrous aircraft designs specified by the Admiralty since the last war. Most were intended to be fighter aircraft but the Admirals, only very few of whom had ever flown or gained experience of naval aviation, could not rid themselves of the conviction that there must be an observer with the pilot in every aircraft and, moreover, the observer must be the senior in charge of the aircraft. The result of this thinking was the production of heavy, lumbering, ugly, slow machines, which were more danger to their crews than they were to the enemy. Most of these aircraft, designed under Admiralty specification, were built by the Blackburn Company.

Hence there were the Roc and the Skua, much the same looking aircraft, with a couple of guns in the wings and a pop gun in the back for the observer and maximum speeds of about 160 knots. And yet the astonishing fact is that in the early days of the war an ME 109 was shot down by a Skua pilot. The latest naval fighter was the large Fairey Fulmar, again with provision for an observer, which had a little Rolls Royce Kestrel engine to pull it through the skies. Downhill, it could reach a speed of about 200 knots. And then there was the Torpedo/Bomber called the Shark. At St Merryn, I was given the task of flying this ridiculous little biplane to tow a large drogue through the air one hundred yards behind as a target. Once the drogue had been launched, the Shark could hardly remain airborne even at full throttle. I doubt if it ever had enough power to carry a torpedo or bomb, let alone drop it on an enemy.

The Shark was pleasant enough to fly, except for the oil spraying from the engine over my helmet and face on take-off, but on arrival over the sea near the coast, the telegraphist in the large rear cockpit had to stream the drogue. This meant almost full throttle again. Two Hurricanes appeared and started firing at the drogue behind us and it seemed to me and my telegraphist that they were firing straight at our bottoms. We could only cower down into our cockpits and hope for the best. The worst part of the exercise was when it came to dropping the drogue because it was rarely possible to wind it in fully and sufficiently close before approaching the dropping zone. I had to approach the zone at very low level and nearly full throttle with this damn drogue hanging down at the back and leaping about in the slipstream just missing trees and hedges. When the drogue was released, the Shark with its relieved crew soared skywards before heading back to St Merryn.

My three particular chums with me at St Merryn, all Midshipmen like me, were Tony Harris who was the tallest and not only with the face of a young boy, but with the enthusiasm and charm of one. He would be killed eighteen months later when the oxygen in his Corsair failed at height.

Bruce Clark had very blond hair with a small strong and compact body which had served him well when he had played as scrum-half for a famous rugby club. Bruce was a naturally gifted pilot with astonishing skill. His log book during every stage of his flying training had the very rare assessment of 'Exceptional' written in it. He survived the war flying mostly Seafires, the most difficult aircraft of all from a Carrier. He remained in the Royal Navy after the war and became a famous trials and test pilot before he transferred back to sea in command of a Destroyer to end his career as a Captain RN. He and I were to meet again many years later and, as a foursome with our wives, spend many holidays together.

My best friend was Basil Bartlett with whom I had shared a cabin at Netheravon and again at Yeovilton. He was the only one of us four who had been educated at a grammar school; a quiet person, more mature than I was and holding firm views quietly expressed about aspects of life to which I had barely given thought. When I had boasted to him about my joust with Jennifer in the hotel at Teignmouth, I had expected his male admiration, but instead he seriously rebuked me and made me feel really rather ashamed of the promiscuous part I had played. Without my quite realising it, the friendship of this more mature boy and his companionship was a factor in my development. But Basil was by no means a dour personality; he was good fun at any party and liked to join in the rough-house games we sometimes played in the Wardroom after dinner. His choice of sport was a bit odd for one of his age; instead of cricket and rugby and all that type of thing, he liked to play golf, usually with his father at their home in Scotland. Basil was the same height as me but not quite so thin with wavy, dark hair and often a rather serious expression on his face which belied his sense of fun and hood humour. I don't think that he was a particularly good pilot but a steady one; a good man to follow. Possibly he would have been better chosen as a torpedo-bomber (TBR) pilot than as a fighter pilot. Having compared his build with mine, I should tell that I was a reedy youth, little more than nine stone and my height was 5 foot 10 inches.

There was no great pressure to fly many hours at St Merryn. Before we four arrived, a number of pilots were already there, elderly most of them, to carry out the various tasks of second-line flying. Some of them had been professional airline pilots, others were amateur pilots, actors some of them such as Laurence Olivier and Ralph Richardson. These chaps left fairly soon to resume acting for which they were more suited.

We were given a long week-end leave and the four of us decided to go in my little Ford car to St Ives where Tony remembered a smart hotel at which he had stayed on holiday with his father and mother years before. We arrived at the Manor Hotel at the back of St Ives and Tony got out of the car to organise the rooms for us to stay there for the week-end.

He came back looking rather flushed and reported that the hotel was fully booked up and he had been told that we would have to go elsewhere. But I had noticed that there were very few cars parked outside the hotel and it seemed very unlikely to me that a country hotel should be full during wartime when petrol was so strictly rationed. I wasn't an Old Harrovian for nothing; I could easily adopt the rude and pompous manner so typically used by many young Harrovians of that time. I stumped out of the car and demanded of the female receptionist that she either booked us into two double rooms for the week-end or to send for the Manager. She could choose which option she liked but, rising to the full height of my pomposity, I told her to do one or the other immediately.

She opted for the Manager who came out of his office and smiled when he saw this irate boy in what, with its maroon tabs on the lapels, looked like the uniform of a hotel bell boy and hopping about with fury in the reception area demanding rooms. 'Look here,' I said still trying to sound important, 'we are four Midshipmen of the Royal Navy and what's more we are fighter pilots (pointing to the Wings on my sleeve) and your receptionist won't give us rooms in your damn hotel. Why not?' The Manager (probably the owner) was a kind man who, trying to stop his face creasing into laughter, apologised sincerely for the terrible mistake of his staff in failing to recognise the uniform and rank of a Midshipman of the Royal Navy. He personally showed us to two large double rooms and then said that for the honour of having four naval fighter pilots in his hotel in wartime and, in some small reparation for the mistake made by his staff, he would charge only one half the normal price, including dinner. He hoped we would have a very happy leave at his Hotel. Fully mollified, we were profuse in our thanks. And pompous little Henry Adlam gained much kudos and standing with his friends for his successful enterprise.

That was a lovely short leave and was the last time we would all four friends be together. We only wore uniform for dinner in the evening and wore holiday clothes during the day when we either went for walks or more frequently played golf at the well-known local course. The only one of us who could really play golf well was Basil and, as I had never played before, I partnered him against Bruce and Tony both of whom knew only a little about the game. The arrangement suited me as I always liked to win and was bound to do so with Basil.

I remember that on one of our walks we sat and rested on the cliff top while the conversation turned to a discussion about our families and fathers in particular. Bruce was the youngest of seven children, five of them boys, and he had very little close contact with his elderly father. But his eldest brother, a successful business man and twelve years older than Bruce, had taken the place of his father and they had a reasonable good relationship. I noted that neither his father nor any of his many siblings were much interested apparently in his success as a young rugby player or in his brilliance as a pilot. His mother had died shortly after Bruce was born. I suspect that he was very much a loner in his family.

It became evident as Tony spoke that, as an only child, he had much love for his father and also a deep old-fashioned respect for him. Tony described how, on his last leave, he had inadvertently used the word 'sod' about someone and his father had been absolutely furious and had berated Tony as if he was still a schoolboy. Tony didn't think such an intense reaction from his father was either unusual or wrong but in line with his upbringing and with a childhood which had been all the happier because of the strict guidelines set by his father. His childhood had obviously been strictly controlled by both his parents but, as he spoke about it, I sensed that it had been a very happy one.

Whereas Bruce and Tony, and myself to some extent, came from wealthy families, Basil did not. His father was a foreman in a large printing company where he earned good wages and, for his ability and good sense, was highly regarded by the management and was well liked by those who worked with him. Father, mother and the five children, of whom Basil was the youngest, lived in one of a row of houses on the west side of Edinburgh. I knew Basil was clever and intelligent but he must have been exceedingly so because he had gained a scholarship to Watsons, a fine school in the City. It seemed that he had an unusually close relationship with his father who, as a well-read man with a wide range of interests, had done much to help and encourage Basil towards the scholarship. The greatest pleasure for both of them had been to play golf together at the nearby excellent municipal course. Two of his three sisters were married but lived nearby. I felt a degree of envy as Basil told us about his family because there was obviously such a close-knit relationship among them and such a strong love between father and Basil, the youngest son.

For my part, there was not a lot I could say about my father because I didn't know him very well or much about him except that he had been Chairman of a large and successful engineering company. I explained about my parents being divorced and how my Mother had worked so hard with those damn bull terriers to provide a home for me and that I was proud of her success with the dogs, however much I loathed them. I shot a bit of a line about the South of France and the parties there and, of course, about driving Father across France to England. That was it really; there was not much more I could say about Father.

When we arrived back at St Merryn at the end of that short leave, signals awaited us appointing Bruce and Tony to join a ship which would transport them out to West Africa where pilots and aircraft were being accumulated for some secret Admiralty purpose. The airfield to which they were sent was called Mackinnon Road and some twenty young pilots with whom I had trained, including Bruce and Tony, languished in that boring and boiling hot dust bowl for eight months waiting for this top secret operation of the Admiralty to take place. Absolutely nothing happened, neither did anyone ever explain what it was all about. And so, at the end of that long period, these pilots all came back to the UK to join fighter squadrons which by then badly needed them. It was just another case of incomprehensible planning by the Admiralty when dealing with naval aviation. At the time, Basil and I were dreadfully disappointed to be left behind at St Merryn and we wondered how much longer we would have to trudge around the sky doing such jobs as towing drogues.

CHAPTER FOUR

890 Squadron

I need not have worried about the prospect of towing drogues at St Merryn. Two days later, signals arrived appointing Basil and me to 890 Squadron, a fighter squadron flying an American aircraft called the Wildcat, and we were to join it forthwith at an Air Station near Greenock in Scotland. How lucky we considered ourselves, to be appointed so quickly to a first line Squadron. We indulged ourselves with one hell of a party that evening before we were flown in an elderly troop carrier to the airfield in Scotland.

The first action on arrival was to meet the Commanding Officer, Lt Jimmy Sleigh, DSC, RN, a South African who had been a Battle of Britain pilot and subsequently had seen further action in one of the early Escort Carriers. But luckily for me, he had been one of my two instructors during my training at Yeovilton. The Squadron was brand new and, as its first Commanding Officer, Jimmy had been given the opportunity to make his own selection of six pilots for it and had chosen from his personal knowledge of us at Yeovilton. We learned to have great respect for Jimmy, as our CO. All through the period of working-up the Squadron during the weeks to come, he demanded a great deal from us in terms of effort and enthusiasm and he expected us to endure long hours of flying each day. We responded gladly; he was just the type of leader we wanted. He made sure that the entire Squadron, not just the pilots, but our aircraft maintenance crews, were fully trained and ready for operations.

The senior Pilot and second in command was Lt. Dagwood Cosh who, as his rank implied, was a few years older than most of us. Although with no more flying experience than we had, he proved to be a most competent leader. More than that, he was a most amusing companion with a fund of ridiculously funny songs and stories; a great chap to have around. He left us after a year to command his own squadron and earned a DSC before being killed in action on an Arctic convoy.

Two of the outstanding characters among us were Winnie Churchill and Jack Parli, both New Zealanders. They were inseparable friends and as a pair they had fought and drank their way through the training period at St Vincent and Netheravon and got themselves into so much trouble that, after gaining their wings, they had been refused their Commissions as officers and had been given the rank of Petty Officers. The story goes that after a short while, the Petty Officers' Mess for the sake of peace and quiet, begged the Captain at Yeovilton to arrange for the rumbustious pair to be taken away and given their Commissions. And so it happened. That reads as if they were a most unpleasant couple of young men. Not so; I had known them since the first days at St Vincent and had found them to be two most likeable people, full of fun and the joy of living and great company. They just loved a fight but only if they considered the size and number of the opposition to be a suitable challenge.

Winnie was a very blond, fair-skinned young man, well over six feet and very strong with a superb physique. He could probably have passed for 'Tarzan' any day except for his charmingly ugly mug with broken nose and overlarge usually smiling mouth containing a couple of broken teeth. In spite of that, he appeared as a handsome man and women very obviously thought so. Other New Zealanders told me that, but for the war, he would have played as fly-half for the All Blacks because he was a truly outstanding rugby player.

Jack Parli had a quite different appearance. He gave the impression of normal height and size and of not being a particularly athletic man. In fact, he was a deceptively and immensely strong man who could be very fast on his feet and with his hands. Deceptive because his body, although broad, was smooth without apparent muscle and almost womanly in its sloping shoulders and yet his strength was phenomenal. He had rather a quaint face, certainly not handsome with his hair cut too short at the sides leaving a tuft on top, a snub nose with small twinkling, kindly eyes. He was not angered easily, even when fighting, but his anger when it came was controlled and ferocious. When he took his teeth out, which he often did for fighting, rugby and beer drinking, his face could look exactly like 'Popeye'. Jack played rugby entirely in the New Zealand manner which is to say that, whatever the Referee couldn't see couldn't be wrong and thus he was a very effective wing-forward on any team and a menace to the opposition. I liked both these men immensely and I am fortunate indeed to have known them as my friends.

The other three pilots to make up the Squadron were myself, Basil Bartlett, and Cliff Nell who was a very nice, rather naïve English lad much given to puns and stories about 'Sam and his musket' which amused us all except the colonials who never did fathom out the significance of Sam's musket but, it didn't matter, we all liked Cliff and enjoyed watching his performance.

The CO outlined the plan for the Squadron to arrive by fast ship in New York and to proceed as quickly as possible by train to Norfolk, Virginia which was a huge shipbuilding port combined with a large aerodrome of the US Navy. Arrangements had been made for the Squadron to borrow Wildcats, with US markings still on them, from the American Navy and we would be provided with a Hangar, complete with offices, large enough for our Squadron to operate. We would have about six weeks to work-up to a fully operational state before we were to receive seven brand new Mark 4 Wildcats under the Lend Lease agreement. At the end of that period we were due to carry out deck-landings on USS *Charger*, one of the first Escort Carriers built in America and operated by the US Navy.

As soon as we arrived at the aerodrome in Norfolk, Virginia, which was in the form of one huge concrete circle instead of runways, we settled into the hangar and offices which had been allocated to us amongst the many other buildings. Without delay, Jimmy Sleigh set the squadron on a programme of working–up and flew the heads off us with usually three flights a day. It was a good thing that we were so busy and fairly tired out at the end of each day because there was little pleasure in a run ashore in Norfolk. (Do I have to explain that in the Royal Navy every Air Station or Barracks is a ship and, when you leave it, you 'go ashore'.) The City abounded in troops of the US Navy and dockyard workers with the result that the restaurants and bars were hugely expensive, well beyond our pockets, and usually very noisy and crowded.

The Cinema on the Air Station was right up to date with the latest films and the meals at the Bachelor Officers' quarters were very good and so, after a first few sorties into Norfolk to have a look at it, we tended to remain at the Air Station. Our accommodation was not good as, except for Jimmy Sleigh, we six pilots were put into huts on our own at the edge of the Officers' area. Since no booze was permitted in the Officers' quarters in the US Navy, we were glad of this separate accommodation because we could hold our drinking parties and gossip about the day's flying in our huts, having bought our own booze back from the City.

The truth is that we handful of British troops were not made welcome in the City.

This was difficult to understand since America was on the brink of declaring war with Germany and Japan, its Government was giving great help to Britain under Lend Lease and the great majority of American people were fully in support of us. And yet there was so much aggression towards us from the lower ranks of the American forces at that time and certainly in that City. It seemed to me that they were imbued with the myths of the Wild West perpetrated by the movies, which they had avidly watched from childhood, and perhaps they came to believe from these childish films that ridiculous brawls and fist-fights in bars were normal manly behaviour? Many men of the American fighting forces were longing to get into the war (of which they had no knowledge) and might there have been a sort of immature jealousy of the UK and its war experience? I never knew how else to explain their attitude.

The other side of the American attitude is the wonderful hospitality we received elsewhere in America. Four weeks later, Jimmy granted ten days' leave for us having accepted the offer from a Sports club to use their holiday camp near Richmond, Virginia. It was an attractive wooded place beside a lake where, in lovely hot weather, we swam every day. Here Jack, who with his apparently lazy, effortless stroke was able to churn through the water faster and for longer distances than anybody I ever knew, took the opportunity and trouble to insist on teaching me to swim. He recognised my fear but firmly helped me to overcome it. I was never able to swim well, but I no longer panicked when my head was under water.

We found Richmond to be an attractive friendly City and most evenings on that leave were spent with local families enjoying their hospitality; usually consisting of strong Mint Juleps followed by a delicious dinner. At first the problem was getting into Richmond and back to the camp because the bus service was abysmal. We were overheard in a bar talking about the problem by an elderly, well dressed citizen. He came round to our table, laid a bunch of car keys on the table and said, 'My Chrysler saloon is just outside, you boys take it for the duration of your vacation here and enjoy it.' Of course, we sprang to our feet to greet him hardly able to believe such generosity. But he meant it and accompanied us there and then out to his lovely new green and cream shining car and insisted that we drove it away. It was difficult to know quite how to express our appreciation for such kindness. However we found a shop selling

Scotch single Malt Whisky and a small crate of bottles was welcomed by the elderly American who had shown us such friendship and trust. In the war years to come, I would not only enjoy the friendliness of American hosts in New York but, later in the Far East and Pacific, I would come to know many aircrew of the US Navy and admire their flying ability and courage.

When we returned to Norfolk after that pleasant holiday in Richmond we had to start preparing for our first deck-landings on USS *Charger*. For the purpose we used a small disused airstrip about twenty miles away to practise dummy deck-landings. Jimmy Sleigh did the 'batting' as well as the instruction and advice after each session of landings. In a few days of practice out on the airstrip, we all felt ready for the ordeal of our first deck-landings and we longed to get it over and done with. Despite all our flying training during the past ten months, we could not consider ourselves properly as Fleet Air Arm pilots until we had landed on a Carrier. 'It must be dreadfully dangerous and difficult landing on a Carrier, do tell me about it?' One of the pretty girls I had met in Richmond typically had asked me only the previous week and how bogus I had felt in admitting that I had not yet landed on. Now, I was about to lay the 'deck-landing' bogey to rest, successfully I hoped.

The USS *Charger* was out in Chesapeake Bay off Norfolk and we were awaiting the signal to go out and land on her. Jimmy had decided that we would use the old Wildcats for our landings; no point in breaking our brand new Wildcats which had by now been delivered to us from the factory. He would fly out by himself and land first because he would have to 'bat' us on. The reason being that the batting signals to the pilot used by the US Navy, on the landing approach, were the exact opposite of ours. It would have been impossibly stupid for us to attempt to adapt to their system just for this occasion and so the Captain had reluctantly agreed that we might use our own batsman and signals. Actually, it would be quite an occasion since it would be the first time that a British Squadron, albeit a small one, had landed on an American Carrier. Yet another reason for some trepidation; we simply must not make a mess of it!

Half an hour after Jimmy had taken off the signal came through that, as expected, he had landed safely and the ship was ready for our first flight to land on. Dagwood Cosh was leading the first flight with Winnie as number two and Cliff Nell number three. That left Jack Parli to lead the remaining flight of three with me in my now customary position as his number two and Basil, who normally flew behind Jimmy. We waited anxiously in the crew room for a signal from the ship to be phoned through to us. Jack as usual appeared calm and relaxed and I thought, as I watched him, how lucky I had been that Jimmy had put me to fly with Jack as his number two. It never occurred to me any longer that Jack had no more flying experience than I. He was a leader I would always be happy to follow.

It was over an hour before the signal came through and we were off at last. Jack led us out over the coast on the course given to him and soon the Carrier was in sight, steaming quietly through the placid sea of Chesapeake Bay. How small she looked. Even as I watched, her wake commenced to boil up into a white foam as she increased speed and began to turn into wind. Meantime, in accordance with Jimmy's careful briefing, Jack had brought us down to eight hundred feet and was aiming for us to fly down the starboard side of the ship as she came into wind. I could see the affirmative flag flying, denoting that she was ready for us to land. It would be up to Jack now to judge when to break away to port from our formation to commence his circuit. Some seconds after he had done so, I would follow him round on to the downwind leg of the landing circuit and, after an interval, Basil would follow after me.

It had been emphasized that there must be a sensible time lag between us on this our first deck-landing and so, while I was still on the downwind leg with the hood locked back and having selected hook and wheels down, full flap and fine pitch, I could see Jack seemingly almost stationary poised on the after end of the deck before his Wildcat, at that distance appearing to alight like a small bird on to the deck. Now, looking down at the Carrier just ahead of my port wing-tip, I must make the critical judgement when to turn on to the cross-wind leg. It was happening too fast; I had failed to take sufficient account of the Carrier moving in my opposite direction and my crosswind turn was late. Thus, by the time I had made my final turn into wind, I was too far behind and having to drag along after it.

Flying straight in line with the Carrier and with the nose up in the aircraft's landing attitude, there was not much of the deck that I could see despite the short stubby nose of the Wildcat. One eye glued to the airspeed indicator to fly at exactly seventy-eight knots (just off the stall). Trying to get a view of the deck, I put on a lot of right rudder and began crabbing towards the ship. Bloody dangerous … nose up with that amount of rudder … at that speed … this was the recipe for a sudden, vicious stall into the sea. Sweating with fear, I was about to open full throttle in an attempt to go round again when … there was

Jimmy in my sight giving me the 'come on you are all right' signal. Seconds later, I was over the round-down, could see to straighten up down the deck, closed the throttle and landed with a thump to be hooked to a sudden halt by the arrestor wire. Flight deck crew disengaged the hook and signalled me to taxi ahead over the crash barrier to the aircraft park on the other side, and to shut down the engine.

I sat there in the cockpit, hearing but not conscious of the sound of the wind over the flight deck, the sound of the ship moving through the sea and the shouts of command around me. I was shocked at the difficulty of the landing and shaking at the thought of the appalling mess I had so nearly made of it. I wanted to think quietly about it because I knew that in a few minutes my aircraft would be pushed back and ranged ready for take-off for at least one more deck-landing. I decided that at all costs I would avoid lining up straight behind the Carrier on the final approach; I would so judge it that I would make a curving approach to the deck, with the aircraft still banked on a turn if necessary. As I concluded this, Jimmy jumped up on to the wing to tell me that I had made a bad approach (as if I didn't know) but next time to keep my circuit closer to the ship and make the crosswind turn much earlier. He told me that he would send me off first and had briefed the other two to keep clear of the circuit for me while they waited for their turns to land. All of his advice confirmed my thinking on what to do next time.

I was ranged ahead of Jack and Basil and took-off first. I was surprised to find how quickly the Wildcat was airborne before reaching the end of the deck and I flew straight ahead up to no more than four hundred feet before starting my turn on to the downwind leg. This time I remained much closer to the ship as I selected hook, wheels and flaps down. I turned crosswind into the ship as I came level with its stern and this resulted in a gentle curving approach, with the port wing slightly down as, at the same time, I brought the nose up into the landing attitude with the speed held at eighty-five knots. I could see the deck and the batsman all the way in until a final straightening up and levelling of the wings, with speed down to seventy-six knots, I cut the throttle just past the round down and the Wildcat settled firmly on the deck and picked up the second wire. No trouble at all, I thought as the flight deck crew pushed me back ready to take off again for another landing. My third landing was as good as the second and I mentally hugged myself with the joy and relief of it. I watched Jack and Basil complete their second landings which, since they hadn't made a mess of their first, was all they were required to do.

We were invited to lunch with the ship's officers and their Commander Air who, in a nice little speech of welcome, congratulated us on our accident-free performance. Little did he know apparently how close I had come to spoiling that performance. I was longing for a couple of large pink gins, as were my fellow pilots, but no alcohol was allowed in US Navy ships. But we all appreciated the welcome and the good lunch.

Why, I asked myself the next day and many more times over the next five years, does everything in the Royal Navy have to happen in a sudden mad rush? Because the day following our completion of deck-landings on the USS *Charger*, there was a sudden signal to pack up all the squadron gear and embark our maintenance personnel in our Carrier. The onus for achieving this fell on the CO, of course, but also on the unfortunate Cliff, who had been designated as the Divisional Officer of the Squadron. The truth is that Jimmy had recognised Cliff from the outset as a quietly competent organiser capable of setting out a clear Movement Order which all our people would understand and follow. There was some advantage, it seemed, in my role as the gormless young Midshipman of the squadron; I was never given that sort of job. Basil, I should have said, had reached his twentieth birthday two months earlier and accordingly had received his stripe as a Sub Lieutenant, leaving me as the only Midshipman.

The situation, we learned from Jimmy, was that our Carrier had completed a defect repair in the Norfolk Yard quicker than expected. This would enable the squadron to have a very brief opportunity to work-up with the ship in Chesapeake Bay before hot-footing it up to New York where we were to join a large convoy about to be assembled for passage to the UK.

I felt considerable excitement at the prospect of landing on and joining our own Carrier and I was entirely confident now about my ability to land on her. I knew that in size her flight deck was slightly wider than the USS *Charger* at eighty feet and the same length at four hundred and forty feet.

A day later, we took off and formed up into our two flights, with Dagwood leading the second one. Jimmy led us out to our Carrier waiting out in the Bay and we kept a tight formation as we flew at two hundred feet over the ship to show ourselves off a bit. A Squadron of eight Swordfish aircraft had joined her earlier from another Carrier, now in dock for repairs, but their aircraft were all struck down now in the hangar and, no doubt, their aircrews would all be watching carefully to see how we performed. As we broke up into two flights, wheeling round to come up her starboard side, so the ship increased speed and turned into wind. I thought what a splendid sight she was with her white bow wave and white wake boiling up astern against the dark bluish grey of the sea around her.

But it was time to concentrate on the landing and Jimmy had warned us not to attempt, at this stage, a close back-up in the landing circuit. Anyway, as number four in the second flight, I was virtually 'arse-end Charlie' of the squadron and the last to land, so I could position myself on the approach exactly where I wanted. I made my curved final approach and could see the batsman clearly plus most of the deck, including the crash barrier with the other six aircraft parked ahead of it. The batsman, evidently liking my approach, gave me the OK signal all the way until a 'straighten-up' signal just before he crossed the bats for me to cut the throttle The Wildcat caught the third wire and I was safely down. Round me came the ship's flight deck crew to disengage the hook, to hold the wing tips steady against the strong wind over the flight deck and, since mine was the last aircraft to land, they signalled me to cut the throttle.

Leaving my parachute in the cockpit, I clambered down the wing and walked to where the others were being conducted to the aircrew briefing room which was just below the flight deck on the port side. Except Jimmy, who had seen it all before, we were chattering away excitedly and rather pleased with ourselves and our landings, when the Lt Commander Air, in charge of all flying from the ship and who had entered unnoticed, knocked on the table for our attention. First he introduced the Lt Cdr 'Ops' whose job it would be to keep us informed of the enemy situation at sea, and then, Lt Pat Heaton, the batsman, who had previously been a Wildcat pilot.

Commander Air commented that the landings had been satisfactory, under the circumstances and informed us that we had the next two days only, plus this afternoon, in which to work-up because after that the ship would be operational. That afternoon, he said, there would be a maximum combined range on the deck for take-off of both Swordfish and Wildcats followed by firing and bombing exercises. Get ready for it, he said, and left. Well, that shut us up all right. Much more quietly now, we put our flying kit away in a locker provided for each aircrew and found our way down to the Wardroom. There I gulped down a couple of pink gins while meeting the Swordfish boys, two of whom had been with me at Netheravon. Not much time for chatter with them; Jimmy would want us all to attend a briefing as soon as we had swallowed a quick lunch. I just had time to find my cabin which, thankfully, I would share with my particular chum, Basil.

We were up and down, off and on that Flight Deck in our Wildcats almost non-stop it seemed to me during the next two days. It was a hectic period during which the Squadrons would learn to work in conjunction with the flight deck teams of the ship's company. We had to learn how to judge our approach to the deck to land ideally within fifteen seconds after the aircraft in front of us. Once landed, we had to taxi fast forward over the lowered crash barrier seconds before the pilot behind cut his throttle to catch one of the arrestor wires. If he missed all the wires, as could so easily happen, it would be catastrophic if the crash barrier had not come up again in time to prevent him crashing into the aircraft already landed. It was all split second timing and co-ordination between the pilots and the crewmen and engineers of the flight deck. All this frantic speed was to reduce the period of time in which the Carrier would have to hold its course into wind. Not only was the Carrier vulnerable to U-Boat attack while operating its aircraft, but the course into wind might take it in the opposite direction and away from the protection of the convoy.

The training and operation of the two watches of the flight-deck crew was the responsibility of Pat Heaton, the batsman, who also supervised every movement and placement of aircraft on the deck. It was hard work all day long every day at sea for the men on the flight deck, including the Deck Engineering Officer who with his team was responsible for the slick operation of the crash barrier, the arrestor wires and the catapult launcher. Ahead of the crash barrier in the deck park and down in the hangar would be waiting the fitters, riggers, radio mechanics and armourers to service the aircraft and ready them for the next sortie. Everything was done in difficult conditions on the deck and very limited space in the hangar.

I didn't fully appreciate it at that time but one of the joys, in an American designed and built Carrier, was the provision of decent cabin accommodation for aircrew. Basil and I took the comfort for granted, as we settled into our pleasant double cabin located on an upper deck with the showers and heads just nearby. I was not to know then how palatial our cabin would be in comparison with the accommodation for aircrew officers provided in any of the Carriers of Admiralty design. Accommodation there, I would find, would be either cramped dormitories for eight young officers and their clothes or cabins for four, low down over the noise of the ship's turbines. Obviously the US Navy had a regard for their aircrews, entirely lacking at the Admiralty.

The steward had found our cases somewhere for us and, as we unpacked our uniforms, there was no foreboding about the future by either Basil or me. We were both excited that, after so many months of training, at last we were at sea in a Carrier and we looked forward with naïve eagerness to operational flying. For me, the companionship with Basil was an important factor in my attitude towards whatever the future might hold. I felt that no harm could come to such a firm friendship and I reckoned also that both of us had become competent pilots, well able to deal with Carrier operations. Full of these cheerful but absurdly naïve thoughts, I led the way along to the Wardroom to join Winnie, Jack and the rest of our squadron at the bar where we met and started to get to know the ship's officers.

On arrival in New York harbour, where there was a mass of shipping, we were told that there was to be a delay of two more days to complete the assembly of the convoy. None of us as aircrew were put on any duty during this short period but I was to find later that usually aircrew were seized upon in Carriers by the Commander to carry out duties and tasks in harbour which normally would be undertaken by the ship's officers. It was a 'fair do' really since, after all, we were naval officers and there was so much for us to learn about naval life. Apart from what we had learned in the initial weeks as sailors, plus a 'knife and fork' course at Greenwich for a week, we had received no training as naval officers. Therefore such duties were as good a way as any to learn our responsibilities and we accepted the need for them.

Winnie and Jack asked Basil and me to join them on our first run ashore in New York and the four of us made ourselves ready to see the sights of the City and for whatever else it might have to offer us in the form of entertainment. The ship was moored in the middle of the harbour, surrounded by other shipping, but liberty boats had been arranged to take officers and men, not on duty, ashore. The first place to make for was the Brabazon Plaza Hotel which was used as a focal point and as accommodation for British officers, of all three Services, who might be on leave or who had some duty in New York. We had been told that many of the wealthy ladies of the City acted as hostesses and arranged parties and dances in their houses with lots of girls all lined up to meet and date with us. So they did, but not on the particular day and evening of our visit because, as this was just a day before Christmas Eve, every event and every potential girl-friend was already booked up. Not all that dismayed because we had plenty of accumulated pay to spend and were determined to enjoy ourselves, we had drinks at a bar before seeing a matinée performance of the 'Rockettes'. These were a formation dance team of beautiful girls who performed on the stage. They were a popular form of entertainment in New York at that time. After a meal of huge steaks in a restaurant, we were joined by four young officers of the American army.

The eight of us began an evening of heavy drinking as a party together with lots of discussion about the war and what our part in it would be and how much we all wished we were having Christmas at home. It was all very amicable which was just as well because these chaps were all Texans, very tall and looked very tough indeed. Earlier experience in Norfolk kept us wary to start with as we knew how easily American servicemen at that early period of the war could take umbrage at some point during a discussion and the whole evening could end up in one of their ghastly brawls. That wouldn't have worried Winnie and Jack but I was of a naturally nervous disposition and Basil, being a normal sort of chap, wouldn't have enjoyed a brawl either. One of the American lads in particular, the youngest, called 'Hank', was the biggest of them all with immense great muscles, buttocks and thighs. He and I got on very well together while he told me about his lifestyle on a Texan ranch and I bragged about life in the south of France. The contrast between us was ludicrous because Hank, fit as he was, must have weighed around sixteen stone whereas I not only weighed in like a weed at not much over nine stone, but even looked like a weed.

Everybody seemed to enjoy this absurd contrast in our appearance and then, Winnie I think it was, suggested that we should exchange names; I would become 'Hank' and the huge Texan would become 'Henry' said in a squeaky English voice. And so that's how it happened. Later, with lots of drink in all four of us, we said farewell to our American friends and only just caught the last liberty boat back to the ship. I went aboard still called 'Hank'; a name which was adopted immediately by all my squadron and shipmates. The ridiculous result is that it followed me into civilian life and now sixty-three years later nobody alive knows me by any other name. But I like it. I often wonder if the real 'Hank' retained his adopted name of 'Henry' and whether he too survived the war?

CHAPTER FIVE

Convoy

It was a large convoy and would be a slow one having thirty-eight merchant ships some of them too elderly and battered to move fast. Consequently, its escort of two Destroyers and three Corvettes had taken a longer time to assemble them into an orderly formation than expected. Our Carrier had its own Corvette in attendance astern and to starboard to provide some anti-submarine protection, but its other purpose was as a rescue ship for aircrew should their aircraft crash over the side when landing. We joined the convoy at dusk and took position near the rear on the outer starboard column of ships.

Life at sea followed a regular pattern of Combat Air Patrols with periods of Stand-By, which would be either at immediate readiness on deck in the cockpit or in the aircrew's Ready room. We patrolled in pairs and nearly always I flew with Jack as his number two. The general intention was that we would fly two patrols on one day and, on the following day, one patrol plus two sessions of Stand-By. But of course the demands of the Convoy situation each day made any such regular pattern impossible and every evening Dagwood, as Senior Pilot, would put up the programme of flying for the next day.

My patrol on the following morning was scheduled for around 10 am but I was up early to watch the first patrol of Swordfish and Wildcats take off just after dawn and to look, as far as my eye could see, at the sight of so many merchant ships ploughing their way through the Atlantic sea in orderly formation. The weather was reasonable with mostly high cloud and the sea was sufficiently rough to give the ship just a bit of a roll, but I had no experience then with which to judge whether the sea was normal for the Atlantic at this time of year or not. On the stern of the flight deck, the aircraft handlers already were ranging our Wildcats ahead of two Swordfish. I made my way across the deck to the crew room where I arrived half an hour earlier than I need be; changed into my flying overalls and sat fidgeting, excited and nervous really, waiting for the pre-patrol briefing to start. Jack came in shortly after and greeted me cheerfully as usual and in a relaxed manner changed into his flying kit and settled down with me to await events.

The aircrew Ready room was arranged into rows of reasonably comfortable chairs with, at the back, sufficient lockers to contain the flying kit of all aircrew. At the front of the room, there was a large plot of the Atlantic and surrounding coastlines which covered half the wall space. This was kept up to date by Lt Cdr Ops to show the position, speed and average mean course of the convoy; the position of other convoys and, from Admiralty intelligence, the known or suspected location of enemy U-Boats in our area. According to the plot, there was a scattering of them marked ahead and to the north of our route and a larger gathering further into the mid-Atlantic. The briefing was started by Ops pointing out all these various factors shown on the chart and Jack and I noted these down on our pads, as did the Swordfish crews who had joined us. I used a small knee pad made for me in light aluminium by my fitter, Mac. It held a card showing a small compass-rose with space for notes and this neat little pad, when I was in the cockpit, would clamp comfortably on my left leg just above my knee.

The next briefing was from the Met Officer, Brian, to whom we listened with careful attention. The weather was always a main factor in our lives but, out here in the middle of the Atlantic, a good forecast was going to be crucially important to us. According to the Swordfish boys, Brian was good at his job and could be relied upon. Reasonable weather with mostly high cloud was expected for the next eight hours although the wind would remain quite strong at force five. The senior Fighter Direction officer, Lt Cdr. Ian Merry, introduced himself and gave us a suggested patrol height of 10,000 ft, if clear cloud allowed. He reminded us of the radio frequencies we should use and that our IFF (Identification Friend or Foe) should not be switched on unless we were in trouble or unless he told us to use it for his team to obtain a fix on us. The Swordfish crews had their own established procedures for anti-submarine search ahead and around the convoy and did not require so much briefing.

It was time to go and I came up from the fug of the Ready room on to the flight deck where the handling crews were standing by the chocks and the wingtips while my airframe rigger and my engine fitter prepared to strap me into the cockpit. Mac, my fitter, a fatherly old chap of some thirty years, talked about the Pratt & Whitney radial engine and how smoothly it had run on test. Then it was time to 'press-tits' to start up and the already warmed engine came to life immediately. I opened up to full power against the chocks, checked the magnetos and reduced to a fast tick-over ready for take-off. Meantime, the ship heeled over as she began her turn into wind while the deck had started to vibrate and shudder beneath the aircraft as the ship gathered speed up to her maximum of sixteen knots to provide the necessary wind speed over the flight deck. There would be plenty of wind for Jack and me in the Wildcats, but the Swordfish were very heavily loaded with depth charges and would need all the length of the deck, plus a full thirty knots of wind over it, to get off.

Looking up briefly I could see the two pairs of aircraft of the first patrol returning and approaching the ship separately, with the Wildcats ahead of the Swordfish, moving to take up position on the starboard side in preparation for their landing. They must so arrange their circuit that the first aircraft should be on final approach to land on the flight deck as the last of our patrol took-off ahead of them. Thus the ship would have to hold its course into wind only for the minimum of time.

Jack's Wildcat was ranged at the front in the middle of the deck with the chocks removed ready to take straight off. The 'Affirmative' was signalled from the bridge as the bows steadied five degrees off the wind. Pat Heaton, the 'Bats', had raised his flag and was waving it in a circular motion above his head. Jack released the brakes as the flag swept down and then opened up to full boost. The tail came up almost immediately and the Wildcat started to gather speed down the flight deck.

Even as Jack started moving, Bats was already waving chocks away and signalling me forward to face down the middle of the deck. This would be my first operational flight and my excitement and tension mounted as I looked down the flight deck and watched Jack jink slightly to starboard as he became airborne so that his slipstream would be clear of my path. Throttle open as far as possible while still holding the aircraft on the brakes, then Bats swept his flag down for me to go and, with full power, my Wildcat began the take-off. There was some roll to the ship with the sea on the port quarter but, thanks to the high wind speed along the flight deck, there was no difficulty in controlling the aircraft and keeping it straight. Seconds later I was airborne and climbing to join up with my leader to commence our patrol.

That first day there were no alarms or excitements and moreover the weather remained good. At the end of the two-hour patrol I gained my first experience of landing when there was some movement of the ship's stern up and down, although I hadn't been able to see clearly the amount of movement until the final stages of my curving approach. But the deck-landing technique I had been taught of holding the aircraft nose-up almost on the stall with a gradual rate of sink-down towards the deck, counteracted much of the pitching movement of the ship's stern. It was a useful first experience which prepared me for the future, when returning to the ship in bad weather and in rougher sea conditions would be more difficult.

Although it had been a quiet day, it set the pattern for convoy work ahead when we would long for confrontation with the enemy U-Boats or for a chance to shoot down their surveillance aircraft which, by their combining together, had so effectively been decimating our merchant shipping. It was difficult for young new pilots to appreciate at first that success should be measured not entirely in U-Boats sunk and aircraft shot down, but in the number of merchant ships convoyed safely through to their destination. The essential purpose of the Escort Carrier, working in combination with the other escorting Destroyers and Corvettes, was the protection of the convoy. But even on that convoy, regarded as a comparatively successful one, we lost two merchant ships. After the horror of witnessing from the flight deck the sudden explosion and sinking of one of them, I tried to dismiss the thought that the Carrier, day and night, was the prime target for the U-Boats.

I don't wish to denigrate the skill, courage and success of the Royal Navy in those small warships escorting the convoys, when I write that the Swordfish aircraft was the most effective single unit for combating the U-Boat in mid-Atlantic. That old-fashioned biplane, designed by Faireys happily without Admiralty interference some ten years before the war, proved to be the very best means of finding and attacking the U-Boats. Because it was so simple to fly, the pilots and crew were able to fly it with great courage from Carriers, both by day and night, in weather and sea conditions so appalling that pilots of other aircraft types could not have even contemplated operating at all. A danger for the Swordfish crews was that some RN Captains of Carriers, in their total ignorance of naval aviation and in their enthusiasm for their own personal success and that of their ship, might order combat operations to be undertaken which were beyond the capability of any aircraft or the skill of any pilot.

The function of the Swordfish was to patrol ahead and on either side of the convoy, usually about twenty-five miles out, using their ASV (Air to Surface Vessel) radar to search for enemy submarines on the surface or at periscope depth and to attack them with depth charges. Even if they could not find and attack the enemy before the boat could dive, the effect of their patrol was to keep the U-Boats down and unable to attack the convoy. By late 1941, however, the U-Boat commanders had become prepared to surface and fight it out against the flimsy Swordfish using both their cannon and machine-guns.

This is where the Wildcats, on combat patrol as a pair could come in fast on call-up from the Swordfish to fire at the enemy gun crews on the deck of the U-Boat who, intent on returning fire against the Wildcats, enabled the Swordfish to continue their depth charge attack. The Wildcat was slightly slower at that time than other fighter aircraft but it had a formidable fire-power of six 0.5 Browning machine guns and was eminently suitable for this situation.

The main purpose of our small fighter squadron, however, was to prevent the surveillance of the convoy by the Focke-Wolf Condors. These were converted four-engine airliners which, hitherto before the existence of Escort Carriers, had been able to range with total impunity over the whole area of the mid-Atlantic, to report the size, speed and course of our convoys to the lurking packs of U-Boats. They had been hugely successful in providing the enemy submarines with critical information but also, such had been their impunity, they had been able to bomb our merchant ships on the edges of the convoys. The Condor was fast and dangerous to attack having a 20mm cannon turret and three machine-gun positions giving them fire coverage from on top and below. The Germans, we knew, were producing these Condors in large numbers as they represented a major weapon in their war against our convoys. They also used for the same purpose a large twin-boomed, three-engine Flying Boat, the Bloemen-Voss 138, which operated more usually in the north Atlantic and Arctic. This was a well-armed and spiteful opponent too, but it was slow and therefore easier to knock down.

At this period of the war in 1942 and '43, the role of the Fleet Air Arm was predominantly a defensive one. Although it should not be forgotten that earlier, eight Swordfish had sunk nearly the whole of the Italian fleet in Taranto harbour. But during this same period of 1942 and '43, offensive strikes were made against German airfields and shipping in Norway and along the coast of the Bay of Biscay and again in the Med. Later in 1944 and '45, in the Far East and Pacific, large strikes of over 150 naval aircraft against Japanese oil refineries, their airfields and shipping, by Avenger bombers escorted by Hellcat and Corsair aircraft as fighter-bombers, were made constantly and daily.

CHAPTER SIX

Some Happenings at Sea

Jack and I were at 'immediate readiness' in our Wildcats, which were ranged as the only two aircraft on deck. The weather was foul with thick cloud from about four hundred feet going up to considerable heights with heavy rain and high winds. Nevertheless the two Swordfish had been sent off over an hour ago to carry out their patrols at almost sea level. It had not been thought worthwhile to send us up on patrol since, with such heavy and extensive cloud coverage, we would be unlikely to see and find anything and neither, for that matter, would a Condor be able to see the convoy. So we all thought.

But it was typical of such heavy and prolonged showers that occasional brief gaps were appearing and, sure enough, the message came over the deck Tannoy from Cdr Air to start engines. Whether for real or just to warm them I didn't know but frankly I hoped like hell that we would not be sent up in this stuff. Then over the R/T came Ian's voice from Fighter Control to report a 'bandit' on the screen, estimated at forty miles and angels six. Stand by to take off and he would give us a vector to steer before we were airborne. OK by me if there really was a bandit, that was a different matter, but I didn't want to get airborne to bog around up in that stuff just on the whim of an over enthusiastic Captain.

Meantime we were turning into wind and, as we did so, there was a heavy sea running against the port quarter of the ship making her roll as well as pitch into it. 'Vector 260, try angels six,' came the voice from Ian. 'Roger' from Jack.

I just had time to correct and set my directional gyro compass before the 'affirmative' was signalled and Jack at full throttle was already moving down the deck. Pat almost immediately was waving my chocks away and lining me up towards the bows.

Down went his flag and with no hesitation I opened up to full throttle ... almost level with the Island and bloody hell ... but I was aiming down into the sea with the bows of the ship smashing into it. I would have to pull her up into the air well before reaching the end of the deck .... I did so ... and of course, with that strong wind over the deck, bless my little Wildcat she came up and airborne well clear of the sea.

Keeping low over that ferocious sea, just below the cloud base, I looked for Jack's Wildcat among the rain squalls. There he was, waiting for me below cloud, turning to port onto the vector given by Ian and enabling me to cut across to join up with him. Maintaining fine pitch of the prop, for I would need quick engine response for the close formation I would have to keep in cloud, I moved to his starboard side as close to his aircraft as possible. Jack signalled from the cockpit with his thumb up to query was I OK and ready, I nodded confirmation and so we started to climb close together up into the thick cloud.

There was considerable turbulence and I had to give maximum concentration to my formation flying and to fight my aircraft in close if I were not to lose him, but how fortunate I was that Jack was such a steady leader. I had total confidence in him. Concentrating so intensely in tight formation, I could not look at my instruments to see what height or course we were on but then, after an age as it seemed to me, suddenly at nearly 12,000 ft, we broke through into a gap between layers of cloud and I could move away from Jack's Wildcat and take stock. First action was to turn on my oxygen as, on the climb up, there had been no opportunity to do so earlier. There was no sight of a Condor, nor of the sea far below us. Jack reported the situation to the ship. Ian, from the ship, replied that the Bandit was on a course heading away and evidently had not been able to sight the Convoy.

The static on the R/T had become bad and communication difficult but we were just able to receive the order to return to base as swiftly as possible because the weather had deteriorated with an even lower cloud base and very poor visibility. Because of the bad R/T reception, neither of us could hear the course to steer for the ship given by Ian but we heard and complied immediately with his instruction to 'make our cockerels crow', which meant that we must switch on our IFF transmitters. Jack circled round before we re-entered the cloud below us so that both of us could check our YG beacons to see if a sector signal might come up indicating our course back to base. Mine came up on sector 'D' suggesting a course of about 050 degrees which, Jack and I agreed on the R/T, would be about right. So Jack started to let down through the cloud on 050 with me in formation close to his starboard side.

After about ten minutes on that course, descending slowly, Ian's voice came through on the R/T now more clearly, 'I have your position on the screen; steer 020 for base. Come in at angels one but no lower because of the convoy.' Jack acknowledged and we turned on to the given course while losing further height down to 1,000 ft but, as we expected, still in thick and heavy rain cloud. Then Ian's voice, 'You are engines directly overhead, turn on to the ship's course into wind at 210 now, repeat 210 now.' 'Roger' from Jack who had already started the turn. From Ian, 'You are clear to descend down to sea level on course 210. Mother will maintain that same course into wind.' From Jack, 'Roger, thanks and now leave us to get on with it, matey.' What a nice way of telling Ian to shut up, I thought. But Jack's laconic, confident reply warmed and cheered me when I needed it.

Jack took us down fast and barely half a minute later we came out of cloud very low over a grey and white sea of frightening appearance. Immediately, although it was difficult to establish any horizon between the equally grey sea and low cloud, Jack went into a steep turn to port on to what should be the downwind leg of our approach to the Carrier. A short pause before I turned to follow him; I must not get too close, yet in this murky visibility it would be too easy to lose him somewhere ahead. If we had judged it right, the Carrier should be coming towards us on our port quarter but, in the dreadful visibility, there was no sign of her that I could see. Wheels, flaps and hook down in readiness and hood securely locked back and open (I always had a dread of being locked in the cockpit if I hit the sea or crashed over the side and unable to get out.) There she was! Just where she should be… Jack had timed it perfectly.

I throttled back to let Jack get further ahead. He was on his final approach and I watched his swoop on to the deck and safely down. Now me and, in a steep turn on the cross wind leg, I could see the pitching and rolling of the Carrier. I had determined from experience now, that my method of landing in such sea conditions was to come in high off an even steeper turn than usual (to give me a better view and judgement of ship movement) and aim to land well up on the middle of the deck … about the fourth or fifth wire. I rarely ever looked at the batsman. I reckoned he would only befuddle me, although I recognised that some pilots were reassured by his signals. I wasn't being cocky about it; by now I had enough experience to establish my own method. Pride before a fall, don't they say?

The landing went as I intended until the ship gave one hell of a roll to port as I caught the fourth wire, slewing me towards the edge of the deck on that side, but I had already caught the wire which, straining at its full extent, held my Wildcat just on the edge so that from the cockpit I looked down on that awful sea. I was sweating from forty minutes of a hairy flight but, at that point, I think I almost wet myself. By now the deck handlers had rushed across the deck and were all round the aircraft securing it.

I was longing to go below to my cabin, have a shower because I had been sweating and then along to the Wardroom to put down some pink gins in company with Jack and Ian, the Direction Officer, who we reckoned had done a good job. But the Captain, with Cdr Air, had sent for Jack and me up on the Bridge. But bless the dear old boy. All he wanted was to say that it had been a good show our getting back. We aircrew liked him; we knew that he consulted our Squadron COs whenever a difficult decision about flying had to be made. We were luckier than aircrew in some other Carriers with Captains ambitious for their DSOs.

Basil was waiting in the cabin with a hot cup of black coffee and our small flask of whisky at the ready. In the privacy of our cabin, perhaps I had allowed myself to look as shaky as I felt after that hairy but useless flight, because he put his arm round my shoulder and gave me a slight hug. 'You really must not go out to play again when it's raining as badly as that, Henry,' he said, 'It frightens me that you might catch a cold, or something silly of that sort.' It was his way of telling me how worried he had been for me on that flight and, by the way, he still called me 'Henry' sometimes although no one else did. Both of us had long since lost our earlier naïve and sanguine outlook on the certainty of our future and of our lasting friendship. We had seen enough now to know that we would be lucky, either one of us, to see the end of the war and the future was always a taboo subject with any of us. The right attitude was to look forward to the next party or, better still, the next leave.

We couldn't foresee then how the Squadrons of the Fleet Air Arm would develop more into a striking force in the years ahead but, right now, we found that the defensive role was demanding enough. Dale, who had joined us recently at short notice, flying in bad weather had misjudged his final approach to the deck and hit the rising round-down of the flight deck. His Wildcat went into the sea upside down behind the Carrier and there was no way he could have got out. Two of the Swordfish crews had failed to return at night in particularly bad weather. For us aircrew, as with those sailors in the Destroyers and Corvettes, it was a kind of war of attrition against the U-Boats without much apparently to show for it. Winnie, with Cliff, had knocked down a Condor and had done well to get back on the deck with part of his tailplane hit by cannon fire. The rest of us, although we had been involved in a number of chases, had not been able to get close enough for effective fire at a Condor. And we had all at sometime given support to the Swordfish to keep the U-Boats from attacking on the surface.

I was finding the Air Patrols combined with the continuous vulnerability of the Carrier to U-Boat attack all rather nerve-racking. But I was thankful to have the type of war job which, at the end of the day, allowed me plenty of whisky, a good meal and a cabin with a comfortable bunk for the night. Best of all was the companionship round the bar with fellow aircrew; the laughter from the uproarious and sometimes ridiculous flying stories that flowed with the drinks. With a few drinks inside, it was usually possible to see the funny side of what had been a hairy situation at the time and generally there was a lot of ribbing and fun between us all. Thank heavens for alcohol.

On a typical start to a morning at sea, I was woken up by the cheerful voice off our young steward, 'Wakey, wakey, sir, 5.30 and a lousy morning but here's a nice cuppa tea.' His voice was enough to drag me back from sleep and to remember that I would be on the first Air Patrol of the day. Take-off would be at about 7am leaving me plenty of time, I reckoned, to sip my hot tea. I glanced down at the lower bunk to see Basil, pretending to hold on to his precious sleep and no doubt enjoying the pleasure of listening to me having to get up while he could stay in his bunk.

'Come on sir, time to be up and getting at it.' The steward was back to chivvy me up as I needed him to do. Anyway, he could afford to be bossy as, being under the T124X contract, he was almost certainly earning much more than me. Since the Carrier was always, night and day, the prime target for the U-Boats, he probably considered that he earned his high pay.

As I shaved, I felt the ship moving in a fairly heavy swell. Well I wouldn't worry about it until I got up top to the flight deck to have a look-see. I felt my bowels revving up as they always did before an early morning patrol, so I finished shaving quickly and dashed off to the heads and to have a shower. Jack was there already having his shower and grinned a cheerful greeting at me. 'Morning, Hank, feels like a nice day for it,' he said as he staggered slightly with the movement of the ship.

A bacon and egg breakfast had become traditional for aircrew before combat operations; it was considered to be a special treat, as indeed it was in wartime Britain, and a booster for the day ahead. But not many of us at breakfast that morning were enjoying the traditional treat. I was having my usual difficulty in swallowing the overcooked and greasy egg with fried bread although Jack was cracking on and seemed to be enjoying it.

At the table with us were the pilots and observers from the two Swordfish that had landed on in the dark fifteen minutes earlier. The crews had just come down after de-briefing. The faces of these four young men were grey and lined from the fatigue and stress of the hazardous flight and from the freezing cold of the open cockpits; no doubt the TAGs (Telegraphic Air Gunners) now in the Petty Officers' Mess looked the same. They were not interested in talking about the patrol as yet, but concentrated on the warmth of the food and the steaming hot coffee. Their two hours of Anti-Submarine patrol around the Convoy had been through low cloud, heavy showers and in pitch black darkness which had not lightened as they found the ship and came in to land on the moving deck. Patrolling for them in such conditions was not unusual. But they had kept the U-Boats down during the night without any loss to the merchant ships in our Convoy.

After breakfast Jack and I came out on to the flight deck and stood together against the wind and surveyed the weather and the grey sea. The weather had improved and was not too bad at all; scattered sixth/tenth cloud at about 4,000 ft and high cirrus above with a cold, strong wind of about eighteen knots which had changed the swell into a lumpy sea, causing the ship to pitch quite steeply. Around us, in the early morning light, the aircraft handling crews were ranging two more Swordfish for take-off with our two Wildcats ahead of them.

There was nothing special to tell us at the briefing and, with the improving weather, there was the prospect of a reasonably quiet patrol ahead of us. Towards the conclusion of it, after we had been circling the convoy at 8,000 ft for nearly two hours, Ian's voice came over the R/T, not as we might have expected, to tell us to join the circuit for landing but, with controlled excitement:

'Bandit at vector 290, angels 6, estimate thirty miles: buster at vector 290.'

Jack steep turned on to 290, and at full throttle and revs, we were on our way in loose formation. This could be a good interception with cloud only at half cover at some 4,000 ft although cloud was thickening up in the west where we were now aiming but, if Ian's angels were correct, we would have a 2,000 ft height advantage. The Condor, as the Bandit aircraft was sure to be out here in mid-Atlantic, was capable of a speed not far short of ours and we would need the extra height for our attack.

'Turn left to Vector 220.' Came Ian's voice.

Then I realised how wise Jack had been to keep our height because we saw the small black speck only slightly below us moving fast across from right to left. But it had seen us too and had turned away heading for the thicker clouds to the west. With full power and some extra height we were gaining but not fast enough. At about 800 yards from us it entered the first wispy clouds.

Jack was astern and to the right of the Condor, but slightly below, where the cannon fire from the top turret could not hit him. He was giving the Condor brief squirts of fire from his six Browning machine guns despite little hope of hitting it at that range. Jack called me on the R/T.

'Go left of the cloud, Red Two; I will follow him; might get lucky to see him in cloud.'

Three minutes later Jack called me again. 'No luck, return and meet me above the cloud at angels six; we must make sure he doesn't double back towards the Convoy.'

Just then, at the edge of the cloud below me, I saw the black shape of the Condor.

Time only to shout in the R/T, 'I see him!' and immediately stuff the nose down and at him with guns squirting and spraying bullets at a distance probably too far for much effect. The Kraut gunner in the top turret had been alert too and he was firing back with a better chance of hitting me with cannon at that distance. But the Condor turned back into the thick cloud immediately where I followed flying at full throttle. I desperately wanted to get him at all costs and, intensely excited and wound up, flew flat out through the cloud prepared to accept the possibility of ramming into him. Meantime my gyro horizon had toppled and I began to lose all sense of the aircraft attitude. As I wrestled with the controls, the speed was building up massively with the engine roaring at dangerously high revs. I shot nearly vertically as it seemed down out of the bottom of the clouds at about 2,000 ft which was only just enough height to pull out of the dive above the sea.

'Go back to flying school,' I thought grimly and sweatily, 'go and relearn to fly on your instruments.'

Came Jack's voice on the R/T. 'Where the hell are you, Red Two, and what the blazes are you doing?' He instructed me to steer 100 degrees and join him at angels six in clear sky. Still at full boost and fine pitch, I climbed and after several minutes caught him up bogging slowly along at about 130 knots. Flying alongside my leader, Jack, there was time now for me to take stock of the situation. With horror I saw that the fuel tanks, as shown by the gauges, to be nearly empty! 'How far do you reckon we are from base, Red One?' I asked, 'I am nearly out of fuel.'

To which Jack replied: 'I reckon as much as eighty miles. Make sure that you are in coarse pitch for the prop and fully weak fuel mixture. Don't formate on me, but keep this same throttle setting and same course until I tell you, then we are going to lose height gradually at this slow speed down to angels three. I shall be alongside you all the way.'

If the Carrier was that far away, as Jack had calculated, there seemed little chance for us to get back to it. And certainly not for me because, even in loose formation during the patrol, I was bound to have used more fuel than Jack. More particularly, I must have used a huge amount of fuel at excessive revs and boost chasing the Condor and then catching up with Jack. I was making excuses for myself really, because my engine handling during the patrol had been bad as I should have been flying at lesser power and weaker mixture.

We were down now to 3,000 ft and apparently had come near enough to the Carrier for Jack to make radio contact and to give our situation report.

'Make your cockerels crow,' came Ian's voice from the Carrier and then, a minute after we had switched on our IFF transmitters, he gave us a course to steer of 070 to the ship.

We turned on to the new course and I tried to assess the state of the sea down there and the wind direction over it. No doubt Jack was doing the same as it was likely that we were both going to have to ditch. Ten minutes later, I could just catch sight of the Convoy ahead. Even as I did so, the engine coughed and spluttered and began to lose power. I thought quickly about baling out and discarded the thought; I didn't fancy a parachute jump into the sea; that would be worse. So this was it; I would have to ditch and I dreaded it. I couldn't swim and I had always feared the sea. This was no time to be asking myself what the hell was I doing therefore in the Fleet Air Arm. I must control my fear and get on with it.

Jack kept near me as I went down; gliding by now with the prop just windmilling and no power. I decided quickly to ditch into the waves, rather than along them, which would also bring me more or less into wind.

Straps extra tight, canopy wide open and securely locked back, full flaps down and trim; about a hundred feet left now and oh hell the waves looked awful and high; nose up a bit, get the speed down; don't stall it; quite wide troughs try to clonk it down in the middle of one. The initial 'CRASH' as we hit the sea flat. Then the real 'BANG' as the Wildcat ploughed into the brick wall of the full sea. The engine and nose went under immediately and the icy sea was gushing into my cockpit. With my fear of the sea there was an overwhelming urge to panic, but I knew I must stay calm if I was to survive.

By the time I had pulled the dinghy out and scrambled into it, the Wildcat was already sinking and I watched as the tail plane sank beneath the waves. Noise of an aero engine and I looked up to see Jack circling above me. He was obviously doing so to give the Carrier a fix on where I had ditched. But by doing so he was using his precious fuel and jeopardizing his own chance of getting back to the Carrier. I waved and shouted stupidly, willing him to go. He did so but only to return two minutes later to dive down on me to show, as I was to realise later, my position to the Destroyer following him.

Jack did get back. He landed straight on to the Carrier, which had turned into wind ready for him. His engine and prop stopped as he opened the throttle to taxi forward just moments after he had landed. Once his wheels were down and he was committed to that landing, he would have had little chance of survival had the engine failed at that point.

Meantime, the Destroyer had come racing up and, almost without stopping, had skilfully dropped a boat and crew to pick me up and then hoist me on board. During the following few days, I watched and learned how well the Destroyers and Corvettes of the Royal Navy performed their job of guarding the Convoy in combination with my Carrier. When I was able to return to my own ship a few days later in Greenock, we in the two squadrons had a super drunken party on board, as was our custom on return to harbour, at which I dared to tell Jack what a silly old git he had been, taking such risks for me, and to thank him. The typically dismissive comment from Jack was 'No problem and no sweat, Hank, you would have done the same.' Basil became unusually drunk and, for a change, it was I who had to help him back to our cabin and to his bunk, rather than the more customary other way round.

Some time later, it was my turn to lie in my top bunk while Basil was woken up by the steward to get ready for the early morning patrol. Half dozing and half awake, I was watching Basil, in his underpants, shaving over the little hand-basin in our cabin, his short dark hair untidy still from the pillow and his slim body tense from the effort of holding steady against the movement of the ship as he shaved. A fine looking young man really, I thought, and I felt a great warmth towards him for the strong friendship and companionship which had grown up between us ever since the early training days at Netheravon, where we had first shared a cabin together. He turned and smiled at me and I realised that he had seen me, reflected in the shaving mirror, watching him so intently. I was momentarily embarrassed at being caught and then I thought, 'What harm can there be if he is aware that I love him like an elder brother, as I do.' I smiled back and turned over in the bunk, away from him, pretending to return to my sleep without a care, as if he was about to catch an early bus to an office job.

But I remember feeling uneasy that morning for some reason, although it was just another day of patrols at sea. I made myself lie there quietly in my bunk until I felt the vibration when the ship increased speed for Jimmy and Basil to take-off. Then I waited to be sure that there was no undue commotion up top, before getting myself up and along to the Wardroom to join Jack with Winnie and Cliff for breakfast. They would be off on the next patrol while Jack and I would be on stand-by for the morning.

After an hour of standing by in the Ready room, I thought I would wander up to Fighter Control to see if anything of interest was going on. I wasn't allowed to be in there really, but Ian would sometimes allow one pilot at a time to stay and watch. Indeed there was something happening; a clear and large blip, obviously a Condor at this distance from land, had just appeared on the edge of the screen. Ian and his team were concentrating hard on the plotting of the Condor and assessing its speed and height so that they could give Jimmy and Basil the information and course enabling them to intercept the Condor. Within a few moments, Ian was able to call Jimmy on the R/T, 'Hello Blue One this is Mother. Bandit at angels six, vector 160, buster. He should be coming from your right on a course probably of 050 and below you.'

I knew that I ought not to be in the FDR (Fighter Direction Room) in the middle of an action but I could not bear to leave it; the excitement was intense. The sailors were plotting the movements of the three aircraft, on the large vertical screen, just as fast as the information could be passed to them from the radar operators below. All eyes were glued to the screen and Ian, standing up with the 'mike' in his hand, was conducting the interception by making constant assessments of the position of our two Wildcats relative to that of the enemy and calling his vector instructions to Jimmy. Then 'Tallyho' from Jimmy, 'he has seen us and we are chasing. Good interception Ian, we have height over him and he has no cloud cover.' This came from Jimmy in almost a quiet conversational tone.

Then from Jimmy to Basil, 'Spread out ready to go for his port quarter as I take him from this side.' 'Roger,' from Basil. Then a few moments later from Jimmy, 'Going in now, go.'

There followed a silence except for the static on the R/T. It seemed a never-ending period of silence and I could visualize the two Wildcats following the classic combined attack astern and from either quarter of the enemy. The question was, what would the Condor do?

Oh, the aching silence; nothing but the single 'Roger' from Basil all this time.

Seconds later we heard a transmission ... a gasped ... 'I'm hit.... can't get ....'

From Jimmy almost shouting, 'We've got him, he's down: tail gone and he's breaking up.'

Nothing more from Basil.

From Jimmy, 'Blue Two has been hit and is down in the sea.' Then, 'I am circling the wreckage looking for him.' And then in answer to Ian, 'Yes, the Condor is finished. I am looking for Basil.' Later, 'No sign of him in the water, just some wreckage.'

Feeling sick and breathless I turned to scramble my way blindly out of the FDR. I should never have gone there and how I wished that I had never done so. Would I ever be able to forget hearing Basil's voice on his final call 'I'm hit ...'? The awful thought of him, probably wounded, striving to get a damaged canopy open and unable to get out of the aircraft as it plunged seawards.

To hell with stand-by. I just needed to find my way down to our cabin and to sit there quietly for a while. At the back of my mind, I realised that the ship had turned into wind and increased speed to receive the Swordfish returning from their anti-submarine patrol and for Jimmy, the sole Wildcat pilot, to land on. I sat there trying to come to terms with the realisation that Basil had been killed and was gone. In those wartime days, the pace of life was such that a month was almost as a year normally would be, and our friendship had been formed eight months ago and sustained over a very long period therefore. Memories of all our good times together went through my mind. And sitting in that empty cabin, I wept for the loss of him and at the awful manner of his going.

A while later there was a tap on the cabin door and Jimmy came straight in. 'I know, as we all do in the Squadron, that you and Basil were very close friends. Although my formal report has been submitted at the de-briefing, I thought you might want to hear directly from me exactly what happened.' It was sensitive and kind of him because the proper pattern of behaviour on such occasions was to go on as normal, as if nothing so significant as the loss of a close friend had occurred.

He pretended not to notice my face with its unmanly tears and spoke about the attack. 'When Basil and I started our attack together, the Condor pilot opted to turn to port, towards Basil, as he dived down trying to get away from us, thus forcing Basil to aileron round and down after him and making himself particularly vulnerable to the cannon fire from their top turret. Leaving me with the opportunity and advantage of getting up close and to fire right up the arse of the thing. As I was closing, Basil was diving and firing and taking the brunt of the cannon and machine-gun fire from the German gunners. He did a fine and courageous job. He enabled me to make the kill.'

I could see in my mind, as Jimmy described it, exactly how in less than a minute of violent action two aircraft had been shot out of the sky and nine men had been killed, there being a crew of eight in the Condor, none of whom had got out either.

I thanked Jimmy for coming to see me. 'Now Hank,' he said, 'be reminded that you and Jack have the patrol this afternoon and it is time for you to sink a couple of gins, if that is what you need, and to get something to eat.' He was quite right, of course, I must show the courage and stoicism to act as other aircrew in similar circumstances always have to do. Moreover, it would do me no good to sit moping in the cabin. I was glad too that I would be airborne without delay. Flying from a Carrier concentrated the mind wonderfully and left little room for morbid thoughts. I washed my face and went along to the wardroom bar where I was greeted by my friends and I drank a couple of pink gins with them as we talked quietly about the events of that morning.

The patrol later that afternoon was uneventful and, after landing, I returned to my cabin. The steward was waiting for me so I asked him to find Basil's two small suitcases and to bring them to me in the cabin. I had decided to have a couple of whiskies in the bar, an early dinner and then to set about the grim task of packing up Basil's uniform and going through his papers, letters and any personal things before having them sent on to his father and mother. Knowing him as well as I did, I considered it very unlikely that I would find anything in his correspondence which could upset his parents. He had a girlfriend, a girl he had known since schooldays who lived close to his home. He had told me about her and of his intention for them to get married when the war was over. I had the impression that their relationship was no great raging romance for either of them but, on the other hand, Basil had held strong views about the importance of marriage and family life. Unusual views for a young man of his age, it had seemed to me, but at least he had made me think about such things.

I sat down at the small desk to write a personal letter to his parents, telling them of our long friendship and how much it had meant to me. Jimmy as his Commanding Officer, I knew, would be writing more formally and he would no doubt tell them of Basil's courage in action. I put all his personal clothes; underpants, vests, socks and shirts into a laundry bag, sent for the steward and told him to dispose of them. Then I went to the Wardroom bar and got drunk. On return to the cabin, after undressing, I started to climb shakily up to my top bunk, with memories of Basil with his hand on my bottom shoving me up there .... then I thought 'no', I wanted to be in his lower bunk, even using his sheets and pillow. I lay face down in his bunk and cried as the full realisation that he was dead and gone forever, hit me.

That was the Squadron's last voyage in that Carrier. We were due to fly ashore to Donibristle in Scotland and the expectation was that we would go on two weeks leave from there. There was an expectation also that we would have more new pilots and Wildcats and, as a larger Squadron, join a Fleet Carrier. It was the autumn of 1943.

CHAPTER SEVEN

Ashore and on Leave

On a bitterly cold day in November, our small Squadron of seven Wildcats flew off from our Escort Carrier to proceed direct to Donibristle, an aerodrome not far north of Edinburgh. We didn't do much of a display over the ship on leaving it; the weather was most unpleasant with low cloud and we were all anxious to get to Donibristle where we hoped a signal would be awaiting us confirming an immediate two weeks' leave. Also, although very cheerful with the prospect of leave, we were all hung over from a farewell party the previous evening while the ship was making her way towards Gourock.

Donibristle was a small aerodrome with a single short runway, no control tower and without even a YG beacon as an approach aid. Because of the low cloud, Jimmy had briefed us to separate into two flights of four and of three to low fly in line astern along the Caledonian Canal to the east coast of Scotland. We arrived over Donibristle, admittedly in rather an ungainly heap, to find that this little aerodrome had an absurd pimple of a 200 ft hill at one end of its single short runway which, in that freezing weather, had black ice on it as an extra hazard. It was not an impressive arrival in the dark of a late winter evening but nothing, not even some of us sliding on the ice off the runway, could spoil our cheerful mood.

Transport was waiting to take us to comfortable cabins near to the Wardroom where we met five new pilots who had been awaiting our arrival during the previous two days. Jimmy Sleigh called us into an ante-room to tell what he knew of our immediate future. First of all he confirmed that we could take leave as from the following morning and unofficially he advised the six of us from the ship to go early before the Customs Officers descended on us to claim their dues on the few 'goodies', silk stockings, watches, etc which we had purchased in New York. It would be nice to be one up on the Customs men, who had to be notified whenever we flew ashore and were merciless in extracting every penny of duty on any purchases we had made in America. Such 'goodies' were packed, together with our clothes, in parachute bags which fitted snugly in the fuselage behind the cockpit. While we were away on leave, five new Wildcats would be flown in to Donibristle to bring the squadron up to a strength of twelve. Jimmy's expectation was that the squadron would be appointed to a Fleet Carrier after a period of four weeks of flying at Donibristle to work-up and integrate the new pilots.

By this time the bar was open in the Wardroom and, other than Jimmy who had paperwork to do, we all moved in there looking forward to meeting each other; the new pilots being keen to find out about the Squadron and what it had been doing and we, the original members, anxious to meet, talk and find out about the new boys. All five of them had been trained at Pensacola in America and had amassed many more flying hours at the end of their training than we had at the same stage. Since their return to the UK, they had all completed deck-landings. They appeared as typical young Englishmen, no Colonials amongst them, and keen to talk flying. One of the five stood out as being rather different from the others; a tall, slim but well-built man, probably a year or two older than the others, having black hair swept back and rather too long and with a very white skin. His name was Johnnie Lowder and he affected a languid manner accentuated by smoking expensive Balkan Sobranie cigarettes through a black holder.

Instead of standing up around the bar with us, Johnnie lay back in one of the armchairs and listened to our talk which, at first, was about the slightly awkward flight we had made in unpleasant weather from the ship and our ungainly arrival at Donibristle. In a brief lull in the animated conversations, Johnnie spoke from his chair, 'I thought your squadron landings were an utter shambles,' he said. 'More like a flock of ugly ducklings fluttering down and skidding all over the place on a bit of ice. Very disappointing,' he added. He spoke in a public school accent and with a slight stammer.

There was a stunned silence. We all turned to look at him. The other four new boys rather shocked but we, of the Squadron, in fury that some damn sprog pilot should dare to criticise experienced operational pilots such as ourselves.

Winnie moved away from the bar, his face red with anger and fists clenching but Dagwood moved quietly in front and stood over Johnnie and introduced himself as the Senior Pilot of the Squadron.

He asked Johnnie politely to describe publicly to all of us the exact extent of his service and flying experience.

We waited. Johnnie's white mask-like face creased into a delightful smile and he said,

'Experience? Other than flying training – absolutely none; especially compared with you chaps whose Carrier experience I envy so much. All the more reason for my disappointment; I had so hoped and expected you to put on a good show.

'As for my service, I started by joining the Marines and transferred to the FAA when they asked for applicants. But I just had time to win the Marine's light heavyweight boxing championship before I left, if you would count such nonsense as service experience.' I noticed that he said this with a glance at Winnie who was still red-faced with anger.

All this was said with his occasional stammer, which he controlled by an intake of breath at the start of each sentence, but with his eyes crinkled up with amusement and accompanied with a most friendly smile. We had to smile with him, stand him up and insist he join us at the bar where he proceeded to put away a vast quantity of gin during the ensuing party. We were to find in the months to come that Johnnie was an entirely fearless pilot, a wild character quite unlike the smooth exterior which he affected and, so like Winnie, he just loved a fight. I had noticed the glance Johnnie had given Winnie when he spoke about his boxing championship. It occurred to me then that these two strong young men, although so different in appearance, manner and background, were extraordinarily alike in their impetuous characters. I wondered how they would get on together.

Before I had too much to drink that first evening at Donibristle, I telephoned my Mother to tell her I was back and coming on leave in four days time. I felt guilty about the delay because I knew how much she and her companion dear Maddie longed to see me. But, truth to tell, I badly wanted a bit of life and excitement before settling down to a quiet leave at home. My plan was to visit Rosa Lewis at her Cavendish Hotel where, provided she could find a bed for me, I could be sure of meeting new exciting people and of enjoying four days in London's west end with its restaurants, dinner-dances and night clubs all of which were going great guns in those wartime days. Rosa Lewis had long been a famous personality in London; having made her name in the Edwardian period as one of the best and most famous cooks of that time before, as the story goes, she was gifted the Cavendish Hotel by Edward VII for services rendered.

In the Second World War Rosa did exactly as she had done in that even more dreadful First World War, she did her best to see that the young fighting Officers, who came to her hotel, had a good time and thoroughly enjoyed the period of their leave in London. If they could not afford the bills when they were presented during or at the end of their happy visit, then 'Put a bit on old So and So's bill,' she would say to Edith, (her long term companion and hotel manager). 'He can afford it.' Usually I had plenty of money at the start of my leave but I should blush now to write that twice, when due to depart the Cavendish, I had to admit that I was broke. 'That nice American Colonel will be glad to help out I expect,' Rosa said as she passed my bill to Edith for her to transfer the amount to the Colonel's. 'But you will 'ave to do better next time, 'Enery.' Although Rosa could talk 'posh' if she wanted to, she enjoyed reverting to her original cockney speech, which she would normally use.

The Cavendish wasn't the type of hotel to take advance bookings. It always seemed to be full anyway. The thing to do was to turn up at the start of a leave and just beg Rosa for a room. If you were lucky, she might remember or think of you as one of her favourites and if so she would turn to Edith and say, 'We can fit young 'Enery in a room somewhere can't we?' Luckily for me, Edith so far had managed to do so. Well, more or less, because on two occasions I came back in the early hours of the morning to find my room already occupied. The bedrooms at the Cavendish were all large, beautifully furnished and all of them were provided with huge double beds, I don't think that there was any such thing as the modern 'twin bedded' room. The first occasion, as I came in, I switched on the light and there was a kind of squeak from the bed and there was this quite small young man, sitting up in my bed, naked, black hair standing up on end, his mouth wide open in shock at his sudden awakening and looking like a startled prawn. 'This is my room,' I snarled unpleasantly and rather drunk, 'Get out of my bed!' Well, of course, I should have realised straight away; Edith with Rosa's approval often had to double-book a couple of young chaps if she was to provide them with the accommodation which they desired so much at the Cavendish. She never hesitated to put them in together to share one of the huge beds.

The startled prawn turned out to be a Subaltern in a famous regiment, his name was Tim and we settled down comfortably enough for a good night's sleep in the bed. He was a pleasant young chap and I liked him but he left the next day. I told Rosa that I hoped I hadn't frightened him off but she said that he had only wanted a bed for the one night anyway. She added with an air of great satisfaction that he came from 'one of the very highest families in the land' which meant nothing to me but I looked suitably impressed for Rosa's sake. I said, 'Next time if you have to double me up, could you make it happen with a pretty girl rather than a chap?' Rosa was really severe with me. 'I would never do that sort of thing; if you want a girl, you go and find your own girls young 'Enery, you cheeky boy!' All too evidently, I had misunderstood the rules of Rosa's house and I apologised humbly.

After I had booked in having travelled from Donibristle, I joined a cheerful group of young officers and women in the main public room, all drinking champagne and chattering. I spoke to a good-looking dark girl. She was Eva, a young widow whose husband, a Flight Lieutenant, had been killed flying Hurricanes. I spent three hectic days with her in London, usually dining and dancing at Quaglinos or the Berkeley every evening and on to a night club afterwards. Eva lived in a little flat in Ebury Street which in those days she had been able to rent quite cheaply. I spent one night with her there but sex didn't really work out well between us; she had not recovered from the loss of her husband and I felt myself to be a very inadequate replacement, even on a casual basis. It wasn't all that important because we enjoyed going out together and we made a good pair at the various parties we attended; it was what she needed to help her through a very bad period and it was good for me too.

After paying an absurdly small bill, probably because Rosa out of habit as well as kindness had hived some of it off on to someone else, I said goodbye to her and Edith and left the Cavendish to return home to Taplow. I had enough money remaining to pop round the corner into Fortnum's before I left London to buy a wartime hamper of very expensive goodies to take home. There followed for me a quiet and very pleasant holiday with my Mother and Maddie; I had sufficient petrol coupons for us to visit friends, to see two or three good films and I enjoyed walking to my local pubs where, wearing civvies, I could feel part of normal life. I realised belatedly that this tranquillity was really what I needed rather than the hectic hubbub of people and parties at the Cavendish, or anywhere else for that matter.

Although London in wartime was always the most exciting place to be on leave, I had enjoyed some other 'runs ashore', as we termed a few days' leave, when the ship had been in harbour in New York or Halifax, for example. But I had once suffered a disconcerting experience during the summer in New York when I had met a pretty

American girl at one of the dances organised where I was staying at the Brabazon–Plaza Hotel. It was at a time when I was still very anxious to prove myself as attractive to women. My last effort had been at the hotel in Teignmouth with the randy young Wren who had quite frightened me off my stroke with the intensity and dominance of her sexual drive.

So I was full of new hope when this nice American girl invited me to her apartment, having arranged for the friend who shared it with her, to be out for the evening. Being a hot summer in New York, I was wearing my No.10 uniform which is white, very smart having gold buttons all the way up the jacket to the stiff round collar with epaulettes to show my rank as a Sub Lieutenant. I had bought this uniform from Gieves who seemed to have made it of shark skin, it was so thick and stiff. It had trouser creases like knife edges, including up the middle so that it felt as if my bottom was being cut in half whenever I sat down; particularly as the trousers were so made that they could only be held up high enough by taut braces. The pretty girl was lying back on the bed, waiting for me, in just her pants, looking absolutely desirable. I felt myself entirely ready to respond handsomely but, as I finally undid all the buttons and struggled free of that shark-like jacket, I was revealed in my vest with trousers held high up above my waist by those bright red braces. I must have looked like a half-peeled shrimp.

There was a great squeal of laughter from the girl. 'Oh my Gawd,' she hooted, 'He's wearing Surrspenders!' In the face of that laughter, all of me just collapsed completely. All I could do was to put the jacket back on and leave her.

The next day I bought a uniform from the US Navy stores; it looked much the same but it was of soft material, the trousers were designed to be held up by a belt and it was not only comfortable where it mattered, but smarter. Too late!

But back to the end of that last leave, on my journey back from my home in Taplow to Donibristle, the train from London to Edinburgh was crowded almost entirely with servicemen but I managed to get a seat in the first class and settled down hoping for a solitary journey; I wasn't in the mood for chat. I had enjoyed a good leave, firstly with all the fun and excitement at the Cavendish and then the quiet pleasure of life at home with Mother. Now as I sat in the train I was a bit low, rather as I had been when a fifteen year-old boy going back for the term to the dreaded Harrow.

Comfortable with plenty of room in my corner seat of the compartment by the window, I began to think about life immediately ahead of me and cheered up as I realised that there were all sorts of excitements and interests in store. Assuming that the Admiralty might keep to its plans for the Squadron, there would be some weeks at Donibristle flying with the new pilots and then the prospect of joining a Fleet Carrier in which life might be different, in all sorts of interesting ways, from that in an Escort Carrier. And so I looked up and around at my fellow passengers in the compartment and became aware for the first time of the ferocious glare directed at me from an RN Commander. He was seated squashed in the middle of the opposite seat and seemed to expect me, horrible little junior RNVR Subbie with wings that I was, to offer him my comfortable corner seat by the window. I smiled sweetly at him and felt better.

On getting out at Edinburgh station, I found that a whole group of our Squadron ratings had been on the train also returning from leave. Some of them called out cheerily to me asking 'Had a good leave, Sir?' I went over to them to ask about their leave and fortunately, as I approached them, they all saluted me very properly. Had they not done so, that boot-faced Commander, who had been watching us, would doubtless have expressed to me in strong words the disapproval his face so clearly showed at my familiarity with the sailors. It must have been difficult, I suppose, for officers of his Dartmouth background to understand our Fleet Air Arm style of relationship with the ratings who maintained our aircraft and who looked upon us, their pilots, as their personal responsibility. They worked hard to ensure our safety. You don't ignore men such as those. It was a bit of luck seeing my squadron people because, of course, the squadron Chief Petty Officer, Carey, had been busy on their behalf and had organised a three-ton lorry to collect them and take them to Donibristle. He told me that he had reserved a seat for me in the front cab with him and the driver, which of course he hadn't since he could not have known I would be there, but it was his nice way of expressing his pleasure at being able to give me a lift. I was glad to be back with my Squadron and my earlier depression lifted as I looked forward to joining fellow pilots in the Wardroom.

There were some changes. Dagwood Cosh, who had been our Senior Pilot since the squadron had formed, had been appointed as Commanding Officer of another Wildcat squadron elsewhere. We would miss him as a good leader but also for the fun and friendliness of his character. The very sad news was that one of the new young pilots, who had returned two days early from his leave in his keenness to fly, had stalled and spun in on his approach to the runway. We, the old boys of the squadron, felt some guilt because we had been emphasising the advantages of deck-landing off a reasonably steep turn on the final approach and maybe he had been trying to do this on his last flight. This may have been the cause of the boy's misjudgement and consequent death.

Later in the week the two replacements arrived, one of whom was another New Zealander. In the meantime, much to the approval of everyone, Jack Parli had been appointed as the new Senior Pilot. I was particularly glad that, instead of being made a section leader, I would continue to fly with him as his number two. Had I no ambition then you might ask? Yes; to stay alive by flying with Jack was the extent of my ambition.

Donibristle was a lousy little aerodrome as such but what a thoroughly pleasant Station it was at which to work-up the squadron again with its new pilots. It was a comfortable Station for all of us, including our squadron sailors, and Edinburgh with all its pubs and restaurants was less than an hour away. Best of all was our local pub, the Star at the village of Aberdour only three miles along the road with a landlord quite willing to stay open until all hours and with the local village policeman equally willing for him to do so.

I telephoned Phoebe, my sister, who was sharing a flat with another widow at Arbroath where they both continued to share in the life of the RN Air Station there. I suggested that she might like to come down to Donibristle and stay at the Star for a few days before my squadron was due to leave for another Carrier. She didn't hesitate and the following day she arrived and settled into the pub. We had seen little of each other over the past three years and it was a happy opportunity for us to talk. She had suffered a very bad time with the loss of Ward, her husband who had been killed in 1941, followed by the death of her fiancé, Pat Humphreys, who had been killed a year later. Both were Observers in the Fleet Air Arm. Anyway, now it was party time for her with me and my squadron chums at Donibristle. And party we did, in the Wardroom, at restaurants in Edinburgh, at parties of highland dancing in some of the local large houses but mostly at the Star where we would drink sometimes until the early hours of the morning.

We did some flying each day too because we had the new pilots to integrate into our squadron ways and also we all had to keep in flying practice. It so happened one morning that Winnie and I were left behind while the others were airborne. 'Come on Hank,' said Winnie, 'I challenge you to a dog-fight.' Whilst recognising that Winnie was a damn good pilot, I reckoned that my flying was smoother than his and that I would be able to steep turn inside him any day and so, laughing, I shouted back, 'Yes, and let's put a quid on it.' We didn't bother to have gun-cameras fitted; we would know who won all right because, whoever had the other in his gunsight, would make a Drrrr noise over the R/T in imitation of our machine guns firing.

Not long after we had broken away from each other at 10,000 feet, I was flying craftily along close under a bank of cloud, quite sure that I would find Winnie just ahead of me round the edge of the cloud, when I heard the wretched noise of Winnie blowing 'Drrrr' into my earphones followed by his chuckled 'Gotcha Hank'. But on the second sortie, I had him in my sights briefly but he saw me and dived and turned madly vertically in typical Winnie split-ass fashion. I followed but he was getting away from me so I was inspired to shout, 'Pocker, Pocker, Pocker' into my mike and 'Gotcha!' 'Don't be daft,' called Winnie, 'you are out of range.' I replied, 'Oh no I'm not. My 'pocker' noise means that I am using cannon and you are well within its range and dead.'

And so it is that my sole claim to any distinction throughout the war is that I invented the word 'pocker'. It came to be used frequently in the FAA for expressions such as 'Go away you Pocker!'. It sometimes caused misunderstandings though and the word has fallen out of use.

Johnnie Lowder appeared entranced with Phoebe, who at age about twenty-six then and despite all the sadness in her life, was still a very attractive woman. They hit it off together immediately. In many ways their characters were similar; Johnnie had a boisterous, careless attitude to life, which matched Phoebe's feelings at that time. He was exactly the type of young man to attract Phoebe. And so, although the time had come for Phoebe to return to Arbroath, I had the feeling that these two would arrange to meet again in the future.

A few days later the signal came for the squadron to prepare to embark in HMS *Illustrious* which was at anchor lying off Gourock. The CO, having made the necessary travel arrangements, gave our Air Engineer Officer and CPO Carey the task of getting the troops on board. We, the pilots, would have to wait a day or two before flying our Wildcats across Scotland for the landing on *Illustrious*. That evening we were all feeling excited at the prospect of joining that famous Fleet Carrier, but rather irritated at the delay and having to wait about before we could do so. None of us went ashore and the evening was spent drinking rather too much as we discussed the prospects for the future and speculated about where the Carrier would be sent and what sort of action we could expect.

At the end of the evening, after the bar had closed, I was sitting in a comfortable armchair in front of the dying log fire, somewhat befuddled with whisky, and quite content to stay there for the night, rather than rouse myself to walk a few hundred yards to where our cabins were located. The others were moving out of the wardroom, when Winnie came back and pulled me out of the chair saying, 'Come on Hank, you can't sleep here, it will be damn cold soon'. But Johnnie stood in his way and started to argue belligerently that it was my decision if I wanted to remain there and he, Winnie, should mind his own damn business. They confronted each other with fists clenched ready to fight. The aggression which had been building up between them since that first evening had reached boiling point. Jack came back into the room and saw the situation; one which we had all been expecting. 'You can't fight here,' he said, 'you better both go up to the cabin block and get it out of your systems there.'

And so this inevitable fight, which we had all been silently dreading, took place in the building of our cabin block. There was a long corridor, about four feet wide, with the doorways of our cabins running down the length of it on either side. We watched from our doorways as each of these two men, marched solemnly to their respective end of the long corridor, stripped their shirts off and turned to face each other; Winnie glaring with red faced anger and Johnnie his grim white face like a mask.

Without any particular signal being given, they started to run full tilt at each other and they met in the middle with fists flying. Johnnie was punching fast with his fists going like pistons towards Winnie's face. But many of the punches were being muffled by Winnie's strong left arm while, with his right, Winnie was swinging great haymaking blows into Johnnie's ribs and stomach. Although both men were big, Winnie was the heavier and Johnnie was having to give ground to the onslaught of the hammer blows to his body and, as he gave ground though still punching fast, so Winnie changed his tactics and began to aim blows to Johnnie's face. With a shout, Winnie then launched himself at Johnnie and crashed him down on to his back on the ground where, with his weight, he was able to hold him down. Finally, he had Johnnie by the throat, holding him firmly down with all the strength in his left arm and the full weight of his body, while he drew back his right arm and fist ready to smash it into Johnnie's upturned face. Johnnie now helpless on his back, his white face streaked with blood, glared up at Winnie and, despite expecting to be bashed unconscious, yet he shouted, 'Get on with it then, you will have to finish me, get on with it you bastard!'

Winnie lowered his fist, got up, turned his back on his opponent lying on the ground and started to walk away to his cabin. He had a badly cut lip and was also bleeding slightly from the nose. Then he stopped, turned round again and extended his hand to Johnnie lying on the ground still. 'Come on chum,' he said, 'We're in the same squadron together, fighting the same bloody war, let's forget it, and anyway you shouldn't be taking on big bastards like me.' Johnnie accepted Winnie's hand to help himself up and without further talk they each went to their cabins.

Jack Parli, to whom this sort of affair was fairly commonplace, had positioned himself during the fight to interfere if necessary had things become really rough in his judgement. He now murmured, 'Well that's over with at last, with blood and gore all over the floor and me without a spoon.' This ridiculous phrase of his, which we had all heard from him before, broke the tension and we all turned in for the night. I have always had a loathing of physical violence and this fight between two of my best friends had been particularly sickening. It has remained strongly in my memory for that reason. But the positive aspect of it, why I have told the story, is that those two young men became from then on the firmest of good friends. I know, don't tell me. It reads like a story from the 'Boy's Own' magazine; but it is true.

In the Pacific during 1945, they flew constantly together in a flight of four Corsairs led by Winnie with Johnnie as his section leader. They had just completed a strafing attack on a Japanese airfield at Sakashima and had started on their way back to the *Illustrious* without any casualties, when Winnie for some unaccountable reason took it into his head to break away from his flight, handing the leadership of it over to Johnnie, so that he could carry out a second attack on the airfield on his own. It was utter madness. It was contrary to all we had learned which was rarely to do two runs over an airfield and certainly never to attack it solo. Of course Winnie was killed; it was inevitable. Johnnie was seen to be in tears as he reported, after landing, that Winnie had been killed.

CHAPTER EIGHT

HMS *Illustrious*

At the ungodly hour of dawn, a time so beloved by the Royal Navy, we clambered into our Wildcats ready to fly in formation from Donibristle across Scotland to the sea off the Mull of Kintyre near where HMS *Illustrious* would be waiting for us to land on. Only the previous day, there had been a sudden flurry of signals reducing our Squadron once again to eight aircraft and pilots so that four of the new boys, who had so recently joined us, would have to remain at Donibristle to await early transfer to another Squadron. Johnnie Lowder, Mike Penhale the New Zealander and Ron Dugdale were the three who stayed with us.

It was a pleasant sunny day as Jimmy led our two flights of four to our rendezvous off the Scottish coast. From low over the sea as we lost height and circled her, the *Illustrious* looked large but also long, sleek and beautiful, so unlike the brick-like appearance of our previous Escort Carrier. I felt really thrilled at the prospect of joining her. Meantime, Jimmy had signalled each flight to move into echelon starboard prior to each individual approach and landing. We were all anxious to put on a good show as there would be many members of the ship's company watching critically as our Squadron landed on.

I was number six behind Jack and I was concentrating on judging how close behind him I could land without having to take a wave-off from the batsman and be sent round again. On my final approach, the very much longer, slightly wider flight deck plus the much larger 'Island' on the starboard side, all provided more sight of the ship so that I found it comparatively easy to line up for the actual landing. Out of the corner of my eye, I could see the batsman kind of cavorting about and waving his bats, but I was concentrating on the landing which I completed comfortably catching the third wire. I was surrounded immediately by the experienced deck handling party who swiftly disengaged the aircraft hook and signalled me on to taxi fast over the now collapsed crash barrier to the deck park in the bows. As I taxied forward, I could see a whole crowd of critical spectators or 'goofers' as we called them, lining the outer galleries of the Island. As for the DLCO (batsman), I hoped he would turn out to be a bit calmer and steadier as he came to know and recognise my style of landing approach.

After visiting the Ready room and finding a locker there for my flying kit, I found my way with the others down to the Wardroom. This was a very large, well-appointed room furnished with lots of tables and comfortable chairs; it had to accommodate a considerable number of officers and to provide a centre for their leisure and social hours. There was a long bar, normally with two stewards serving behind it and a Petty Officer steward was there to show us to our cabins. Opposite the Wardroom, he showed us the dining-room with its spotlessly white tablecloths on long mahogany tables sufficient to dine over one hundred officers.

Aft of these two main rooms, the steward led us along passages with officers' cabins on either side, down another deck where there were more cabins and the junior officers' heads and showers, then further down to another half-deck where we were shown the accommodation allocated to us. Here at the very stern of the ship and two decks below the Quarterdeck were six cabins, basically single ones, located just one deck above the huge revolving shafts driving the ship's propellers. Some of the cabins were already occupied by aircrew from another squadron. We were to become accustomed, to the turbine noise but were inevitably woken up by the vibration whenever the engine revolutions increased to give extra speed for aircraft operations. Our basically single cabins all contained a second bunk which could be lowered from the bulkhead and in addition a camp bed was provided so that three aircrew could be accommodated in each cabin. It was an exceedingly cramped arrangement, leaving very little room for our clothes. I shared with Johnnie and Mike and we took it in turns each week to use the camp bed. As there was no space to move about, whoever was sleeping in the camp bed had to get up first to use the small hand basin, shave and get out.

The extraordinary thing is that we aircrew accepted the situation. It never occurred to us to complain of the discomfort or lack of sleep. I think that we were overawed by the grandeur of the Royal Navy and its traditions. The ship's officers, in their larger double or single cabins on the decks above us, thought of the ship as their home and this apparently justified their occupation of the best accommodation. We were regarded as temporary members of the ship, which was unkind as we too were so proud to be serving in her. Amazingly, it never seemed to occur to people that the ship and its whole complement of fifteen hundred men existed for the sole purpose of enabling fifty-five aircrew to fly from the ship on operations against the enemy. We never reminded them of this fact because, surprisingly, the thought of it never occurred to us either. Although I did make this very point when, as a Senior Pilot in the year 1945, eight of my pilots were crammed into a small dormitory provided specifically for aircrew in the latest Admiralty design of Light Fleet Carrier. I dared to have a row with the Commander about their accommodation, but got nowhere.

Despite our disappointment with the cabins, we found the *Illustrious* to be a happy ship and it was a pleasure to serve in her. Most of the officers had remained from the previous year when the ship had played a major part in the Mediterranean convoys and had suffered much bomb damage in fighting her way through to Malta. They had justifiable pride and confidence in themselves as a result and we, as new aircrew in the ship, respected their experience. These officers, nearly all RN, suffered the presence of aircrews maybe not gladly but pleasantly enough and enjoyed watching, or joining in with, our hectic and drunken games in the Wardroom when in harbour. We were at that time very much of a new breed to them; being almost entirely RNVR, mostly from grammar schools and many of us from the Colonies. We lacked knowledge and experience of the Royal Navy and its procedures, but it should have been apparent how anxious we were to absorb its ways and traditions.

Among all the ship's officers, there were those who were particularly involved with our air operations from the ship. Firstly, the Captain, who was well liked by all the ship's company. He had never flown an aircraft, of course, but he had captained the *Illustrious* through the battles in the Mediterranean and had acquired some experience and knowledge of Carrier operations. But the first in our aircrew order of priority was 'Wings', the Commander Air in charge of all flying operations. He never found time to come ashore with us and to fly any of the types of aircraft under his command but we all assumed that he must have had much Carrier experience before he was appointed to such a vital aviation job. The ship's Commander was really the number two man in the ship second to the captain and he too affected our aircrew lives considerably. He would give aircrew horrible duties to do when in harbour, such as Officer of the Guard to control the men ashore or Officer of the Watch in harbour. But, if we made a mess of it, he was tolerant of our naval shortcomings.

The officers of particular importance in our lives were the four in Fighter Direction. The senior, an RNVR Lt Commander, was Michael Hordern. A charming man, quietly efficient at his war time job in the Navy but normally a superb actor who was later in life to receive his 'K' for services to the theatre. The other three, all RNVR, were also ex-members of the acting profession in their normal lives; Robert who was a very well known Shakespearean actor with a gorgeous fruity voice and the other two were delightfully amusing and more in the genre of comedy in their previous profession. They were great characters and did much to keep the ship's company happy by using the internal radio system to put on comic sketches and interviews with characters such as the Bosun's Mate, the Commander, a pilot, etc. It was an initiative which other ships in which I later served tried to follow but not with the same success. But the main thing as far as we were concerned was that, as a team of Aircraft Directors, they were first class.

The two DLCOs, Deck Landing Control Officers (batsmen), were an odd pair. The senior one was a Lt Cdr RN, no less, who had established himself as the doyen of the batsmen fraternity in the Air Arm. Before him, the signals by 'bats' to the aircraft coming in to land on to the deck had been done probably by one of the squadron pilots. But this man had foreseen a need to train pilots specifically for the job. All well and good, really, but what a to-do he made of it. He made a tremendous show of pirouetting and dancing about at the side of the flight deck while waving his bats about at the oncoming aircraft. Unlike the majority of the pilots, who paid little regard to his antics, he took himself very seriously indeed. The Barracuda pilots told me that he was much better during night landings, probably because signals had to be given slowly and positively for the pilot to interpret them. In later years, his ultimate pomposity was to insist that he have a Midshipman to carry the bats for him across the flight deck to his batting position! His colleague in *Illustrious*, also RN and inclined to take himself too seriously as a batsman, was nevertheless good at the important and difficult task of organising the constant movement and ranging of aircraft around the flight deck. Both of these DLCOs wore wings but I never saw them fly.

In my opinion the batsman as a deck-landing aid was over rated. His signals, under the RN system, were supposed to be imperative, i.e. if he raised the bats high, the pilot was being 'told' to go higher.

This was the opposite to the American system in which, with the bats held high, the pilot was being 'advised' that he was too high. However, to most pilots, the batsman served as a check that their approach was correct but they would not necessarily follow his signals if they were confident of their own judgement. The only signal from the batsman that I ever regarded as imperative and to be obeyed was the wave-off, otherwise I might land on the aircraft ahead of me. But the batsman could be a help to inexperienced and nervous pilots and, certainly, his signals were essential for deck-landings by any pilot at night. Unfortunately, it was rare for the batsman to have flown and deck-landed the type of aircraft he was batting which would have given the pilots so much more confidence in him.

The immediate programme for HMS *Illustrious* was to work up the four new Squadrons which had just joined her. For this, she would remain in the area near Greenock, generally off the little pimple island of Ailsa Craig, and anchor sometimes for the night in Lamlash. There were two Wildcat squadrons, the other one having twelve aircraft to our eight. There was a Seafire squadron of nine aircraft. As they were unable to fold their wings for hangar storage, five of them had to be shuffled around on the deck park while four were parked on outriggers aft of the Island. Then there was a Squadron of twelve of the new Barracuda, the first time these aircraft were to be used operationally.

The Seafire, which was a normal Spitfire with the attachment of a hook for deck-landing, was in reality entirely unsuitable for Carrier operations. The narrow track of the undercarriage, its fragility and that of the whole fuselage made the Seafire unable to cope with the constant stresses of Carrier landings. The big wooden propeller constantly shattered because it had too little deck clearance. The aircraft had a very limited range, no bomb load and, with the extra weight of the hook, was not all that much faster than the Wildcat and with lesser fire-power. The in-line engine, with scoop-type coolers under the wings, made a successful 'ditching' in the sea difficult. But also, although a beautiful machine just to fly, it was very difficult to deck-land because of its tendency to 'float' over the wires when the engine was cut. Over the years, in the process of operating from Carriers, the Seafire seriously hurt or killed many pilots. Yet there were a few pilots of above average ability who loved the thing, despite its many faults as a Carrier aircraft.

It is worth mentioning, relative to the Admiralty's love affair with the Seafire and their continuous use of it, that in 1941 while in New

York, I joined my squadron CO on a visit to the Grumman factory. One of the Directors told us that there was no limit to the number of Grumman aircraft quickly available under Lend Lease payment. But the Admiralty pressed on with ordering the Seafire; presumably for some good reason of their own, which has never been divulged.

The new Barracuda was made by Faireys and, in consequence of the Admiralty specification, was a monstrosity. It was a high-wing monoplane, which inevitably meant that the undercarriage, located in the wings either side of the fuselage, had to be strong and very long to reach the ground and thus of massive construction. The Rolls Royce engine was inadequate for the final size and weight of the aircraft and so, although it could stagger into the air with a comprehensive array of weaponry, it could not carry it very far. The Observer was placed in a bubble type canopy under the wing giving him visibility at both sides and limited sight downwards. It was also difficult for the poor chap to get out quickly in an emergency. For the pilots, dive-bombing was a problem when re-trimming the aircraft while pulling out of the steep dive. This manoeuvre and the re-trimming had to be done with great care to avoid pulling the wings off.

There were some good aspects of the design. The pilot was placed right on top and at the nose of the aircraft giving him superb visibility, especially for landing. Despite its rather menacing appearance, The Barracuda was nice and gentle to fly and easy to deck-land, as I was to find a couple of years later. But aircrew never liked it as an operational aircraft.

I was so thankful that, except for a short period in Hurricanes, I flew American aircraft from Carriers throughout the war. They were all superbly designed for the purpose of Carrier operations, including even the radial engines which, having no extruding coolers under the fuselage, gave the pilot a good chance of survival, if he had to ditch. The Hellcat, for example, which came into service about the same time as The Barracuda was basically a fast fighter aircraft with heavy fire power, yet it could not only carry as big a bomb and weaponry load as the Barracuda but take it twice as fast and twice as far. The American Corsair fighter was equally good; I believe that either of these superb fighter aircraft could have been made available under Lend Lease at that time in 1943, in place of the Seafire. But Admiralty seemed besotted with using the Seafire.

I have described the ship, the officers and the aircraft. The next three weeks were to be spent sailing up and down that area off the Scottish coast to work them all up into a competent fighting unit. Each day and sometimes at night, there were flying exercises. Full ranges on the flight deck of up to thirty aircraft with engines running ready to take-off, catapult launches, strafing and formation exercises for the fighters, dive-bombing and night flying for the bombers, constant deck-landings all day. A busy time and not without its quota of accidents, particularly for the Seafires with shattered propellers and write-offs from hitting the barrier. Fortunately, the pilots were unharmed. Two Wildcats were written off too, one stalled and slewed off to starboard wrecking two Seafires parked on outriggers, the other caught the top of the barrier trying to go round again from a bad approach and ended upside down on the deck park. The pilot, not in my squadron, wouldn't be able to fly again. A Barracuda hit the stern of the deck (the round-down) on a night landing and fell into the sea. It was not possible to recover any of the crew.

At the end of two weeks, the ship anchored off Greenock for some days to take in stores. It had been a bad and sad start to a new commission for the ship. Everybody had been reminded or had learned, if they hadn't known it before, that continuous deck operations under pressure, even in a large Carrier, are always going to be difficult and dangerous.

Meantime some pilots were sent ashore to pick up replacement aircraft, particularly Seafires, to fly them on board when the ship would leave harbour. In the absence of anything exciting happening ashore in Greenock, I found it preferable to remain on board to enjoy the comforts of the Wardroom and its bar, talking flying and chatting with fellow squadron mates and making friends with the ship's officers. There were plenty of duties to keep us occupied on board in a new ship, including the harbour duties inevitably given to aircrew, such as Officer of the Watch.

A Dining-In night was held and it was my first experience of such an occasion. All officers had to attend, unless on duty, and I wore my 'bum-freezer' dress uniform for the first time. I had only just bought it as one of the effects (as they say) of the pilot who had been killed in the recent Barracuda accident. It may seem grisly now as I write it, but it's no good being silly; I needed the uniform and the parents had preferred not to have it sent to them. I had only met him once briefly round the bar and he must have been smaller than I thought, as the uniform was a bit of a tight fit.

The dining-room really was a magnificent sight for the occasion with all the officers present and seated at spotless linen covered tables groaning with silver candelabra and trophies. Stewards, also wearing their best square rig uniforms, were standing behind the chairs of every three officers. The whole affair was conducted faultlessly by the Commander, as President, assisted and organised with the utmost efficiency by the Chief Petty Officer of the Wardroom who remained in the background quietly hissing orders to his stewards. The 'Chief' of the wardroom was a most important character; he received a budget based I believe on 1/6d per day per officer plus much the same additional sum taken from our Mess bills. With this budget he was responsible for all our catering. It involved his negotiating in every harbour, particularly in foreign countries, with local tradesmen. A good Chief was worth his weight in gold. Indeed, that could well have been his true worth. I remember decommissioning in my last ship after two years abroad to see the Chief drive away from the quayside in a not all that elderly Rolls.

For a Dining-in night, guests could be invited from other ships in harbour so that the tables were all filled with about a hundred officers. Masses of drink would be taken in the bar first, followed by very good wines during the dinner ending with the port circulating at the end of the meal. The most junior officer would toast 'the King' which in Royal Navy tradition was given sitting down. The President would give a brief speech followed maybe by a senior guest. The whole thing was very formal and new to most of us and we all loved it; particularly our colonial colleagues in the squadrons. After dinner everybody went traditionally mad as we played violent physical games in the Wardroom. The naval grandeur of the occasion was spoilt for me to some extent as it was my turn for the camp bed. Trying to erect the damn thing in my drunken state and in the confined space of the single cabin with two other chaps reeling about in it was a disaster. I gave up and went to sleep on the deck (floor) in what was left of my bum-freezer uniform. How fortunate that I had bought it second-hand. So ended my first Dining-in night.

Two days later, HMS *Illustrious* left the harbour at Greenock accompanied by a Destroyer and sailed over the top and around into Scapa Flow which was filled with ships of the Royal Navy, alongside masses of merchant shipping. And there was one large Battlewagon of the US Navy anchored in the harbour too at the time. I had never been to Scapa before and, once I had been ashore, hoped not to do so again. What a dreary place it was as a base for thousands of sailors. I remember large canteen sheds there to provide beer for the sailors and acres of playing fields for football and rugby.

As 'A' for Adlam, I got caught again as the very first aircrew Sub Lieutenant to be put on the awesome duty in charge of the Guard ashore. The essence of it was to keep control of the heaving mass of sailors on the quayside as, after copious pints of beer in the canteens, they struggled to board the tenders which would take them across the harbour back to their respective ships. To make matters much worse, our sailors began to fight on the quay with the American boys who were aiming to get back to their Battlewagon.

Fatuously standing there wearing gaiters, with my guard of eight sailors and a Chief Petty Officer around me, all similarly gaited and each armed with a sort of cudgel, I assumed that I must somehow stop the fighting. I started to utter an order to them to move forward, in a voice squeaky with anxiety and fright, when the Chief stopped me in time. 'Don't,' he said, 'Don't even think about it Sir. If we get into the middle of that lot, one of the sailors will surely take a swing at you and we would have to take him to jail. Now you just rest here easy, Sir, with a couple of the lads and leave it to me.' Then he moved with six of his chaps quietly round the outskirts of the shouting, fighting sailors, picked on a couple of the most vociferous and arrested them. The word went round immediately. 'The bloody Provos are arresting people.' The fighting stopped. The Chief, with me walking along with him, established control. An hour later everyone was back in their ships and I was in the bar sinking a huge pink gin. As I sank my gin, I thought how damn stupid it had been of the Commander to send such an inexperienced naval officer as me out on such a task. I would have been in deep trouble without the Chief Petty Officer. And then I realised that the Commander had to send an officer in charge of the guard according to regulations, but he knew that he could rely on the CPO to keep me right.

During the next three days in harbour, a convoy was assembled around us and made ready for passage to Murmansk, the Russian port. The convoy, with its normal escorts of frigates and corvettes, left harbour early in the morning and some four hours later we followed accompanied by a Battlewagon, two Cruisers and four Destroyers; we were a formidable small fleet in fact. The intention, according to our briefing was for our fleet to sail separately but some twenty miles out of sight from the Convoy. From there our fighters would provide air cover for the convoy as well as for the fleet and the Barracudas would join with the escorting ships of the convoy in their anti-submarine operations. There was also the hope of inducing some ships of the German Navy out of their harbours in Norway in pursuit of what they might think to be an inadequately protected convoy. The third aim, we were told, was to act as a diversion to engage the attention of the Germans away from the Allied landings in Sicily.

The weather during those first days was not too bad with scattered layers of cloud at medium and high level. The sea, cold and grey, looked to be quite rough but it caused little movement on the flight deck of a Carrier this size. Flights of four Wildcats were flown off on Combat Air Patrol every two hours during daylight to cover the convoy and the Fleet. The patrols were limited to the two-hour duration to retain sufficient fuel at the end of the patrol in case combat action became necessary; my experience of some six months earlier when I had been forced to ditch out of fuel, proved the point. The Seafires could only patrol for an hour with their limited endurance and so were rarely used for this purpose. Sometimes patrols of Wildcats or Barracudas were launched by catapult, instead of ranging them for normal take-off, but the minimal propeller to deck clearance of the Seafire made it unsuitable for catapult launching.

There was excitement on the morning of the second day when the first bandit appeared on the radar screen. It was a small blip, assessed by its slow movement across the screen, to be a BV138 German flying boat. Four Wildcats of the other squadron were on patrol and two of them were despatched to find and attack the BV 138 while two circled awaiting further instructions or vectors from the ship's Fighter Director Control. It was essential to prevent the enemy aircraft from sighting our separate fleet, which we were so anxious to keep as a secret force. Our CO and his flight were at stand-by in their cockpits with engines warmed, ready for immediate take-off, just in case of an attack by bombers.

Those of us in the crew-room had heard the ship's Tannoy announcing the presence of an enemy aircraft and we made our way quickly up to the Goofers' gallery where we might see what was going on and could watch for the return of the Wildcats. A short while later, the Captain announced to the ship's company that the enemy aircraft had been shot down. It was a good start to the operation provided the enemy aircraft had been hit before sighting and reporting upon our 'secret' fleet or the convoy. The next few hours would tell whether the German crew had been able to send a message back to their base.

At gin time before lunch, we crowded round the two pilots who had landed from their successful attack on the German Flying boat. None of us so far had any experience of this type of enemy aircraft and we were keen to learn as much as possible about it and the best method of attacking it. Naturally enough, the two pilots who had been successful in knocking down the enemy aircraft enjoyed telling their story, but rather excitedly and not too clearly to us round the bar although, of course, they had given a proper factual account earlier at their formal de-briefing. Jack Parli signalled to me, Cliff Nell and Mike Penhale, the members of his flight, to join him in a quiet corner of the Wardroom where he discussed with us how best to attack the BV 138 from what we had learned.

Being a flying boat it was slow, but it had a formidable armament of two turrets of 20 MM cannons, one at each end of the top fuselage and one machine gun turret located between them. The rear Cannon turret could fire downwards and backwards below the tail boom. It was an unusual aircraft in its design having three engines, two being located in the wings with a third larger engine on top of the main hull. The tail unit was at the rear of two twin booms. Jack pointed out that, contrary to our previous experience with the FW Condor, we would have the big advantage of greater speed over the BV 138; we wouldn't have to be tail chasing the thing round the sky. He reckoned that our speed would enable us to make frontal attacks and that its vulnerable area was underneath particularly at the bow of the hull which appeared to be unprotected.

We had been briefed that the BV 138 with its long range and its excellent search radar had proved to be very successful from the German point of view in finding our convoys in the Arctic and Bay of Biscay. The trick was to get at it before its radar could spot the convoy and, on that day, it seemed that Mike Hordern and his Fighter Direction team had done well in launching the Wildcats at the BV 138 in time before it had come near the convoy. More of this sort of action could be expected because it was known that the Germans had produced this Flying Boat in large numbers and seemed to regard them as expendable.

The next morning all four of us in red Flight were in our cockpits ready to take off on patrol as soon as it was daylight. At the pre-flight briefing we had been told that the weather, which so far had been quite good, was deteriorating and I wasn't too sure what that would mean in this Arctic area, which was new to me. In this month of July, it was not so exceptionally cold as I had expected and I presumed the weather would be much the same as the Atlantic had been. I hated this sort of thing; waiting in the cockpit to start up before taking-off into a dark sky and unable to see what the conditions were like. Truth to tell, I had become more worried about weather conditions than anything else in flying. I was keen to have another bang at the enemy, that didn't worry me, neither did flying operations from a Carrier cause me any concern, especially not from this large Fleet Carrier. But I had suffered a few unpleasant experiences with bad weather in the Atlantic and was a bit twitched about it. Moreover, flying operationally over a sea known to be freezing cold was an unpleasant thought; there would be no likelihood of surviving from a ditching. Sitting in the cockpit like this, waiting, was conducive to what I thought of as the premonitions syndrome to which I had become prone in the previous Carrier. 'This is the flight which is going to be my last one.' Such would be my thoughts as I climbed into the cockpit. Fortunately, they were usually dismissed from my mind as soon as I lined up down the flight deck and opened the throttle for take-off.

Came the call from Wings over the Tannoy, 'Start up engines.' They had been warmed up earlier and so, as the great ship increased speed and heeled over to begin her turn into wind, four Wildcats and two Barracudas were ready to take off. Dawn had just about crept up into the sky and I could begin to see an overall cloud cover at about six thousand feet; not too bad weather conditions after all. When airborne, the three of us in Jack's flight caught up with him and moved into a comfortable 'finger' formation to commence our patrol. Under instruction from the Fighter Control room, we kept just under the cloud base and in position between the Fleet and the convoy. So we settled down to the usual boring two-hour patrol, sitting on the hard and uncomfortable seat of the combined dinghy pack and parachute. Maybe we would have a bit of luck in that there would be a Bandit to attack. Neither should we dismiss the possibility of a bombing or torpedo attack by Junkers 88s, in case the BV 138 yesterday had radioed a report of our presence before it was shot down. So we were very alert in spite of the boredom of patrol.

Suddenly the voice of Michael Hordern on the R/T, 'Hello Red One, this is Mother. I have a bandit for you at angels eight, vector 120, repeat vector 120 and buster he is moving towards the convoy.' 'Roger,' from Jack, 'Red Flight turning on vector 120 now.' As we turned, so we moved into two separate sections with Cliff Nell as Red Three leading Mike Penhale but following astern of Jack and me. Fighter Control estimated the bandit, which they assessed to be a single aircraft and probably a BV 138, to be about thirty-five miles away. They gave us continuous vector alterations to cut across its path. Jack was taking us below the cloud base at 5,000 ft but, after some ten minutes by which time we should have sighted the Bandit, the sky was empty.

Jack called to Mother, 'I am separating into two sections; Red Three and Four will remain at angels 5. I am going up through cloud to your angels 8 see if he is lurking up there in a gap.' 'Roger, understood and agreed,' from Fighter Control. I checked my oxygen on and closed up tight on Jack's Wildcat as we circled up together into the cloud above us. But it was thick cloud all the way up to angels 9. Just before we reached that height there came the call from Control. 'Hello Red One, Bandit below you has turned towards Mother. He is moving fast.' 'Your course back to us Red One is 280; lose height and buster, repeat `buster.' Jack, with a quick look at me, started his turn on to 280 and to dive at full throttle to get below the cloud where we now expected to see the Bandit. The probability was that his radar had picked up the blip of our fleet and now, having turned towards it, he had to come down below cloud to have a visual sight of what his radar had found. Sure enough, as we broke cloud, there he was nose down and heading on course for our fleet.

It was a BV138 and we were overtaking it very fast. On the R/T from Jack, 'Go to line astern Red Two, I am going under and up.' Jack dived down below and then rocketed up, in an area out of the initial firing sight of the rear turret gunner and, with the full force of his six Browning machine guns, absolutely shattered the end of the port boom and tail unit of the target. In fact, he very nearly flew into it, he was so close. The enemy aircraft reared upwards rolling to starboard, out of control, presenting me with the perfect target of its starboard engine, hull and cockpit. I just had time for a quick burst from my guns before I had to rudder and aileron violently to the right and down to avoid smashing into the huge machine which filled my windscreen view. By this time, I was down to a mere thousand feet above the sea. I pulled out of the dive and turned sharply back in time to see the BV 138, all control gone without the tail unit and with thick smoke from its starboard engine, crash headlong into the sea.

We had come down on the BV138 from out of the cloud so suddenly and so fast that the wretched German gunners had barely been given the chance of a shot at us before we were attacking them from below and clear of their firing line. Jack had done the damage that was necessary and the final squirt of fire from my guns would not have made much difference to the inevitable end of the enemy aircraft. Nevertheless, my heart thumping with the tension and excitement of the attack, I had felt slightly sick as I watched that huge and rather lovely looking flying boat plunge full tilt into the sea and smash into pieces. There had probably been eight men on board but, as we circled the wreckage, it was evident that none had survived. The whole business since we had first sighted it had taken no more than about two minutes. So there was a good possibility that, in such a short timescale, the crew had not sighted our Fleet to send back a report to their base on its presence and position.

In that case it had been a successful operation due to Jack's good leadership of his flight in combination with the excellent directions from Mike Hordern back at Fighter Control. The other two of our flight rejoined us as Jack led his flight of four Wildcats back to the Carrier, already turning into wind preparing for us to land on. My initial feeling of nausea at the violent end of the BV138 was being replaced by elation at our success and I was looking forward to landing back on board, knowing that many Goofers would be out there to watch our return. I was feeling such a fine fellow that I over-did my steep turn on to the flight deck and, just in time, corrected a stall which would have put an end to me into the sea. As it was, I was able to bang the Wildcat down on to the deck in what must have looked like a deliberately exciting style of landing. In a way, I suppose that sort of hairy approach and landing was the FAA equivalent of the slow roll, which an RAF fighter pilot might execute over the aerodrome after a successful combat. Both were equally stupid and unnecessary.

I enjoyed a cheerful session of drinks at the bar at midday chatting with fellow pilots about the events of the morning. But, later, on my own in the cabin, how I missed my late particular friend, Basil, with whom I could have spoken quietly about my sick feeling of horror when watching the violent end to the German aircraft and its crew. It had seemed to be such a one-sided engagement, with little chance of escape for the crew, and yet it had been easy only because our attack had been well managed. Had some circumstance compelled us to attack from above, for instance, which would have given their longer range and more powerful guns full scope, then it might have been a different story. Anyway, that's what I imagined Basil would have comforted me by saying, if only he had been there. Later in the afternoon of that day, it was business as usual when Red flight was back on stand-by in expectation of another patrol before dark.

We parted from the convoy near Murmansk, where other escort ships came out to join it, and our Fleet turned back for the home run.

This time, without the convoy to worry about, it had been planned apparently to make our presence known in the hope of bringing out some part of the German Navy. When nearer to the Norwegian coast a major sortie of twelve Barracudas with a protective cover of eight Seafires and eight Wildcats, from our other squadron, was launched against shipping anchored in a near harbour. My squadron was detailed for boring patrols over the Fleet ready for any counter attacks. At least we had some action because Winnie, with Johnnie Lowder in his section, was vectored away to find and chase yet another BV138 which they shot down, although Winnie's aircraft did receive some hits. Our strike aircraft returned from the successful attack on the harbour without loss; apparently the Germans were surprised and quite unprepared for any attack on the shipping there.

On the return of *Illustrious* to Scapa, all four squadrons flew ashore to the Naval Air Station at Hatston near Kirkwall. One of the tasks while ashore there was to learn and practise flying as a Wing, which would consist of several squadrons, with the fighter aircraft acting as cover for the bombers. In effect, the Fleet Air Arm was learning to operate as a major striking force, rather than maintaining the defensive role which hitherto had been most of the requirement of the early years of the war.

Controlling a Wing of some sixty or more aircraft was a new craft to be learned by our leaders and a right cock-up they frequently made of it. But it was no easy task to lead, say, thirty-six Bombers together with another forty-eight Fighters to a target maybe two hundred miles away. The fighters would have difficulty keeping station over the bombers whose flying speed was much slower. But the major problems would arise if this gaggle of aircraft, taking up a large area of sky, were to run into cloudy conditions on the way to the target and then again over it. Constant, quick decisions had to be made by the Wing leader to give changes of height or direction as necessary to the various squadron leaders who, in their turn, could not move their whole squadron fluidly around the sky as quickly as the Wing leader needed them to do. The bad tempered language over the radio between the Wing leader, Squadron and Flight leaders could be sometimes very ripe. To most of us pilots it was to say the least an interesting new flying experience and I, for one, used to chuckle sometimes at the ripe language and at the general chaos going on around me. I rather enjoyed those early 'Balboes', as we called them, but the time would come when in the, Far East and Pacific, all of us would have to be much more competent.

During that short period at Hatston, there were a couple more interesting and amusing events. The first was that all the fighter pilots, three or four at a time, were told to attend at a remote office building at the far side of the aerodrome. It was all very mysterious. I was one of the first ones to go and arrived to find two middle aged gentlemen, rather well dressed in civvies, surrounded by cardboard boxes and each holding tailor's measuring tapes. To start with I was asked gravely which side did I dress. Well, I had no idea what the man was talking about until he explained that I was to be measured as for a very tight pair of trousers, which, rather to my embarrassment, he proceeded to do.

In fact, we were being measured for the new, highly secret, 'G' suits. These suits were a typically British, brilliantly simple idea. Let me explain that when a pilot of a fast aircraft pulls out of a steep dive, or executes a steep turn, the weight of his body can double or even treble. The blood in his body is forced downwards into his stomach and legs and away from his brain and he 'blacks out.'

The boffins had come up with the clever idea of making a strong suit of a type of canvas material, which fitted from ankle to just below the heart, but with pockets on its inside, which were to contain water. Therefore, as the pilot pulled out of his dive, the water being heavier would be pressed downwards also, thus preventing much of the blood from draining down from the heart and brain. It was brilliant. We tried it out having mock dog-fights with one of us without the suit and the other wearing it. There was no doubt about it; the chap wearing the suit could out dive and out turn the other.

As with so many brilliant and simple ideas, there were unexpected snags which were not apparent until we came out to the hot Mediterranean climate. As the pilot and his blood became hot, sitting with little movement in his hot cockpit, so the water became heated which, in turn, increased the pilot's temperature yet more. I remember feeling as hot as a boiled egg after landing on, jumping out of the cockpit as soon as I had switched off the engine and turning the small tap on my leg so to release the steaming hot water from my suit. Oh the relief as the hot water poured out of my suit and ran steaming across the flight deck. But there were hoots of laughter from the sailors on the flight deck, unaware then of our secret 'G' suits, who thought I was having a desperately needed pee!

Another much more serious snag occurred when a pilot was the first to ditch wearing the suit. The water in the suit, more buoyant than the sea water around it, forced the legs and bottom of the pilot up and his head therefore down into the sea. He drowned before he could be rescued. It seems that these suits were discarded shortly afterwards, because we never wore them in action.

After another sortie in *Illustrious* on the Arctic run, acting this time purely on convoy protection, we returned to Hatston to learn that an escape exercise had been organised for the aircrews. It was an exercise to see how we, the aircrews, would cope in trying to escape after a crash landing in enemy territory. It was also a test of the security arrangements throughout the Orkney Islands as the Army was alerted that a number of enemy agents and saboteurs were known to have parachuted on to the main Island. The Soldiers were briefed to be on their guard and to search for an unknown number of enemy agents who, when found, were to be brought to army headquarters unharmed, for immediate interrogation.

In other words, they were not to be bashed into submission first. When I heard this, I thought Heaven help any soldiers who tried to rough-handle Winnie or Jack; they would never know what hit them.

Dressed in plain blue trousers and jerseys, some thirty junior aircrew officers were bundled into the back of a large lorry on which the tarpaulin cover at the back had been firmly tied down so that they sat in the dark interior unable to see anything outside. The lorry was then driven across and around the main Island of the Orkneys, stopping from time to time to drop one officer at a time, each one in a most desolate and wild area of countryside, to find his way back to the Air Station. Two days were the maximum period allowed for each aircrew to report back to base, with the warning that the Army would be out searching for them and their arrest might not be gentle since the soldiers had not been told that this was an exercise.

I was dropped out of the lorry in high country and was able to see for many miles around me. There was not much to see except hilly scrub land with no roads visible and not so much as a single cottage or farmhouse in sight. This really was not my type of scenario at all; I was not a tough outdoor person and had never even been a boy-scout. It was no good just to stand there, I had to move in some direction. A bleak sun was breaking through grey clouds and at mid-morning I guessed it would be vaguely in the area of south east. The Air Station I knew to be on the southern tip of the main Island so I took a line and marked a point vaguely again to the south. And started walking. From all the cowboy films I had seen as a little boy, I knew I should keep off the skyline on the hill tops, such knowledge being the sum total of my escapology skills.

By early afternoon I was beginning to see an occasional habitation and getting hungry. I was thinking about approaching a farm, either to pinch some food or risk asking for some when I was startled to see a man move just near me and then duck down into the long grass but I had seen that he was dressed in blue and therefore must be one of us.

I called to him and we met for a chat about our situation. I had seen him before, of course, in the Mess although I didn't know him. He was older than me and rather a big burly chap so when he suggested that we team up and try to get back to Hatston together, I was considerably relieved and only too glad to do so. I thought, he just couldn't be as clueless at this boy scout type of activity as I was. His only plan, he told me, was to try and steal a car from a village or farm which seemed very optimistic to me since, in those days, the population was told, not only to lock their cars, but to remove the rotor arm of the distributor as well. On the other hand, it was better than having no plan at all, as in my case. However, he did agree that I was walking in the right direction.

It was hilly countryside but he insisted that we kept to the tops and, as we walked on, we began to see more houses scattered around on the lower ground. We noted one house in particular; quite a grand looking place on its own with a wide drive and courtyard in the front of it. We moved down, keeping in the cover of bushes and trees, to take a better look. A large black Humber car drove into the courtyard as we watched and a smart young sailor jumped out of the driving seat to open the rear door for his passenger who, with his cap and overcoat covered in gold scrambled eggs, could not possibly have been anything less than an Admiral. After the very senior officer had gone inside the house through the open front door, the sailor made a brief pretence of polishing the car bonnet before he chucked his cap on to the car seat and waked round to the back of the house, no doubt for a cup of tea. Dick, my companion, said, 'Come on let's get out of here, where there's brass like that, there bound to be lots of staff and guards.'

But I had been watching carefully; I hadn't seen the sailor put any keys in his pocket or even appear to lock the car before he left for his tea. I had the idea in mind to sneak down there and just see if the keys were still in the car. If so, what the hell could we lose by trying to drive off in it? The whole exercise was supposed to be about showing our initiative and there appeared to be nobody immediately around to stop us. Dick hesitated only for a moment when I explained my thoughts. 'You're right,' he said, 'let's go for it!'

When we got down there, treading carefully and skirting the gravel drive, we found the main door still wide open. So we looked into a large empty hallway and there, at the far end, was a stand with the Admiral's coat hung on it and his scrambled egg cap on a table alongside it. I left Dick looking down the hallway, watching the doors leading off it, to give warning if anyone came out while I crept quietly across the gravel to the car. Oh the joy and excitement of it; the car ignition keys were indeed still there. I signalled the fantastic good news to Dick who promptly disappeared into the hallway. Ye gods, he was going to pinch the Admiral's cap and coat; what a wonderful idea! In seconds he came hurrying out clutching them while I slipped into the driving seat. The car started immediately and very, very quietly and slowly I drove it round and back up the driveway ... and out through the open gates.

We stopped briefly for Dick to put on the Admiral's coat and cap and I wore the sailor's cap. No one had come out to chase us and so I drove sedately to the Royal Naval Air Station at Hatston by following the signposts to the town of Kirkwall adjacent to it. Dick looked every inch an Admiral and I, sitting well down in the seat and wearing the sailor's cap, could surely pass for his driver. And that is what happened when we drove up to the main gates of the Air Station. The two sentries saluted very smartly and the Petty Officer came out of his office to wave us through, with consternation writ large on his face at the sight of an Admiral making an unscheduled visit. As we went, I saw him double back into his office in a panic to notify the Commander. I drove straight to the main office block where Dick took off the Admiral's uniform to put it on the back seat of the car with my sailor's cap. Then we reported our return formally to the Commander. We were the first to return by several hours.

The Admiral, who must have been a pompous ass, played hell about the theft of his car and wanted us to be formally and severely reprimanded and punished. Until our Captain of the Air Station and the Commander pointed out that the exercise had been signalled to him and that, 'With respect Sir, your security arrangements at the house were shown to be very lax indeed.' Nine others of the aircrew made it back to the Air Station over the next twelve hours. One or two were given a hard time when caught by the Army, especially dear Winnie who without the usual restraining influence of Jack Parli with him, lashed out at the soldiers. Cliff Nell didn't get back for two days;

he was so cautious that he had laid up in a barn somewhere and lost all sense of time.

But it was fun, especially for Dick and me, and the exercise was regarded as a great success except by the boot-faced Admiral.

CHAPTER NINE

The Mediterranean

In early June 1943, fun and games at Hatston were over as all four squadrons were now due to fly back on board HMS *Illustrious*. None of us in the squadrons knew with any certainty where we were due to operate but there was a clue when our squadron ratings were issued with tropical uniforms. Moreover, we were aware from the BBC of the major preparations being made for the Allied landings and assault on the south of Italy. Sure enough, *Illustrious* joined a convoy going south across the Bay of Biscay to the Mediterranean and the routine of Combat Air Patrols for us and Anti-Submarine patrols for the Barracudas began. The Focke-Wulf Condors, our old enemy of the Atlantic, were known to operate on surveillance for the Germans over the Bay of Biscay and there was the possibility also of attack from French airfields by German bombers, probably Junkers 88s. Perhaps *Illustrious* might launch a pre-emptive strike on those airfields. We aircrew would have to wait and see what was in store for us.

The convoy was comparatively small, about sixteen large merchant ships, with an average speed faster than usual. There was some urgency, we gathered, to get the cargoes of mainly munitions to the Mediterranean area to back up the assault on southern Italy. I found out later on, but not at the time, that our ship was in a hurry to replace HMS *Indomitable* which had been badly damaged by a bomb from a Junkers 88. It was extraordinary how very little information junior aircrew were given at any time about what was happening and what the plans might be for our ship. During much of my time at sea in a Fleet Carrier, I often never knew precisely where the ship was going or the general situation in which my ship was involved. Such information more often came from the lower deck via my steward or my aircraft maintenance crew, and it frequently proved to be remarkably accurate.

During the first days crossing the Bay of Biscay, the weather and sea conditions were bad but I was fortunate to spend them on stand-by in the Ready room. By the time my turn came for a patrol, the conditions had improved although there was still a heavy sea running which gave some considerable movement to the flight deck despite the size of the Carrier. At this stage of our progress, we were further from the French airfields with correspondingly less likelihood of possible bombing attacks, therefore patrols were reduced to just two Wildcats instead of four. The convoy already was steaming close into the wind and so, to avoid the Carrier having to turn fully into wind for a normal take-off, Jack and I were to be launched from the catapult for the last patrol of the day.

I hated catapult launches. I had witnessed one accident when the hydraulics of the catapult had failed and the Wildcat, with the engine roaring as the pilot had tried to get airborne, had inevitably stalled at the end of the flight deck and fallen under the bows of the ship. The crunching sound as the ship rode over the sinking aircraft and its pilot, remained in my mind. As usual, everything had to be done at breakneck speed and here I was, a mere twenty seconds behind Jack, who had been launched ahead of me. My head and body was braced back ready for the tremendous kick as the aircraft would be pulled suddenly from static to a speed of seventy-five knots in a distance of eighty feet. The acceleration would be such that momentarily I might black out and yet, within split seconds, I would have to recover and take control of the aircraft as it was literally flung off the flight deck into the air by the catapult.

I raised my left hand with the thumb up, to show I was ready, and then opened to full throttle while placing my fist behind the throttle in case, had I been holding it, the sudden acceleration should cause me to pull it back. The aircraft, while vibrating and straining at full power to shoot forward, was held back and immobile by an attachment at the tail of the fuselage. The DLCO dropped his flag, the tail attachment was released and the Wildcat was hurled forward and into the air. How quickly the body and brain reacts. By the time the aircraft was just clear of the deck and sinking down towards the sea, I had recovered all my senses and was flying the aircraft through that difficult moment of near stall, getting the wheels and flaps up and fast gaining the safety of full flying speed. Just another take-off, really.

It was almost dusk by the time we had completed our patrol without incident. The ship had turned into wind and Jack, ahead of me, was on the downwind leg with wheels, flaps and hook down about to land on when, Robert from Fighter Direction, called on the R/T, his usually fruity Shakespearean voice rasping with urgency,

'Abort landing Red One, I say again abort landing. Bandits approaching at angels ten, thirty miles. Vector 110 degrees, buster.' 'Roger, vector 110,' acknowledged Jack and immediately he and I, winding our aircraft wheels up, turned on to the vector and climbed at full throttle as we did so. 'Bandits' must mean an attacking force of bombers and all our fighter aircraft at this dusk hour had just been struck down into the ship's hangar. There must be an almighty panic down there on the flight deck, I thought, as everyone would be rushing to re-range other Wildcats and the Seafires ready for take-off to meet the expected attack.

Meantime, the two of us already in the air would have to deal with the bombers and we were at full throttle desperately trying to gain height. Robert from Fighter Control called again; this time his voice was back to its well modulated fruity tones, 'Hello Red One this is Mother, bandit now recognised as single and a Condor. Bandit has turned away and your vector now 080 degrees.' My heart gave a thump of relief; the prospect of the two of us trying to fight off half a dozen Junkers 88s had been daunting, although I don't suppose it had caused Jack any fear. Then we could see it; the Condor flying fast with plenty of height above us. There was little hope of catching it but, at least, we had chased it off before it could report the exact position and course of our convoy.

At 10,000 feet there was still some light in the cloudless sky and we could see the Condor as a far off speck. Although we chased for a short while, it soon disappeared into the gloom. 'Mother' called and, after telling us to switch on our IFF, gave us a course back to the ship. By this time it was getting dark but, at sea level, darkness would have fallen entirely, necessitating my first deck-landing at night. It would be the same for Jack. I moved into close formation on his starboard side as he began losing height on course for the ship. The ridiculous factor was that there was a whole battery of light switches down on the right of the cockpit which I had never before had occasion to use and, as I flew, I had to fumble about to find the right switch for the aircraft lights on the wings and fuselage. Down at low level, it really was a black night and I could see nothing yet of the Carrier or the convoy as we followed the course given to us and yet we must be close to them by now. I had never lost my fear of night flying after my prang at Shrewton and I felt no better now, bogging around in the dark over the sea. Thank heavens for Jack, I could rely on him to lead me to the Carrier but, after that, I would have to cope with the new experience of a deck-landing at night. I didn't fancy the prospect at all.

Suddenly we were over the convoy and I could see the wakes of the ships and a few faint glimmers of light from them. The Carrier was near the convoy but very difficult to see until, at five hundred feet, we flew over the top of it and I could look down and see the form of the ship from the line of her deck-landing lights. She was already into wind and gave us clearance to land. Jack led me in a tight circuit to bring us flying parallel along her starboard side. At least the trigger-happy gunners on the merchant ships were not firing at us, thinking we were enemy aircraft, as could easily happen at night.

I followed Jack as he broke away to port on to the crosswind and then downwind legs of his circuit and then I throttled back to stay further behind him, not to be too close as he landed. He seemed to go too far astern of the ship for his final approach and I would have to do the same. But then I realised he was quite right; we would be unable to see and line up on the flight deck lights unless on final approach we were in a direct line with them. My usual daytime method of turning on to the deck would not be practicable. For the first time since my early deck-landings, I was now reliant on the signals from the batsman. I hoped it was not the senior one of the two DLCOs, the one who tended to dance about as he batted, as I had little confidence in him. But I must press on now with the landing regardless.

It was not too difficult to line up on the lights looking over the short, stubby nose of the Wildcat but ... was I too high? No, apparently not; the batsman was signalling for more throttle; telling me to hold my rate of descent. He was right and seconds later I was past the round down and received the 'cut' engine signal from the batsman to thump down on the deck. With the relief of getting down in one piece I could stop holding my breath. Two days later, after two more uneventful patrols, *Illustrious* came into Gibraltar harbour, leaving the convoy to continue under the protection of Destroyers, Corvettes and an Escort Carrier. This would be my first of many visits to Gibraltar and I was delighted with the little streets of the town and its long history of connection with the Royal Navy. For instance, I liked the little naval cemetery in the middle of the town for officers and men killed in the Napoleonic wars. It was a sailors' town, full of bars and brothels in the little streets and good restaurants for the officers, assuming the latter would have disregarded the former type of entertainments.

There was mail waiting for me from my Mother, Maddie, Lalline and, unexpectedly, from my sister Phoebe. What she wanted, it transpired, was my old but still favourite brown civilian suit to convert into a skirt since, of course, new clothes were almost impossible to get under rationing at home. I went ashore and sent an immediate telegram via the British Post Office saying simply: 'Negative brown suit.' The meaning should be quite clear to Phoebe with all her naval connections.

Two or three days later, by which time I had completely forgotten the telegram, I was told to report to the Commander whom I found talking on the quarterdeck to a Chief Petty Officer wearing a naval police armband. The CPO had come to escort me as, apparently, I had been summoned to appear before the Provost Marshal of Gibraltar.

I had no idea whatsoever what the summons could be about even when we arrived at the Governor's Residence where I was marched into the Marshal's office. I had to stand to attention in front of his desk whereupon he harangued me about the telegram and its meaning which, he said, was deeply suspicious. He questioned me about my schools, my service in the RN, indeed on almost every aspect of my adult life.

I began by being very scared of this ferocious looking Commander, an ex-gunner's mate I learned later. Eventually, I became angry and barked back at him that, if he really thought I was some sort of spy sending secret messages, then his first action should have been to check my credentials and character from the Commanding Officer of my squadron with whom I had served for the past eighteen months at sea. 'At sea, Sir', I repeated pointedly and I glared at him sitting there behind his desk Then I drew upon my background at Harrow to add with the immense pomposity I had learned there as a boy to add, 'Properly Sir you should have obtained the permission of the Captain of HMS *Illustrious*, the ship in which I serve, before summoning me to your office in this manner.' Absolute bull, of course, because I had no idea of proper procedures. I stopped; feeling rather frightened of my deliberate rudeness. His ruddy, weather beaten face broke into a broad smile. 'Calm down son,' he said, 'I accept what you have told me and you can go, but use your loaf in future and don't send silly messages like that in time of war. And you should know that authority for my actions comes directly from the Admiral. Also, incidentally, for your personal information, I have served at sea continuously since 1939 until three months ago.' I left his office feeling a bit silly and quite shaky from the confrontation, to seek a large gin from the nearest pub.

I dined well on the story, as the saying goes, on board that evening when it was an excuse for a squadron party. Just before we all staggered off to our respective bunks, the CO called Jack, Winnie, myself and Mike Penhale aside to tell us that he had selected us four to go by bus from the harbour, leaving at five am, to the Gibraltar aerodrome. There at the main naval hangar we would find four Hurricanes, fuelled and ready for flight. We were to fly these Hurricanes from the aerodrome to meet the Carrier later that morning at sea off Gibraltar and land them on board. It being eleven o'clock at night, at the end of an evening of heavy drinking, I thought Jimmy must be joking, since it seemed such an extraordinary requirement. But no; it was serious. Someone of high rank had made a very sudden decision that these Hurricanes were needed on board the next morning for some reason. It all seemed so dotty that I just giggled and stumbled off to bed.

A light went on in the cabin and I was being shaken awake by our steward who had already given a shake to Mike whose turn it had been to sleep on the camp bed. I looked at my watch which showed four o'clock and remembered the extraordinary requirement to fly the Hurricanes from the Aerodrome. I had dismissed it from my mind, when falling into my bunk last night, as some sort of joke. Fortunately Jack, before he went to bed, had arranged for us all to be woken up at this time. Good thing he did because, had he not done so, I would have nursed my awful hangover asleep in the bunk for several hours more. When dressed, we had to fetch our parachutes and flying kit from the Ready room. These we dumped outside the Wardroom before getting a much-needed cup of coffee and something to eat from a couple of duty stewards, morose at that early hour.

I began to feel better and listened sensibly as Jack, who before going to bed the night before, had been briefed in detail about our flight in the Hurricanes. The essence of it was that we were to carry out an hour of dummy deck-landings at the aerodrome before a rendezvous with the ship at sea in the straits of Gibraltar at midday. In due course apparently, these Hurricanes were to be delivered to Malta and we would have to fly them ashore there. It would be rather fun and exciting, I now began to think, to fly a Hurricane again and particularly so to deck-land it. There was no problem therefore to the projected flight as far as I could see.

The aerodrome at Gibraltar appeared to be a huge expanse of white concrete, of triangular shape with its broad base at the inland end of the rock of Gibraltar and with the concrete right up to the very foot of the towering Rock. This widest part, close as it was to the Rock, was in effect the main runway and the prevailing wind meant that aircraft took off and landed facing towards Algeciras, across the bay. The commercial buildings and hangars were at the narrower end of the triangle and we were driven over a mile or so of concrete to one of them. Parked outside were the four Hurricanes which we now noted were Mark 11c's with a cannon barrel protruding forward from each wing. The sun was well up by now and the aircraft cockpits would be unbearably hot if we delayed.

The Petty Officer in charge of maintenance gave us the Form 700 to sign showing that the Hurricanes were fully serviceable, fuelled and armed. At our request, he found a copy of the Pilot's Notes for us to study. The first thing to do was to re-familiarise ourselves with the cockpit and its layout and we wasted no time starting on this before the hot sun would make sitting in the static cockpits unpleasant. How strange and cramped the Hurricane cockpit seemed after the orderliness and space of the Wildcat but, after a while, I remembered the feel and place of all the various controls and instruments. After signalling to the ground crew that I was ready to start the engine, I listened to the old familiar deep note as, with puffs of black smoke from the exhausts, the RR engine started up. The other three were ready too and Jack received permission from the control tower for all four of us to taxi out on to the huge expanse of runway.

We had decided that we were going to take as much time as possible over re-familiarising ourselves with these aircraft. None of us had deck-landed a Hurricane before, it was two years since we had flown one, the 11c was a new mark and we would have no more than an hour to become accustomed to flying it. To deck-land the aircraft later that morning was going to be a considerable challenge. To make matters more awkward, we would have to fly all the way round the Rock after each landing, instead of flying a normal short circuit.

Jack took off first and I left plenty of time before I opened the throttle to follow him. The sun was already very hot by this time and, as there was a fairly strong wind blowing as well, a lot of turbulence was created close to the Rock; very noticeable even on the take-off. I didn't feel comfortable flying this Hurricane; it seemed to lack the natural flight of those earlier Marks I had flown at Yeovilton. Perhaps it was the turbulence, I thought. Normally, I would have taken the aircraft up to 10,000 ft and done a few stalls and slow flying with wheels and flaps down to get a better feel for it. But there wasn't time. So I pressed on, grinding my way round the Rock until I turned into wind as I came round the highest point of the Rock, to make my final approach. The turbulence was bad and that, plus the effect of the two cannons protruding out of the leading edge of the wings, made the aircraft feel unstable compared with my memory of the earlier Hurricanes. It was dangerous to bring the speed down to deck-landing level in that turbulence and there was no question of attempting to fly just above the stall to do a dummy deck-landing under those conditions. However, I completed the landing, selected the flaps up and opened the throttle to go round again for another go.

My approach for the second landing was no less difficult so, once down, I stayed down and called Jack on the R/T. 'Red One, these dummy deck-landings here are a waste of time and give me no confidence for the real thing on the ship, sorry but I think we should pack it in.' From Winnie on the R/T, 'That goes for me too Jack, bloody waste of time this is.' 'Right, I agree, everyone back to the hangar for coffee,' replied Jack. And so we all taxied back to the hangar to await the call from the ship. Great leader was Jack; never hesitated to make a decision or take responsibility. If any of us were to make a mess of the forthcoming landing which, as we all knew, was more than likely then sure enough the Commander Air would point the finger of blame at Jack for not insisting, as leader, that we complete further dummy landings.

An hour later the signal came for us to take-off and rendezvous with the Carrier. We formed up in close formation on Jack who took us on a low, fast pass at deck level down the port side of the ship first, before we turned round and moved into echelon on the starboard side in readiness to break away individually for the landing. I had not had time or opportunity in close formation to worry much about it but now the time had come for me to put the Hurricane down on the deck. Jack, in front of me, was already safely down as I approached on the turn, just as I would have done in the wildcat, but at faster speed and flying the Hurricane automatically and unthinkingly as I had done two years earlier at Yeovilton. I flew past the little chap dancing about and waving his bats and I caught the third wire nicely. The deck party released the hook from the wire and I taxied grandly past the Island with its galleries filled with Goofers who, reasonably enough, were expecting to see at least one of us hit the crash barrier or worse. I took off my helmet as I passed and gave them a royal wave of my hand. I felt rather pleased with myself.

Although, under all the circumstances, it had been an exciting triumph to fly the four Hurricanes on board without mishap, there was a slight disadvantage to it. As the wings were non-folding, the Hurricanes could not easily fit below into the already crowded hangar and consequently they would have to be shuffled back and forwards along the flight deck during flying operations. Instead of shuffling them about, Commander Air decided that it would be easier for our flight to fly them on patrols.

The Mediterranean by that time had become a comparatively safe area since the Italian Navy had been hammered and tamed by the Swordfish at Taranto in the previous year. But there was always the possibility, even probability, that German aircraft might attack from Italian airfields. Our four Hurricanes alternated therefore with the Wildcats in putting up a CAP during daylight hours so that, in effect, we flew two patrols each day for the short period before the ship reached Malta. I found that the Hurricane, with its tight little cockpit smelling of glycol and fuel, was more tiring comparatively to fly on two-hour patrols than the Wildcat. But the patrols were without incident.

However, flying the Hurricane over the sea, I could not get out of my mind the fear of engine failure if it should ever occur at a level so low, such as in the landing circuit, where it would be impracticable to bale out. It was well known that to ditch a Hurricane safely was impossible because of the huge cooling radiator located like a scoop under the fuselage. The radiator, as soon as it touched the sea, would inevitably cause the aircraft to bunt upside down and hard into the sea without possibility of survival for the pilot. Engine failures did occur from time to time among all aircraft in those days, but the certainty of being killed if it did occur in the Hurricane, made me look forward to the return to my Wildcat with its radial engine which gave the pilot a good chance of surviving a ditching.

Three days later I missed the pleasure of coming into Valetta harbour when the ship arrived at Malta with the ship's company paraded on deck and the marine band playing. HMS *Illustrious* had played such a big part in the Malta convoys two years earlier that she was well loved by the population of the Island and crowds had turned out to welcome her back. Our flight of the four Hurricanes had to take-off and fly ashore to one of the two aerodromes. However, the four of us wasted no time in getting back to the ship to join the celebrations on her return to Malta. As always there were harbour duties for aircrew to do and, this time, there was the extra one of being detailed off in a motor boat to chug round and round the harbour, dropping very small depth charges by hand into the harbour waters, throughout every night. This was in case Italian frogmen should succeed in broaching the harbour defences with the intention of fixing limpet mines to any one of our many Warships. The Italians had proved themselves to be brilliantly good at this form of warfare since they had succeeded in damaging four of our Battleships, two in Alexandria and another two in Gibraltar. Although the Admiralty regarded damage to their beloved Battleships as disastrous, they were in reality no great loss in modern warfare and it was fortunate indeed that the frogmen had been so foolish as not to have concentrated on Carriers or Destroyers. Apparently our small depth charges were effective because no ships were damaged but two bodies of frogmen were washed ashore.

When off duty, most of the daytime ashore was spent as a group of chaps lying in the sun and swimming although, for me as a non-swimmer, the rocky coast was not particularly attractive. I liked wandering about in the narrow streets and steps of Valetta and, in need of more tropical shorts and shirts, I found a particularly good tailor's shop. Particularly good perhaps, because the young Maltese girl who served me was strikingly attractive, slim with dark hair and lovely wide, brown eyes. Like most Maltese people, she spoke good English and we chattered easily together as she packed up my purchases. I simply felt very much in need of female company and thought, why not try? And so I asked her if she would like to come out with me and maybe have drinks and dinner together at a nice restaurant, or anything else really that she might like to do? I did so want her to say yes, that I was absurdly shy in my manner of asking. She took her time, looking me in the eyes before she smiled and thanked me saying that she would be happy to go out with me.

I met her that evening at her parents' house, quite near the shop. Unlike English girls who tend to dress in bright colours in hotter climates, Marie was wearing a black blouse with a knee length straight skirt of a russet red material. I took her by taxi to an hotel just outside Valetta and why I can remember so well what she was wearing is because, in contrast to the few European women there, her dark outfit and olive colouring made her stand out. She looked beautiful, I thought. Most of the other people in the restaurant of the hotel were very senior officers of the three services and I enjoyed being there amongst them in the company of such a pretty girl. She was composed and conversation with her was relaxed and easy. Her parents, she told me, ran a small restaurant quite near the harbour and their business was beginning to recover from the bombing which had so badly affected all their lives. She asked me if I would like to have an evening meal there and maybe, if I liked, to have a preliminary drink at their house first. I didn't hesitate to accept both invitations.

Marie had asked me particularly to wear uniform again, otherwise I would have worn casual clothes, so I arrived resplendent in my 'whites', those which I had bought in New York, complete with epaulettes and wings. The small terrace house was off the street, cool and dark inside with a pretty and sunny courtyard at the back where Marie had arranged two glasses of cold beer. I had expected that one of the parents would be there but we were alone in the house and, as we talked, I began to realise that the intimate situation thus created was deliberate. She was older than the teenager I had first thought her to be and certainly she was making all the running when she suggested that we go inside where it would be cooler. Once inside, she began undoing the collar clips and gold buttons of my tunic. 'We must take off your uniform, she said, or it will become creased.' She kissed me hard and passionately with a competent composure which left me gasping as I felt her hands undoing the belt of my trousers.

There followed a happy hour, both of us lying naked on a long and comfortable sofa, where I believe that I may have learned more about joyful sex from Marie than in all my previous experiences put together. I could have happily continued for the whole evening but the time came when we had to get dressed for we were expected at the restaurant. Although exhausted and groggy with the excitement of our close encounter, I was elated and proud of myself. In a way it had been almost equivalent to earning my 'wings' at the end of flying training. However, I thought it odd that so pretty a girl would go out with service men, who were just passing through Malta. Her explanation was simple; she liked men. But, if she had affairs with any of the local men of Malta, her fiancé would soon know about it and there would be trouble.

The restaurant was in what should have been a good location near the harbour but the buildings around it had been badly damaged by the bombing and the area still appeared desolate There had been no attempt to make the restaurant appear grand but it looked neat, very clean and cheerful with attractive coloured tablecloths and flowers on all the tables, some of which were set outside.

Mother came to greet me and Father came bustling out of the kitchen at the back also to do so. Mum was nearly twice the size of her daughter Marie but I could see the likeness in their pretty faces. Four of the tables were occupied by civilians inside but I suggested we sit outside for an aperitif first. I wasn't all that stupid because I realised that the reason why I had been asked to wear uniform was possibly to promote the restaurant as suitable for other officers who might be walking past from the Grand Harbour to the city. It worked too because four of the Seafire squadron from my ship stopped, said hello to me and came back later for a meal. Our dinner, for which I insisted on paying in spite of protests from Marie and her Mum, was superb; so much better than the hotel meal had been. I said good-bye to Marie with a chaste kiss and, as I was doing so, four more officers entered to have dinner there. I felt that I had done my duty for Marie. I visited the restaurant with my chums twice more because the food was so good but I did not see Marie on her own again: I didn't like the thought of the big dockyard fiancé catching me with her!

In early September, HMS *Illustrious* and HMS *Formidable* with a complement of about eighty aircraft between them, steamed out of the grand Harbour with an appropriate retinue of Cruisers and Destroyers en route for …. Where and for what purpose?

As usual, I had no certain knowledge of the situation and the purpose of such an obviously strong task force, other than that Landings were expected to be undertaken by the Allied Army somewhere on the Italian coast. My fellow pilots and I presumed that we would be taking some part in support of those Allied landings. In due course at pre-flight briefings, we learned that we would be covering the assault at Salerno.

The essential role of the Royal Navy would be to provide air cover over the Salerno beachhead where the Army were facing a German force very much more powerful than anticipated. Airfields at Sicily or Malta were too far away for the RAF to provide such cover and thus it was an ideal job for the Fleet Air Arm.

A task force of four Escort Carriers, with a complement of some eighty Seafires, had been chosen by the Admiralty to provide air cover over the beachhead throughout the hours of daylight for as long as necessary, i.e. until an aerodrome could be captured by the army ashore when the RAF could take over. These Carriers were to operate close inshore so that the Seafires would have only a little distance to fly to their operating location and height. This was important because the Seafire had a patrol endurance of little more than one hour and twenty minutes. In effect, therefore, a patrol of Seafires had to land back on their Escort Carrier every hour.

For the Seafire to land on the small deck of an Escort Carrier, even under ideal conditions, calls for considerable skill and experience on the part of the pilot. But at Salerno, the wind conditions were no better than a zephyr breeze and almost a dead calm, conditions entirely to have been expected at that time of year. Thus the Seafires had to operate with a total wind speed over the deck of only sixteen knots, being the maximum speed of the Escort Carriers, whereas they needed a total wind speed over the deck of at least twenty-eight knots. These were desperately difficult landing conditions for the Seafire pilots; conditions which surely should have been anticipated at the outset when the whole Salerno operation was being planned by Rear Admiral Vian who, despite never having flown an aircraft or having served in an Aircraft Carrier, had been put in charge of this, the first multi Carrier Fleet of the Royal Navy.

After two days the four Escort Carriers had virtually run out of Seafires, no less than forty-eight of which had been written off as the pilots attempted to land in those windless conditions. The situation was made worse by the limited sea space available for the Carriers so close to shore; this limitation must have created a frantic situation with so many crashes occurring while other Seafires were waiting to land on. How many of the Seafire pilots were killed or seriously hurt in this fiasco does not seem to be recorded. Nevertheless, in spite of the appalling crash rate, many sorties were flown in that short period from the five small Carriers. It was a courageous performance by the Seafire pilots under dreadful conditions. Unfortunately, another ten Seafires were shot down by German fighter-bombers largely due to the lack of radar in the Escort Carriers preventing the Seafires reaching an advantageous combat position.

Meantime, further out at sea, the second task force of two Fleet Carriers, HMS *Illustrious* and HMS *Formidable* were stationed with the secondary purpose of providing air cover over the Escort Carriers. Their complement of fighter aircraft for this task was thirty Wildcats and fifteen Seafires and these aircraft flew about four hundred sorties on patrol over the Escort Carriers and the beach head. On the second day, *Formidable* sent some of her Seafires to join in with the crashes taking place on the Escort Carriers. When there were no more Seafires, the Wildcats from *Illustrious* and *Formidable* were sent to land on the

Escort Carriers to take over the task of patrolling the beach head. It was no problem for the Wildcats to operate continuously from these small Carriers. Moreover, since the Wildcats could patrol for a full two hours and more, the Carriers needed to turn into wind only half as frequently as for the Seafires.

Even with hindsight it is difficult to see how or why the Admiralty came to rely upon Seafires for this particular task. Either a deliberate gamble was taken that there would be adequate wind conditions or, more likely is my guess, Admiral Vian, in charge of the Salerno show, simply had no experience of naval aviation to make the right decisions. Any junior Sub Lieutenant pilot could have told him that the plan for Salerno was a potential disaster. A disaster salvaged by the skill of the Seafire pilots who, despite the wind conditions and the crashes on deck, managed to fly many sorties.

To summarise Salerno: neither of the two types of fighter aircraft procured and provided by the Admiralty at that time, either Seafire or Wildcat, was adequate for the task against the faster German fighter-bombers. The Seafire 11c, with the weight of the landing hook together with its supporting structure, was no longer a particularly fast fighter; very little faster than the Wildcat in fact. The two Fleet Carriers and the four Escort Carriers were adequate to operate the available fighters, if only they had been used knowledgeably, i.e. Seafires for the Fleet Carriers and Wildcats for the Escort Carriers. At least that way the air umbrella over the beachhead of twenty or more Wildcats could have been sustained for as many days as necessary. And our appalling losses of Seafires (and how many pilots?) need never have happened.

My personal part in the Salerno operation was very minor as just another Wildcat pilot flying twice-daily patrols from HMS *Illustrious* to cover the air space over the Escort Carriers plus a small part of the beachhead. We chased about the sky after the faster German bombers none of which seemed bothered to attack our Escort Carriers. It seemed that the Germans were aware of our difficulties and were content to let the Seafires write themselves off, at a high rate each day. The Germans seem to have thought, 'Why bother to attack the Escort Carriers when they are doing such a good job in writing off the Seafires and their pilots for us.'

At the end of the second day, when the supply of Seafires was exhausted, our two squadrons of Wildcats were ordered to land on the Escort Carriers and continue patrol operations over the beach head from there. My squadron flew off early on that third morning and formed up ready to land on whichever of the four Escort Carriers indicated that it was ready to take us. The first flight with the CO had landed on and, while there was some sort of delay on the flight deck, we were told to orbit and patrol overhead at 5,000 feet. It was an intensely hot day with the sea glassy like a millpond and, looking down, I could see the Isle of Capri like a jewel sitting on a bright blue cushion. I was idly thinking of Gracie Fields, whom I believed still lived on the Island, and of her cheerful songs, when there was a kind of hiccup from the engine which then began to run roughly.

I looked down at my instruments to find that the engine temperature gauge showed at red and the oil pressure was just about nil. I certainly didn't want to ditch again. The mirror-like surface of the calm sea would make ditching difficult and this was a further factor which encouraged me to attempt a landing on a deck. I was still getting some power from the engine and I reckoned to land on whichever deck would take me. I pressed transmit on the R/T and in a voice cracking with anxiety called out 'Mayday, mayday, this is Red Two and I require immediate landing.' I squeaked this message out twice more. Down below one of the Carriers was already turning into wind preparing to take our flight on board anyway and, when I saw this, I made up my mind definitely to go for a landing on it.

Meantime, I was getting very little power out of the engine and by now was down to about three thousand feet. I was ahead of the ship and more or less on the downwind leg calculating that I had sufficient height to circle round to position myself reasonably well for the final approach. I glanced quickly round; no other aircraft near me or in the circuit, they were all keeping clear. I decided to assume that there would be no power at all from the engine should I need it, so I closed the throttle completely to concentrate on an engineless landing. I would have to come in very high on the final approach and might have to do an old-fashioned side-slip to get down. Also I must remember how very little wind speed there would be over the flight deck, sixteen knots no more and therefore the deck would appear to be rushing at me twice as fast on my final approach.

All this had gone through my mind but now, at some two thousand feet, I selected wheels down, half flap, hook out, straps very tight and hood locked open. I had already put the prop into fine pitch as soon as the engine had started running rough. There was no going back now; the decision to attempt a deck-landing instead of ditching was made. If I missed the deck, it would not be possible to ditch safely as the wheels would catapult the Wildcat on to its back as soon as they touched the sea and, whether I could swim or not, I would be drowned. Meantime, over the R/T from the Carrier, which was now into wind, I had received the affirmative to land.

I was turning on to the final approach, prop still rotating, speed at eighty-five knots, selecting full flap now, very high up astern of the Carrier with the batsman frantically signally me to 'come down'. Everything was happening very fast. Yes, I was too high; would fly straight over the crash barrier at this rate; side slip down to port, red Very light from the DLCO platform, meaning 'Abort landing, go round again.' A second red light with the batsman waving me off furiously. Straightening up from the side-slip, speed eighty knots. Oh dear Lord, I had overdone it, I was now slightly lower than I should be and I might not quite make it to the deck. I opened the throttle for the first time but only a brief response from the engine for a second before it expired, then I was over the deck to stall and thump down catching the first arrestor wire. Somehow, I was down and safe.

The propeller had jarred itself to a halt as soon as the aircraft landed and I lay back in the cockpit gasping with relief as the handlers pushed me forward. As they did so, a furious batsman jumped on to my port wing and harangued me for not taking his 'wave-off'. I looked at him; I didn't know the man; I said nothing but gave him a couple of fingers sign and so he jumped off again. As usual, the flight deck was all activity preparing for Jack and the rest of the Flight to land. The Tannoy blared out, 'Pilot to report immediately to Lt Cdr 'F' and the Captain on the Bridge.' That's me, I thought and, without any hurry, I undid my straps to climb slowly out of the cockpit then made my way across the deck to the Island and up to the Bridge.

I was confronted by the Lt Cdr 'F', red-faced with anger and, a few feet behind him, the Captain also with a boot-face. 'You stupid man,' the Lt Cdr 'F' shouted at me, 'you deliberately disobeyed a clear instruction not to land; you were likely to crash on to the deck and put the Carrier out of action; you were even more likely to have killed people on the deck park; and don't tell me that you had no engine power because I heard it. You are a menace and I personally shall see to it that you are court-martialled.' The Captain nodded his agreement.

I waited a little before I said anything; not because I was frightened of them but because I needed to contain my anger and to be sure of giving them a quiet, composed answer. I knew that I had just completed an astonishing feat of airmanship; a forced landing without engine on the deck of a small Carrier in conditions of nil wind, could be regarded as nothing less. I was not prepared to be brow-beaten by these two non-flyers.

I replied, 'Sir, you were aware that I was in a forced landing situation from my Mayday call, you gave me the affirmative to land; by the time of my final approach I had no engine power available. I suggest you wait for the report of the Air Engineer Officer, who is now examining the engine, to confirm that the engine had no power.' The Captain interrupted the confrontation immediately and agreed that the Engineer's report must be obtained before anything further was said.

I took my leave of them and the Bridge and went to look for my CO. He had not seen the landing as he was in the Ready Room being briefed by Cdr Ops on the Squadron's role in future operations from this Carrier. 'Leave it with me now, I will consult with the Engineer, see Wings and discuss it with the Captain.' he told me. Well, except for the Seafire pilots, it was a busy time for everyone and I never heard anything more from anyone about that forced landing. It was confirmed that there had been a broken oil pipe in the engine. It was replaced and I flew the aircraft from the Carrier, in some slight trepidation I might add, the next day. I am still a bit miffed, even now as I write, that my feat of astonishing airmanship went unrecorded except in my own Log Book. Everyone was far too busy to give it a thought.

During the next two days, we carried out two patrols each day with all eight squadron aircraft airborne combining with the other Wildcat squadron in another of the Carriers.

There were no problems, neither was there any action except chasing fruitlessly around after much faster enemy bombers which were difficult even to see in the thick hazy weather conditions. It was not a pleasant few days in that ship. The few remaining serviceable Seafires had been able to move to an airstrip ashore, but those pilots who remained on board, with nothing to fly, were miserable. Understandably so; they had suffered a very bad time with the constant crashes of the first two days and it must have been galling to see how easily our Wildcats coped with the deck-landings on their Carrier.

Our Squadron returned to HMS *Illustrious* and the ship's company were given the cheerful news that we were returning to the UK, via Gibraltar.

We paid only a short visit there but it enabled me to buy some goodies to take home. In particular, I bought half a dozen bottles of good Sherry as a sort of peace offering to Father.

In November 1943, HMS *Illustrious* returned from the Mediterranean to Scapa Flow, but before entering harbour there, her four squadrons flew ashore to the Air Station at Hatston. It had been rather a subdued farewell party on board on the final evening mainly, I suppose, because the ship's officers didn't drink much alcohol at sea, as we often did. Truth to tell, I wasn't all that sorry to be leaving HMS *Illustrious* although it was a justly famous ship and I was proud to have served in her. The ship's officers had been an admirable bunch of chaps on the whole but I had never been able to rid myself of the feeling that they regarded us RNVR aircrews as rather below par for the Royal Navy. If these chaps were going to continue serving in Aircraft Carriers, they would have to come to terms, sooner or later, with the fact that the Fleet Air Arm had become composed of ninety-five percent RNVR officers. Another factor was that I had in time become altogether fed up with the bad accommodation.

Two days later, I left Hatston for the long train journey home to Taplow on leave.

CHAPTER TEN

The Far East

I arrived home at Taplow after a long journey by train from Hatston. Mother and Maddie were so very happy to see me that I was embarrassed to remember how, in the past, I had usually spent the first days of my leave in London. They were very pleased with the goodies I had brought them from Gibraltar, mainly jars of unusual types of food, but any food would have been welcome really because rationing had become very stringent. I telephoned Father at 'the old Hell House' to tell him that I had some good sherry for him and he immediately took the opportunity to invite Mother, me and Maddie to his house at Coffinswell for a short visit.

I was surprised at the invitation, bearing in mind that my parents had divorced with some acrimony many years ago, but Mother accepted and next day we trundled down to Devon in the old Austin. The short visit was a success and Father and Mother got on surprisingly well, which gave me great pleasure, so that we returned to Taplow two days day's later on a wave of good feeling. Altogether it was a quiet and pleasant week's leave and, after taking Mother and Maddie for dinner on the last evening to Skindles hotel, for I had plenty of cash remaining after such a quiet leave, I set off on the long, tedious train journey to the Orkneys and back to the Air Station at Hatston.

The biggest surprise when I arrived there was to find that a new Commanding Officer had been appointed to our Squadron, Lt Cdr. Barnett RN. I regretted that I had not had the prior knowledge and opportunity to say goodbye to Jimmy Sleigh, a superb leader, but he had been pier-head jumped to another squadron where his experience was needed. Our new CO came to be known as 'Boot' Barnett: I never knew why unless it was because he appeared always to be rather serious and anxious in his manner. Being a Lt Cdr and RN, he had been given our squadron to command based upon the seniority of his rank although he had little flying experience compared to ours. But that is the way the RN worked and always had done; command always depended upon seniority not experience. It must have been a difficult situation for him and no wonder he appeared constantly anxious. However, he was a reasonably good pilot and never lacked courage.

Also there were four new pilots appointed to the squadron to bring us up to twelve again. Two of them were huge tall chaps; Joe like a long beanpole with a fund of horribly rude stories to tell and Martin, not only tall but big with it and he would survive to play rugby for England after the war. Needless to say that Martin got on particularly well with our two rugby playing New Zealanders, Winnie and Jack. The other two new boys, Ricky and Steven, were quieter characters but both of them good company. I continued to fly with Jack but as the section leader in his flight.

We had to do night flying during that working-up period at Hatston. I knew it to be necessary since in the future I might have to repeat at any time my one night deck-landing at sea. But I loathed flying at night and the truth is that I was still scared of it. Unlike the TBR boys who flew regularly at night, we Fighter boys rarely did enough of it to become confident at night flying. This became apparent when a good friend of mine in the other Wildcat squadron, Stan Brett, was killed hitting high ground on a night exercise.

Christmas came and went while I was at Hatston with the usual round of parties in the Mess. There were not enough WRENs or other local females to jolly the place up so we relied upon boozy parties, plenty of good food despite rationing for the civilian population outside and a plentiful supply of films for the station Cinema. And there was physical recreation, of course. I ought really to have written about the range and type of sporting activities usually available to aircrew as I must have given the impression that, when not aviating, we lay about in our cabins or in the Wardroom perpetually sozzled with pink gin.

On board a Carrier, at sea or in harbour whenever it was practical, the favourite sport was deck hockey. This was played with curved sticks and a puck made of rope rings which had been hardened with aircraft dope. Every department in the ship would produce its own six-man team and the matches were played with the utmost ferocity on the forward flight deck. The other game was volley-ball and, for this, one of the aircraft lifts would be half lowered and a net strung across at the right height. It would sometimes happen, not in many ships thank heavens, that the Captain would make the lordly decision that the aircrews needed organised physical recreation. This would entail our running about the flight deck, in the freezing cold in our shorts, throwing a heavy medicine ball at each other or doing up-downs under the eye of the ship's PT instructor. What a typical bit of RN nonsense that was.

When ashore at an Air Station, my own particular pleasure was to play squash and I had been able to maintain a reasonable standard because there was nearly always a good opponent and a court on most of the aerodromes. Rugby and football matches were arranged frequently and, since most aerodromes were surrounded by fields, there was plenty of space for pitches. My squadron 890 could field an unusually strong rugby team, especially at Hatston when we had three absolutely top players then with Martin joining Winnie and Jack. My engine fitter, Mac, was also a good rugby player. I had managed to disguise from Winnie, our team captain, my natural inclination to funk a tackle but I could handle the ball and kick well and so I played occasionally in the team at centre three-quarter. But really I preferred football which, being much more of a prissy sort of game, suited me better. Moreover, the squadron had a good football team, composed mainly of the ratings, in which I liked to play.

The only other occasion of significance was my birthday in mid-February of 1944 which brought me to the not very grand old age of twenty-two. I had been flying now for three years and, having been commissioned as a Midshipman at age nineteen, I was still only a Sub Lieutenant with no high expectation of becoming anything else. Indeed, I was content to remain as just another 'squadron bog-rat' provided I could continue to be led by people of Jack Parli's quality. As for my flying ability, I had lost my earlier zing and was now no more than a competent pilot with some operational experience. I had a particular dislike of flying in bad weather, which was ridiculous of me, since such weather was a fact of aviation life almost every day. Night flying I hoped to avoid like the plague. I suspect that other pilots had fears about certain aspects of flying which they kept strictly to themselves, as I did. For instance, it was obvious that some chaps never happily came to terms with landing on a deck.

That last paragraph reads rather like a half-term school report and it could well be just that because, while people in England were thinking seriously then about the probable end of the war in Europe, my squadron mates and I were about to start again on a different type of naval warfare in the Far East and Pacific. The confirmation of this came with a signal ordering all 890 Squadron pilots and personnel to embark at Portsmouth in HMS *London*, a Cruiser. We learned that the ship was to give us passage to Ceylon where the Royal Navy was beginning to build up and base much of its entire fleet resources. But a week of leave had been granted before embarkation; probably the last one for a long time: it could be another two years before our return.

Towards the end of that leave, I arranged for all the family to stay at the Park Lane Hotel in London for a farewell dinner party. Father agreed to come up from Devon, Mother and Maddie were only too delighted to stay for a night at the Hotel; Phoebe came too and paired up with Johnnie Lowder and dear Lalline came to keep me company for the night. Entirely unexpectedly and to my pleasure Father said he would host and pay for the dinner party. It had been a very good farewell party and, as such, a cheerful send-off for Johnnie and me to Portsmouth on the following day to embark in HMS *London*. We were to be accompanied on the passage by another Cruiser.

Life on board the Cruiser in the following days was tedious, to say the least. There was nothing in particular for us to do, no duties other than the censoring of letters written by men of the ship's company. Through our CO, Boot Barnett, we asked if we could take on duties on the Bridge as second officer of the watch, for instance. But the response to this was negative although Boot, being an RN officer with a watchkeeping certificate, was welcomed on the Bridge. The normal life at sea for the ship's officers seemed to me to be nearly as boring. Day after day they followed the same routine of watchkeeping, silent gunnery drills, divisional duties and the inevitable supervision of cleaning ship. They had nothing exciting to do each day. Except that, on one special day, there was a gun practice with live shells. The prospect of this shoot had generated great excitement throughout the ship and, when it happened, everyone seemed to enjoy it except me as the noise was appalling and I hate 'bangs.' I spent the half hour of the shoot, therefore, in the heads away down in the bowels of the ship. All their excitement was understandable since, after all, the main purpose of the ship was to fire its big 6-inch guns accurately.

By comparison, life in an Aircraft Carrier, as indeed it must have been also in the small ships of the Royal Navy, was exciting and buzzing with activity. Aircraft landing and taking-off day and night meant that everybody on board a Carrier was actively involved all the time; not just the aircrews but the engineers, the seamen, the aircraft maintenance crews, the flight deck crews, the radar operators and including the cooks and stewards who had to provide them all with continual meals. People had to work fast and hard all the time day after day and mistakes could cause loss of life. Such constant activity generated excitement and enthusiasm; it gave meaning to wartime life for everyone on board a Carrier. It was noticeable, for instance, that the sailors who normally worked below decks in a Carrier and were off duty would find space, if they could safely do so, somewhere around the flight deck to watch the landings and launching of aircraft.

After a long passage, as it seemed, we arrived at Ceylon to disembark the squadron in Colombo. From there the squadron was transported in trucks eighty miles up the west coast to Puttalam, a naval air station consisting of a single runway, made of interlaced metal tracking, cut out of thick jungle. Accommodation for everyone was in 'cadjan' huts of various sizes according to their purpose and located about a mile from the airstrip. These large huts were mostly formed into dormitories or officers' cabins but with one converted as a canteen for the ratings and another as a Petty Officers' Mess.

The whole Air Station was surrounded by jungle but with the front overlooking a salt marsh to the sea. The one really good and attractive building was the Officers' Mess where the bar and lounge looked out through rather grand portals over an open area of gardens on to the main tree-lined highway. Beyond the highway, with its native people constantly passing on foot or driving ox-carts, was the marshland and the sea. I don't know what use the building originally had but I guess it was probably a Rest House, a typical form of small hotel to be found in the Ceylonese countryside. We were very lucky to have this pleasant building to enjoy as our Mess.

During the next two years, I would come to know Ceylon very well indeed, and flying over it daily, would boast that I knew every damn tree. I wrote 'every damn tree' probably because I could never make up my mind what I would do in the event of an engine failure; bale out and become entangled in the top of a tree or crash land into the tops of them? In either case I would never be found in that thick jungle. In the end, as I would be a dead loss whichever I decided, I stopped thinking about it. We had a new batch of Wildcats to fly, which had been delivered straight from America and more new pilots to work-up, so we were going to be busy.

The aircraft were kept in the shade of palm trees as much as possible before flight because, out in the sun, the metal could became too hot to touch so that climbing into the cockpit could be a problem. However, I became used to the heat when flying, as we all did. I wore light flying overalls over just underpants, a tropical flying helmet and, in that strong sun, nearly always flew using sunglasses which the US

Navy had issued to me when I was in America. Light coloured suede half-boots, known as 'brothel creepers' were the only other items normally worn. In spite of the light clothing, I sweated profusely when flying, as we all did. Unfortunately, when we hung our flying kit up on hooks at the end of the day, the various types of huge beetles and particularly the scorpions would infest our sweaty overalls during the night. Our flight office was just another cadjan hut and there was no way of keeping these horrible scorpions and bugs at bay. Before first flight each day, therefore, there had to be a careful and cautious examination of our flying kit before putting it on. I remember we counted four scorpions one morning. Eventually I discarded my flying overalls and wore just shorts, shirt and underpants for flying which could be washed every evening by my 'boy' back at our accommodation block.

My 'boy' was in fact an elderly Ceylonese man who had spent half his lifetime in the Indian army as an officer's batman. I have never known a man dress as smartly as this 'boy'. I cannot remember his name, as I write, but having asked him his name, I remember that I was meticulously careful always to use it correctly. He was quite small and very slim with dark brown leathery looking skin, little beady brown eyes in a strong narrow face surmounted by an immaculate white turban, his body encased in a gleaming white shirt and Sari from which only his brown neck, face and arms protruded. He kept my cabin meticulously clean, guarded it during the day from the many thieves about and spent most of his day 'dhobieing' all my clothes and uniforms.

Once I had arrived back at my cabin from the aerodrome, whether in the morning or evening, he would not allow me out again and to the Mess until I had showered and changed into the freshly dhobied uniform which he had laid out for me. Whenever I tried to skive off to the Mess for a preliminary gin, he would shake his head and say firmly, 'Master cannot go to Mess in dirty clothes, Master must change first.' He was so firm and intense about it that I dared not argue. But how lovely it was to have clean freshly laundered clothes every morning and evening. Whenever I returned to Puttalam during that year, he contrived to act as my 'boy'.

During the monsoon rains, the airfield could become like a quagmire of mud. Elephants were used to move and position the aircraft, which they did much more effectively than tractors could ever have done. We all became rather fond of our elephants, particularly our maintenance crews who, without the elephants, would have been pushing the aircraft around in the mud.

I had a chat with the young mahout of one elephant whom he called 'Lulu.' I asked if I could have a ride later on when he would be passing by our Officers' Mess on his way home. In fact, I had a nasty plot in mind which was to bring Lulu into the Mess if, after a two rupee tip, the mahout was willing. My excuse for this childishness is that, by then, we had been at Puttalam long enough and silly tricks such as this were undertaken to keep ourselves amused; there being not many other forms of entertainment available. The mahout agreed and I clambered on board Lulu's back but, unfortunately, she became stuck halfway through the archway into the main room of the Mess and, in the throes of extricating herself backwards, Lulu left a massive poo in the doorway. I was not the popular figure I had expected to be after that.

Occasionally, we would take one of the two Jeeps allocated to the squadron and dash down to Colombo for drinks and a meal, probably at the lovely Galle Face Hotel. Sometimes we would foolishly decide to go to one of the harbour restaurants, renowned for very hot curried chicken. As I came to realise later, the chicken invariably consisted of meat from the black crows which flocked so noisily and in abundance among the palm trees. I remember with shame now the typical British manner in which we drove to Colombo and back; always much too fast along the eighty miles of that narrow highway, hooting at the lumbering ox-carts and scattering pedestrians as we went.

How aggressive and unpleasant we British must have appeared to the local population. On the other hand I noted, later on when I travelled more in Ceylon, that everyone else seemed to drive in the same manner, hooting their horns aggressively as they screeched their buses and trucks round the bends of the dusty little roadways. But maybe they had learned to drive that way from us?

In a search for entertainment in the evenings, Jack and Winnie would put on their by now famous show of realistic all-in wrestling. Both stripped down to underpants and each grunting and groaning under pressure from dreadful-looking head-locks and arm twists and all that kind of thing. But they made it very funny to watch. Then to my dismay, Johnnie Lowder suggested boxing matches which could take place after dinner in the space near the bar. The next evening he arrived in the Mess equipped with boxing gloves which he had borrowed from the PTI. To start with, he and Martin bashed away at each other and I hoped the whole affair would be limited to the big

*Hank Adlam, a cigarette
between flights* ▶

◀ *In the cockpit of
a Miles Master*

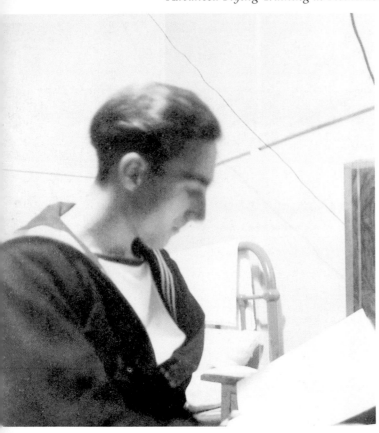

◀ *In a comfortable cabin, mulling over some ground subjects*

With Lalline ▶

▲ *Above, Fraser Shotton, showing how to shoot a line. From the left: Ernie Gaunt RCN, Tony Harris, Fraser, Ian Henderson, Pat Cowan and Bud Sutton RCN*

▼*Below: Hurricanes, with Hank and Harry Beeston*

890 Squadron, 1942

▲ *From left: Hank Adlam, Basil Bartlett, Dagwood Cosh, Jimmy Sleigh CO, Jack Parli, Winnie Churchill and Cliff Nell*

Winnie Churchill, Hank, Jimmy Sleigh, on leave in Richmond, Virginia ▶

◀ *Chrysler saloon loaned to us by a kind American gentleman*

▲ *Group of pilots and ship's officers. Hank, second from left, Winnie Churchill, third from left*

◀ *A Wildcat, with Hank aboard, being ranged for take-off*

Swordfish, having just landed from patrol ▼

◄ *Party time on return to Trincomalee harbour. From far left, Chittenden, Rikki, Hoagy, Jack, Timo, Hank, Cliff, Pat, the Captain and Winnie*

Seafire lands over the crash barrier and dives on to parked Seafires. There were many casualties ▶

▲ *Wildcat, a bad landing*

Seafire, an all-too-common arrival into the crash barrier ▶

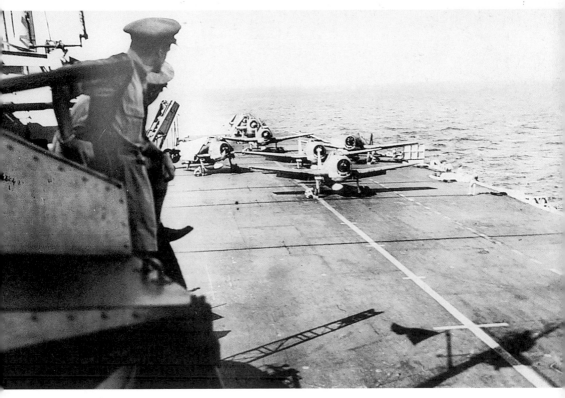

Hellcats about to take off on Combat Air Patrol ▲

Hellcat just landed and folding its wings before going onto the lift ▼

HMS Indomitable, *1839 Squadron, 1945*

◄ *Bombing up*

▼ *Pilots on Stand-By off Sumatra, prior to strike on Palembang, January. From left: Timo Schwenk, Gammy Godson, Neil Rankin, Dick Mackie, ?,?, Stan Farquhar, Fraser Shotton CO*

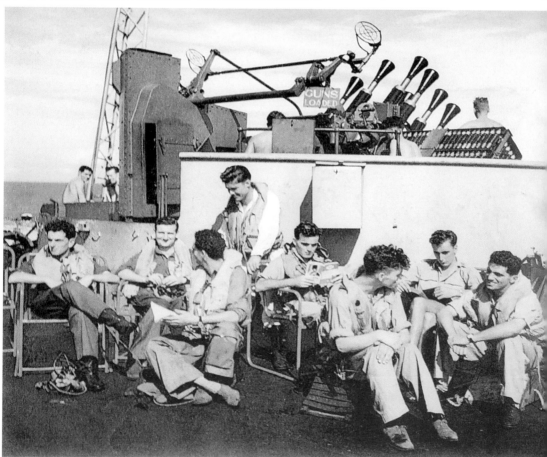

Flight of four Hellcats being ranged for take-off. HMS King George V *in background* ▶

◀ *Noel Mitchell, Senior Pilot, in cockpit at readiness*

◀ *Corsairs ready for take-off*

Leo Budd with his
maintenance crew ▶

Hank, as Squadron Flight Leader with his Corsair number 122, ▶ *and as DLCO batting in a Barracuda* ▼

▲ *The Squadron in Ceylon before going home at the end of the war. Top row: no record of names*
Middle row: Mike Brewer, Peter Ashford, ?,?, Harry Harmsworth, Geoff Higgs
Seated: Thump Orr-Ewing, Jimmy Green, Donald Dick, Hank Adlam and Harry Baines

◀ *Pam, second left,*
and Hank at a
Squadron party in
Cape Town

Engineers Officers' conversion course to service aircraft

◀ *Pupils of my first course, on a Firefly. From left: Rooter Wood, Ace Bailey, Lucky Luckcraft, Jumbo Crammond, Johnny Haines and Jag Mares*

Heather, just before we were married in 1948, with the MG and Tinker ▶

Hank and Heather. These photographs were taken in 1942, before we met ▶

▲ *Two Wildcats chasing a German Focke-Wulf Condor over an Atlantic convoy. The Condor was a well-armed, spiteful opponent*

Two Corsairs on Combat Air Patrol entering the circuit to land-on ▼

men like them and I lurked in the background, out of sight, just in case someone might call upon me to perform. And, of course, they did so. 'Hank' was called for several times and I had to emerge from the shadows pretending enthusiasm.

My opponent was to be an equally light-weight New Zealander who, characteristically, appeared keen on the prospect of the match, dancing about prodding at the air with his gloved fists. I don't remember his name. After we had done a little circle around each other while bobbing about, he suddenly leapt at me and dealt my hooter a frightful blow which caused blood to spurt from it and knocked me on my back to the floor. Gamely, of course, I appeared to struggle with great difficulty to regain my feet for the fight back when, thank heavens, Jack stepped in and, pulling the gloves off my hands, uttered his well-known phrase 'blood and gore all over the floor and me without a spoon,' and suggested, 'We had better finish for now and give boxing a go on another evening.' Dear Jack, knowing me only too well, he had recognised my reluctance to continue. That evening was the end of Boxing as a form of entertainment; men like Jack and Winnie only fought for real with bare fists and were not interested in 'playing' at fighting. Johnnie was the only one disappointed at the conclusion; I think the silly ass was half-hoping for another go at Winnie, no longer with malice but just for the hell of it. He was that sort of chap.

One evening, when we had been at Puttalam for about four weeks, Johnnie walked to the Mess with me and told me of his scheme to go hunting for a leopard skin and of the arrangements he had already provisionally made to do so. He wanted me to join him on a hunting expedition. He proposed to borrow one of the small vans from the transport office, for official recreation purposes of course, and we would drive to a local village about thirty miles into the jungle with his 'boy' to show us the way He had also borrowed two shot guns and battery torches. 'Don't be so daft', I said, 'nobody in their right mind goes shooting at an animal as wild and dangerous as a leopard with a shot-gun.' Then he explained in more detail that the cartridges would be emptied of normal size shot and refilled with nine large shot balls; 'Far more lethal and effective than a single rifle bullet,' he said.

The idea was that we would arrive at the village late in the evening and trek, accompanied by the village tracker, to the water holes. The torches would be fitted on a band round our heads and these we would switch on as we approached the water hole. All we had to do then was to identify a leopard by the width of the eyes reflected in the torchlight and shoot it. This whole idea of Johnnie's was so typically and utterly loony that I was intrigued by it and, on consideration, I reckoned it might be fun. I very much doubted if we would see any animals at all and certainly nothing so exotic as a leopard. But it would be fun, I thought, pretending to be an intrepid hunter and it would make a good story afterwards.

It was Johnnie's show and he made all the arrangements and fixed a date for us to go in a few days time. I was quite looking forward to the little adventure when the unexpected signal came through that the squadron was to embark in HMS *Unicorn* and the pilots were to fly on board on the very morning after Johnnie and I were due to go on this dotty hunting expedition. Well, it was all off as far as I was concerned but Johnnie argued on and on that we could still do it and be back in plenty of time to fly on board the next morning. Eventually, idiot that I was, I agreed to go with him. Our main baggage was packed and would travel with the stewards to the ship in Colombo and, on the face of it, there seemed no reason not to go on the leopard hunt, except maybe for a shortage of sleep before having to land on an unknown Aircraft Carrier. So, regardless of good sense, on the afternoon beforehand we signed for the borrowed van and set off with the 'boy' for the distant village.

It was dusk when we arrived at the village where we met the villagers and the three men who purported to be experienced trackers and would lead us to the water holes. So started the night of total disaster. It was hard going through the jungle tracks over rough ground on a dark night and, two hours later, we had only travelled about three miles when the senior tracker stopped suddenly and signalled for silence. He pointed up towards the tree branches just ahead of us and whispered 'Leopard.' Johnnie immediately shone his torch up there, where certainly two eyes were momentarily reflected, and blasted off with his shot-gun in their direction. Something came to ground (it could have been a monkey) and appeared to bound into thicker jungle ahead of us. I dare not move as I was having sudden trouble with my bowels. But the two youngsters of the three trackers could certainly move and they bolted back the way we had come as fast as they could run. Never mind where the animal went, be it leopard or not, I kept my eye on the remaining older tracker because, if he did a runner too, we might not find our way back for days. I need not have worried on that score; the old boy was a professional and intended to stick with us, for the money if nothing else. So the three of us pressed on.

We came to a sluggish stream. Our guide indicated that we would have to wade along and across it and warned us, 'Masters beware of water snakes, Masters take a stick to keep them away,' and saying this he picked up for himself a broken branch for the purpose. After tucking up his sari tightly round the top of his brown legs and wizened little buttocks, he walked slowly into the dark water up to his waist and turned to wait for us, meanwhile keeping the branch moving around him to ward off the snakes. We had both dressed appropriately for this jaunt into the jungle in long sleeved shirts and long khaki trousers which tucked into the jungle boots with which we had been issued. These boots were made of brown canvas with thick rubber soles and laced right up over the trousers half way up the calf. They really were well designed and just the job for keeping out the myriads of creepy crawlies. By this stage, without them, our legs would have been covered in repulsive blood-soaked leeches. To put it mildly, I was fed up with the whole enterprise but Johnnie, with his press-on spirit, still showed plenty of enthusiasm. So on we went into that stagnant, foul water in which I imagined poisonous snakes swimming round my legs and middle bits. However, what at first I had feared were snakes touching me, turned out to be long weeds and grasses.

After leaving the stream, our guide cautioned absolute silence because, with torches dimmed, we were at long last approaching a water hole. We could hear animals moving and drinking not far away. Creeping nearer, we loaded both barrels of our guns in preparation. Johnnie and I stood up together and switched on our lights .... and there I stopped because there seemed to be scores of reflected eyes turned towards us. How to know which pair might be a leopard?

But Johnnie had no doubt apparently because he blasted off again with his gun.

There were bellows from at least one of the beasts which, as one now came towards us, we could see were mostly buffalos, huge beasts and angry. Our elderly tracker looked very frightened and, clearly furious with these two nincompoop 'hunters', pulled at us quickly to run down a track away from the water hole.

When we were clear Johnnie swore that he had identified and fired at a leopard and wanted to go back to follow it. 'Don't be so ridiculous,' I told him, 'enough is enough of this nonsense; it is nearly one o clock in the morning and already we shall have to move fast to get back in time. And anyway you should break and unload that gun, as I have done, before running any further with it.' With that, I gestured to the tracker to get us back to his village as quickly as possible. There does come a time in dealing with madcap warrior personalities like Johnnie, who are so often like children, that someone has to call a halt to their obsessive desire for excitement. In this case, I ought to have done so much earlier instead of agreeing to go with him on this idiotic hunt. Johnnie, somewhat chastened because the rebuke about the gun had been a good line for me to take, followed meekly as the tracker started the return journey.

We arrived back at the village after three in the morning. The boy remained there, as it was his home village, while I drove off fast along the only road back to the Airstrip. The squadron was due to take-off for rendezvous with HMS *Unicorn* off Colombo at eight-thirty a.m. so that, in reality, we had time to spare and might even catch a couple of hours sleep when we got to the Air Station. It was an uncomfortable journey in our wet clothes but I was relaxed, reckoning that we had no more than another five miles to go. At that point, the engine of the van began to fail and then stopped.

We checked; there was no petrol. The village people must have siphoned out half the tank. Nothing else for it; we would have to take the guns, leave everything else in the van and walk the remaining distance – fast.

The time was nearly 7.30 when we returned to the Air Station, a couple of dirty and bedraggled figures. At the guard-room, Johnnie ran off to return the guns to the armoury, leaving me to cope with the Transport Officer and his inevitable tantrum when he learned that we had left one of his vans unguarded on the road. He wasn't there; presumably still having his breakfast in the Mess. Good; so I briefed his Petty Officer where we had left the van and ran to my cabin to change my filthy clothes. My 'boy,' bless him, was waiting for me with clean shorts, pants shirt and stockings all laid out waiting for me and a bag already packed of long khaki trousers and tunic for on board the ship. I could have kissed his wizened old mug but instead, after I had enjoyed a lovely cold shower, I gave him a huge tip and a sincere 'thank you' for all his good service to me. Then I ran like mad with my overnight bag to catch the bus just leaving for the Airstrip.

Johnnie and I arrived breathless at the squadron office as the CO was half-way through his briefing but we got the main gist of it. Jack whispered to me the correct radio frequency we would be using and, since I would be following as number three behind him anyway; that really was all I needed to know. In fact, I was ashamed of myself for having behaved so irresponsibly. It was maybe acceptable for idiotic and childish characters like Johnnie to go on silly adventures the night before the squadron joined a new ship, but I was a normal kind of chap and should have known better. Nevertheless, despite all the rush and kerfuffle of the recent hours, I was in the cockpit at 8.30 am ready and waiting for the signal to 'press tits' to start up the engine prior to squadron take-off.

Boot Barnett took us in close formation low over the *Unicorn* and a few minutes later, feeling very definitely tired and dozy by now, I found myself on the downwind leg selecting wheels, flaps and hook down prior to the landing. As I locked the canopy back, I had a first good look at the *Unicorn*. She was noticeably higher in the water than other Carriers, having two hangar decks, because her primary function was as an aircraft repair ship. Although I remembered her as having been operational at Salerno where she had operated some Seafires in combination with the four Escort Carriers there. She would not be capable of much more speed than them but the length and width of her flight deck was almost similar to a Fleet Carrier. But there was a good wind to-day out here at sea off the coast of Ceylon and so, with all these good factors in mind, I was not worried about the landing in spite of my lack of sleep. Nevertheless, I kept well behind the Wildcat ahead of me to give myself plenty of time on the final approach. In the event, I plonked my Wildcat down on the deck, comfortably catching the second wire without really noticing whether a batsman was there or not. After some pink gins and a good lunch, I was able to collapse into my bunk and sleep until the evening as there was no further flying that day.

The *Unicorn* was a lovely ship being comfortable even in that hot climate, competently run and happy. Moreover, it had one enormous advantage which occurred in very few other British Aircraft Carriers during the whole course of the war, as far as I am aware. It had as its Captain an experienced naval aviator; one who not only knew about aircraft but could actually fly one. Captain St John Fancourt, DSO, RN had been the Commanding Officer of the Skua squadron which he had led from Hatston to attack German shipping in a Norwegian harbour in 1940. It is known that those ridiculous Skua aircraft made an effective attack but, more astonishingly, most of them succeeded in getting back to Hatston. The distance to the target and back was really too far and only by brilliantly precise navigation did some of the Skuas return without ditching. It does seem such a pity that this 'flying' Captain RN was not given one of the more operational Fleet Carriers to command. I can only suppose that, according to Admiralty procedure, he had not sufficient seniority in rank as a Captain over all the other non-flying Captains.

The Squadron remained on board *Unicorn* for a period of about ten days before our troops were disembarked at Colombo and we flew back to Puttalam. During that time, we carried out some strafing exercises at sea on other warships, such as Battlewagons, Cruisers and Destroyers, which had recently come out from the UK. There was no doubt that the Admiralty was building up a huge presence in this part of the world in preparation for attacks on the Japanese. However, regardless of the unknown original purpose of our joining *Unicorn*, it was a pleasant period on board her and there were no flying accidents. In retrospect, I guess that it had been a useful ten days all round. Our strafing attacks on the Warships had been good practice for us, training for their gun crews, and our landings had kept the flight deck organisation of the *Unicorn* up to scratch.

On return to Puttalam, I was so pleased to find that my same 'boy' was ready to look after me. But Johnnie and I learned that the van which we had abandoned on the road, on the night of the 'hunt', had been stripped down to the chassis in the short time before the Transport team came to rescue it. We had to face the wrath of the irate Transport Officer who swore that he would have us court-martialled for our criminal negligence. It was quite funny really because signals followed Johnnie and me from ship to ship for months after, demanding that we attend at a formal enquiry in Colombo. These signals were sensibly ignored on the authority of the Captains in the ships since our purpose in life was to make war against the Japanese. I suspect that all the fighting services, not just the Royal Navy, contained chaps like the transport officer. Officers in charge of stores, men doing those kinds of jobs who, some of them, never seemed able to come to grips with the abnormal demands and events arising from war. They lived in a world of indents, lists and signed chits without which nothing could be moved or done.

A week after our return to Puttalam came the very welcome and surprise signal that the squadron was to join the Escort Carrier, HMS *Atheling*. All of us looked forward to joining an operational ship again. It was now May 1944; we felt that we had been flannelling around in Ceylon, waiting for something to happen, for far too long.

CHAPTER ELEVEN

HMS *Atheling*

O ur CO, Lt Cdr. Barnett, was ordered to Colombo, to SEAC, I
think it was called, being South East Asia Command of the
Admiralty, to be given a briefing about the Squadron's future
movements. He wasted no time the next day, bless him for that, in
calling us pilots together to give us as much information as he had
obtained. He told us that HMS *Atheling*, another American-built
Escort Carrier, was already on its way from Trincomalee, the huge
harbour on the other side of the Island, to Colombo where our
squadron personnel would embark. The Carrier would have two
fighter squadrons allocated to it, our Squadron 890 with ten Wildcats
and Squadron 889 of ten Seafires. The ship would be classified as an
Assault Carrier although exactly what it was to assault with two
fighter squadrons was not yet clear. No doubt we would find out in
good time. But such information as had been given was very
welcome; everyone in the squadron had become fed up with hanging
around without having a known objective. The pilots, in particular,
were excited at the prospect of joining a ship again.

The Fleet Air Arm was building up into a major striking force
using Ceylon as a training area and as a base for operations against
the Japanese in the Bay of Bengal. There were now five Naval Air
Stations on the Island, the biggest being at Trincomalee alongside the
harbour which, being so very large, was to become known as the
Scapa Flow of the Far East. Already in May 1944 the harbour was
becoming full of Royal Navy ships, including Battleships and Cruisers
together with their attendant Destroyers all in support of the Aircraft
Carriers. Supply ships in large numbers were also making an
appearance. This was going to be a new form of sea warfare for the
Royal Navy which hitherto had become accustomed to being
dependent for its supplies, in the European and Atlantic theatres of
war, on nearby harbours.

But out here in the Indian and Pacific oceans, the Royal Navy would have to transport its own fuel, ammunition and all other supplies at sea with it. Not since the blockade of the French during the Napoleonic war culminating at Trafalgar had the Royal Navy needed to keep a fleet at sea for very long periods without the support of nearby harbours. It would be a major logistic problem which the US Navy had already solved by using large fleets of supply ships. And so the Royal Navy would have to adapt quickly if it was to fight alongside the Americans in the Pacific.

I had become aware over the past few weeks of the general situation and the reason for our presence in Ceylon but, in the slack period of recent weeks with the squadron tucked away in the jungle airstrip at Puttalam, I don't believe that much thought had been given by any of us pilots to the naval developments taking place around us on the island. Our interest quickened now that we knew of the more active role the squadron was about to take and a fresh surge of eagerness to get going could be felt among all the personnel.

In the past weeks Puttalam had seemingly become full of Wildcat aircraft and pilots; our own number was twelve plus two other spare pilots and anther squadron of twelve Wildcats was also based at the Air Station. But now, 890 Squadron was to be reduced to ten aircraft and pilots before flying on board *Atheling*. Of the ten pilots, only Jack, Winnie and I now remained from the original squadron.

A few days later, the squadron was airborne to rendezvous with HMS *Atheling* off the east coast of Ceylon opposite Colombo. We were a bit untidy as a formation, having ten aircraft, so that we had to fly a normal flight of four with the CO and then two flights of three with Jack and Winnie as the leaders. As usual, I was with Jack. I felt genuinely excited at the prospect of joining an Aircraft Carrier again. I liked being at sea. I had confidence in myself as a deck-landing pilot, I reckoned I was as good as any and better than most at putting an aircraft down on the deck. As for the sea, well it could be as safe an environment as any other on which to be forced down for any reason. There was always my particular fear of bad weather and out here, particularly in monsoon conditions, the weather could be frighteningly bad with turbulent cloud going up to great heights. On the other hand, if in thick cloud, it was always better to let down over the sea, rather than over mountainous land. With these thoughts, as we flew low in formation over our new home ship, I was on the whole a right cheerful little chap, strapped down tight into my cockpit ready for the first landing on *Atheling*. The Carrier was the same to look at as any other of the American built Escorts and it would, I knew, be much the same below decks. The important factor would be the ship's officers and whether they and we in the two squadrons would get on and work well together.

In this confident mood, I flew down the starboard side of the Carrier, ready to break away to follow Jack to port on to the downwind leg. 'Concentrate,' I told myself; 'This first landing is no time to be over-confident and to make a mess of it; so no showing off.' On this first approach, I am also watching the batsman as I turn in towards the stern of the ship. I like him; he is nicely steady and positive with the bats and no dancing about. I think to myself that his signals could be worth following on a bad day. Whoops; it is a bad day NOW! I had forgotten the much slower wind speed over the deck of a small Carrier and I am there before I know it. I had misjudged it and already I am almost over the round down. Quickly straightening the aircraft level from the turn, I lose sight of the smaller 'Island' and the short flight deck ahead of me. My normal certainty of the aircraft position relative to the flight deck is gone. In a near panic, I am about to jam the throttle wide open in an attempt to go round again, hoping to miss the crash barrier ahead, when I see the batsman giving me the 'cut engine' signal, which I obey gratefully.

The Wildcat thumps down on the deck and the hook picks up a late wire. The flight deck handlers are there fast to disengage the hook and wave me over the crash barrier to park and switch off the engine. Phew; that was frighteningly close to disaster. As I clamber out of the cockpit, I determine never to be so cocky again and to remind myself constantly how very small is the margin for error when deck-landing. A small mistake and a few seconds can be the difference between a comfortable thump on to the deck, (followed by a nice glass of pink gin in the wardroom) or the aircraft crashing on its back into the sea … and you are dead. Another thing, I told myself, don't be so damnably disparaging in future about the batsmen and their signals; you might not have made it down this time without such help. Suitably chastened, I left my flying kit in the Ready room and made my well-known way down to the Wardroom.

And then the joy of having a decent cabin again. Admittedly rather dourly decorated in grey paint on the metal bulkheads but, in the US Navy style, having everything nicely designed for comfortable living with hand basin, mirror, including plenty of cupboards and drawers for uniforms and clothes, a small writing desk and a comfortable chair. A retreat for occasional solitude when it was needed where I could read, write or just have a quiet kip on my bunk. I am sharing the cabin with Johnnie Lowder and, from custom I suppose, I opt for the upper bunk. Sharing a cabin with Johnnie was an experience in itself; we were such different characters. I would tend to do everything in plenty of time; rise out of my bunk early if I was due to fly, get changed into flying kit with ages of time to spare, that sort of thing.

Johnnie, on the other hand, to start the day would not even open his eyes until he had groped for a cigarette from the table next to his bunk, stuck it into his mouth and somehow lit it, seemingly still with his eyes shut while ignoring the hot cup of tea the steward had brought, until his fag was finished and the tea cold. I used to watch him fascinated, as he went through this morning ritual. If he was on an early flight, he would never make a move from his bunk until the very last minute. Discarding any thought of breakfast and often cutting the pre-flight briefing, he would climb into his cockpit just in time as the call to 'start engines' was given. And off he would go to fly brilliantly.

We were quite different characters, but we got on very well together in spite of Johnnie's sometimes alarming rages. Using a small sharp knife, he could carve aircraft models in wood or sometimes just make interesting shapes of the wood pieces. I remember he had all but finished the model of a Wildcat which it seemed to me to be beautifully done. But he made a slight fault at the very last and, in an absolute fury, he crushed the model in his great hands and hurled it against the bulkhead of the cabin then ground his foot over the remaining pieces. He was a perfectionist model maker.

In the meantime, *Atheling* was making her way round to the other side of the Island towards Trincomalee where the Seafire squadron was based and from where the Seafires would fly out to join us and land on. With experience and memories of the unfortunate Seafires crashing all day and daily on Escort Carriers at Salerno, it was unfortunate that the Admiralty had not provisioned something better than the Seafire to operate from our small, slow Escort Carrier. Their expectation and hope (assuming that they had given it any thought at all) was that in the Indian Ocean the wind conditions would be strong enough to favour the Seafire landings. However, as I had enough experience out here now to know, the weather could behave very oddly, especially during the monsoon. There were times when, in spite of low cloud and heavy rain, the wind nevertheless could be almost entirely still. It would seem as if the thick, dark grey massive cloud, reaching up to 30,000 feet sometimes, was squatting down like a gigantic elephant with its bottom over the land and sea, but unable to make any wind. Such weather conditions would cause real difficulty for the Seafires and they wouldn't be much fun for us in our Wildcats either.

The next day off Trincomalee, waiting for the Seafires to appear, everybody who could do so was in a Goofing area ready to watch them land on. Being reasonably early in the morning, the weather was bright and breezy, just right for the Seafire boys to make their first landing on *Atheling*, but big cumulus clouds would build up later on over the land as happened each day once the hot sun had risen. They arrived in formation flying low and fast over the Carrier then streamed up into echelon with the first flight ready to curve round on to the downwind leg. It was well done and we waited anxiously for the first approach and landing, hoping it would be a safe one. Indeed it was a beautifully smooth landing by their CO who, as we found when we met later, was a Lieutenant Schwenk RNVR, a small dark cheerful man usually known a 'Timo' being apparently a synonym of Timoshenko, a famous Russian general at that time. One or two of the landings were a bit dicey, but they all got down safely. As soon as they were all landed on, the ship proceeded into Trincomalee harbour and came to a mooring somewhere in the middle, surrounded by a host of other warships.

There was a party in the Wardroom that evening at which the pilots of both squadrons combined with the ship's officers not on duty. It was a most cheerful occasion which augured well for a happy ship with aircrew and ship's officers getting on well together. The Captain came to join in the party after dinner. This was the first opportunity for him to meet squadron pilots since his ship, which had arrived only recently from the UK, had been used non-operationally as a ferry to bring new aircraft out to Ceylon. I think he was rather bemused at first at the very boisterous nature of the party but he evidently enjoyed our Fleet Air Arm songs. To us at that time he appeared as an elderly old chap of about sixty, but a friendly and likeable man. He knew little or nothing, of course, about aircraft or Carrier operations.

The subsequent working up period went reasonably well with eight aircraft at a time ranged for take-off, provided there was sufficient wind, followed by strafing exercises at targets towed astern of the ship or at selected locations ashore. Two Seafires hit the crash barrier on landing and were write-offs although the pilots were more or less unhurt. One of our Wildcats made a bad approach and, trying to go round again, caught the top of the crash barrier with its tail-wheel and crashed onto its back. The pilot was hospitalised on return to harbour and had to be exchanged. The weather had been good with adequate wind speeds over the deck most of the time, except on the one windless day when the crashes had occurred.

A few days later, we left Trincomalee harbour accompanied by a Cruiser, two Destroyers and two Frigates on the first of several sorties to attack Japanese supply ships and their protective airfields along the coasts of the Andaman and Nicobar islands. The aim of our small force, we were briefed, was to cause such havoc as we could among the Japanese shipping, relying mainly on the Cruiser and Destroyers for this purpose and for *Atheling*, with her complement of twenty fighter aircraft, to deal with the expected opposition from enemy aircraft and to strafe the airfields. Although no major warships were expected in that area now, there was an abundance of these supply ships serving the Japanese army in Burma and under the protection of the Japanese-held airfields. But, from the formal briefing in the Ready room, I rather gained the impression that in reality we had very little information about the target area. Usually, on these sorties, our Wildcats formed the continuous Combat Air Patrol over the target area or over the little Fleet since, with their limited endurance, the Seafires were less suitable for such work.

We in 890 Squadron were irritated that we had to continue the Patrols while Seafires were launched more often than us to carry out specific attacks on such 'targets of opportunity' or enemy aircraft as they might find on the coastline. It was poor thinking really because the Wildcats, with their six 0.5 Browning machine guns, had the greater firepower eminently more suitable for strafing ground targets. When flying over Japanese-held territory, there were always in my mind the lurid stories of the barbaric treatment known to be given by the Japanese to any aircrew shot down and taken prisoner. At one time aircrew had been provided with cyanide tablets; the choice of a quick death being preferable to the treatment they could expect to receive from the Japanese as their prisoner.

We did not have cyanide tablets now but we were extensively equipped to cope with being shot down over jungle type territory held by the Japanese, including a waterproof medical kit containing four strong morphine phials. One of these could be used if badly wounded or all four phials in place of the cyanide tablets. We had light-weight flying suits with the jungle-type boots such as Johnnie and I had worn on that daft leopard hunt. The suit had pockets designed to take special escape equipment which included an astonishing little combination of a shotgun cum 0.22 rifle for shooting small game, an essential machete for hacking a path through jungle terrain, a lethal-looking knife with an eight inch blade, a kit containing a small torch and waterproof match-box and, finally, a holster and belt containing a huge 0.45 revolver and ammunition. Clever little compasses were contained in such things as buttons or pencils. 'Blood chits' as they were called, i.e. letters written in the language of the area guaranteeing sums of money to any native who gave help, were also provided. Climbing into the cockpit, festooned with all this equipment, one could feel like a knight of old mounting his charger. In practice, many aircrew, myself included, discarded items such as the revolver and combination gun as being too heavy and cumbersome in the cockpit.

On these sorties, the Cruiser and Destroyers banged off their guns on targets along the coast which were selected for them by two of the Seafire pilots. These two pilots had been trained in the technique and specialised jargon used for 'spotting' and reporting the fall of shot from the guns of the warships. These operations, minor as they were, seemed to have gone quite well and undoubtedly adversely affected the Japanese military supplies to their army in Burma.

It was decided that the Seafires should take their turn about with the Wildcats at patrolling over the fleet and, although we pilots in our Wildcat squadron were glad to be sharing the task, it seemed to be rather an unnecessary risk for the Seafires. In fact, it proved to be a disastrous decision because, during the early part of a return passage to Trincomalee, the wind speed began to fall while the Seafires were still airborne.

One of the Seafire pilots, a young New Zealander of rather small stature which did not help him in seeing over the long nose of his aircraft, had difficulty on his first approach to land and had to open up the throttle to go round again. He barely did so in time and nearly hit the crash barrier as he pulled away over the top of the Seafires already landed.

I was watching these landings from a small gallery half way up and at the side of the Island and I felt nervous and worried about the young pilot as he came round again for a second attempt at a landing. He was coming in much too fast, I thought, and so evidently did the batsman who was waving him off and again the pilot opened the throttle, although before he reached the ship's stern this time, so that he went round well above and clear of the deck on this second attempt. I don't know why I stayed to watch, I dreaded any crash on the flight deck which could so often result in the aircraft going over the side. But there was always the expectation that 'it would be all right'; the pilot would master his difficulty and get down safely. Nobody else seemed to be worried, other than me and the batsman and no doubt Wings too was anxious about the situation up on his bridge, although I couldn't see him. It was on the face of it, no more than a pilot having to go round again from a bad approach to his landing. But this was unusual because it would be the pilot's third attempt.

Three Seafires had already landed and were parked in the bows in front of the crash barrier with the usual number of maintenance crews and deck handlers milling round to secure the parked aircraft. The last pilot to land was still fiddling about with something in his cockpit, for some reason, something I personally would never have done. For me the first essential action after landing was always to get the hell out of the cockpit and to the side of the flight deck as quickly as possible. Other men had to be there working in front of the barrier, but there was no reason for a pilot to stay there.

Meantime, the Seafire had gone well ahead of the ship and was just turning, quite far out, on to the downwind leg. I could imagine the young pilot, girding up his courage for the next attempt to land on the deck. I had seen his head as he went past last time, barely above the side of the cockpit with his white face looking down. I felt strongly that temporarily he had 'lost the plot' of how to land the thing and that he was desperate. Oh, why can't Wings, I thought, just pick up the radio telephone and tell the guy to go up high enough to bale out and be picked up by the Frigate? Who could care about the value of the Seafire; heaven knows scores of the wretched things had already been written off trying to land on Carriers; not to mention the write-off of pilots.

It was just a thought, a longing for good sense. But, of course, it was impossible; how could the Captain and Wings write their report afterwards to say 'Very sorry, but the pilot was having some difficulty landing so we told him to bale out.' A fighting service could never be run in such a manner. And so here he came on his third approach to the deck. Too straight he came, too low and much too fast. The batsman was trying to give him corrective signals, but on he came hopelessly wrong. The pilot swooped up fast over the round-down, ignored the batsman's frantic 'wave-off' then he must have put the nose down, desperate to get down somehow onto the deck and he flew, in front of my eyes, fast over the barrier and directly on to the Seafires parked forward. He landed right on top of the Seafire with the pilot still fiddling about in his cockpit.

There was an explosion, although not a massive noise from it, but I could see sheets of flame and many large pieces of metal flying out from the explosion in all directions. These pieces of metal caused casualties and wounds among those men working ahead of the barrier. The 'emergency on deck' siren was blaring out and people were cascading up from below decks to see what was the emergency and prepared to deal with it. The fire crew were joined by the two RNVR doctors who were both at the crash almost immediately to organise stretcher parties to help the injured. I came down from the Island to join the stretcher parties but I was not good at it. I helped one of the two sick berth attendants, on the edge of the bloody shambles, to deal with a young sailor of the deck party whose leg had suffered a huge gash down to the visible bone and was pumping blood. But that was my lot, I had to go below to my cabin where I lay on the bunk feeling shaky. Both of the Seafire pilots had been killed; the one flying and the other who had stayed in his cockpit in the deck park. Three sailors working ahead of the barrier had been killed, two more had been shoved over the side by one of the aircraft, almost on top of them, and were picked up by the Frigate. A further ten men were very seriously injured and some in a critical condition. I had seen a good many crashes on a flight deck, but that was the worst.

The ship had already turned away from the north Sumatra coast and now headed straight back towards Ceylon at her best speed. The next morning, I was feeling rather queasy still but had to rouse myself for the dawn CAP with Jack leading. I reckoned that I was probably suffering from too much of the whisky I had needed after the awful crash of the previous day but, even as I lined up for the take-off, I felt a pain in the gut and a reluctance to get airborne. I decided that it must be one of my 'bad premonition' days which usually I could disregard as soon as I became airborne. The pain in my gut continued, however, even after I had joined up with the flight and indeed it became so severe that I had to do something about it. The only thing I could do was to contact the ship asking for permission to land. What an embarrassment; they would ask me for a reason and all I would be able to say was that I had a bad tummy ache and needed to go to the heads. Moreover, for me to land back on board meant that those aircraft already ranged at the stern of the flight deck, ready to take-off later, would all have to be pushed forward ahead of the crash barrier.

The pain was getting worse; I reiterated my need to land; reluctant approval was given and the ship started to turn into wind for me. I don't remember much about the landing, only scrambling out of the cockpit and racing down below to the heads while ignoring the Tannoy ordering me to report to Wings. Almost immediately, the two Doctors came to examine me in my cabin and concluded that I had appendicitis. These two young RNVR doctors had enough on their plate already with ten men, very seriously injured from the appalling crash on the flight deck of the previous day, in need of their greatest care and attention. Meantime, while *Atheling* was making full speed back to Ceylon, a signal had been sent to the hospital ship in Trincomalee harbour to prepare for the injured men. A second signal was sent to advise the hospital ship of two more surgical operations needed; one an appendicitis case (me) and the other a sinus operation which Jack Parli required. That tough man, Jack, had been suffering for the past two years with dreadful sinus pains while flying. He had never complained but I had seen him, climbing out of his cockpit after landing, his face ashen with the pain of it.

After transfer to the hospital ship in harbour, I had been slightly apprehensive on being greeted and examined by the Commander RN Doctor, because I had the notion that the limit of a regular RN doctor's experience of surgery was lancing boils on sailor's bottoms. But this was an unfair nonsense, of course, because this man completed major surgery with success on those badly injured survivors of the dreadful Seafire crash.

As for my appendicitis, he had whipped that out without any trouble and also had dealt successfully with Jack's sinus problem although Jack, lying in the hospital bed next to mine, was still in some pain after the operation.

Our comfort in this old hospital ship, efficient as it was, depended upon the speed of a never-ending army of ants which menaced that comfort. Their determined approach across the old decking of the ship and then up the four legs of my bed had to be combated by the speed of the orderly in coming to sweep them away. Each leg of the bed was standing in a tin of very strong disinfectant which killed immediately the advance guard of the ants but, as they expired in their hundreds in the tins, so the main body of the ant army would stream over their corpses and up the legs of my bed. I remember watching their menacing progress with fearful fascination, ready to call for help if they started to mount the legs of Jack's bed or mine.

While lying there, I gave some thought to the sailors in the next ward, whom I hoped were recovering from their serious wounds, although I had heard some cry out in pain from time to time. Sailors who worked on the flight deck, were often at risk from whirling propellers, flight deck equipment, or from crashing aircraft, as the awful injuries from the recent accident in *Atheling*, bore witness.

After three days in the hospital ship, Jack and I were transferred by ambulance to a hospital in Colombo and there followed a period of three weeks of care and cosseting such as I had never thought to expect from the Royal Navy. After three days in the hospital ship, Jack and I were transferred by ambulance to a hospital in Colombo and thence, after one week, to an hotel in Galle. This was a lovely old town on the southern tip of Ceylon which, before the Japanese had threatened the Island with their bloody war, had been a major tourist attraction. The hotel was the best in town and we shared a large and well-furnished room. All this was apparently for free and paid for by the Navy so that these two naval aviators could convalesce from their minor surgical operations.

We spent the ten days there quietly enjoying the comfort, the abundant good food and bottled beer. We swam every day from the beach, contained within a wide bay and surrounded by tall palm trees. Jack swam and surfed, using a tiny board, entering the rough sea from far out at the edge of the bay which gave him a run of some four hundred yards to the long, wide beach where, usually in the mornings, I would be paddling about and attempting to swim or just lying in the sun.

During the afternoons, I had found another and different interest in the lovely form of the girl receptionist at the hotel. She was a local girl, small and slim of body having a strikingly beautiful face, and I made every excuse I could find to talk to her at the reception desk. It was unusual in Ceylon for a girl to obtain that sort of job but she spoke very good English with a delightful lilt to it and her father, so I learned, held some management job at the famous Galle Face hotel in Colombo and, being in the trade, had been able to help her. Her name was something like Senaika Pereira but she didn't mind if I called her Sennie. She was engaged, she told me, to a boy who worked as a clerk at the bus station in Colombo. They could only meet once a month and both were waiting until they could save enough money to get married.

Sennie was nervous at being seen talking to me too frequently at the desk and, if I wanted to talk 'seriously' she said with a smile, then we could talk together in the privacy of her room. Her room, where I spent the first of four happy afternoons, was tiny and not much bigger than a box room, but it was cool, being shaded by a hill and trees at the back of the hotel, and there was a small loo and wash-basin next door. For her job, she wore European style clothes of a cream blouse, dark blue skirt, white socks and sandals. She wasted no time at all in taking them all off together with her bra and short silk knickers, turning away from me as she did do to reveal her gorgeous little brown bottom and legs. I trembled so much with desire to touch and hold her that I could hardly fumble my trousers and pants down, but I did.

How very fortunate I was because Sennie brought such a sense of fun and laughter into our lovemaking. Although she did not actually hold up a 'no-entry' sign for me to see, yet it was clearly there for me to understand and to observe. Instead, with close cuddly hugs and busy hands, we kept each other happy and satisfied. I was due to return to Colombo and, on what was to be our fourth and last afternoon together, I told Sennie as I kissed her goodbye that I had so much wanted to buy her a nice present but I had not been able to find something she might like. I hoped she would not feel hurt, I said, because instead I intended to leave a good contribution towards the money she needed for her marriage. How pleased she was and indeed, how I had grown up. At last I had learned to do the right thing gracefully.

With very little boozing and apart from my happy little joust with Sennie, it had been a quiet idyllic holiday which I knew that I badly needed and it wouldn't have done Jack any harm either. In the evenings, we had talked quietly about our home life and I learned in confidence about Betty, the girl Jack had met in Scotland and had promised to marry, if he should survive the war. He was seriously engaged to her hence he had not been interested in finding female company during our holiday, as he normally would have done. The only other person to know of his engagement was his closest friend, Winnie Churchill.

CHAPTER TWELVE

HMS *Indomitable*

The comfortable, quiet and very pleasant convalescence which Jack and I had enjoyed at the hotel in Galle was over. A car was sent to the hotel to collect and drive us to the Officers' Mess at the Racecourse aerodrome in Colombo. We barely had time to settle into a cabin before we were summoned to the office of Commander Air where we were astonished to receive the news that our Squadron 890 had been temporarily disbanded. Some of the pilots, mostly the latest to join 890, had been flown by transport aircraft back to England where they would join a group of new squadrons destined, in due course, to be part of the Pacific Fleet. Both Winnie Churchill and Johnny Lowder had been sent to join 1838 Squadron in HMS *Atheling* again, but flying the American designed and built Corsair aircraft. Jack was to join them in *Atheling* as soon as he had obtained experience of the Corsair, flying from China Bay aerodrome at Trincomalee.

It seemed so natural and obvious to me that I should go with my three best friends to the same Corsair squadron. But no; I had been appointed to 1839 Squadron in HMS *Indomitable* flying Hellcats, the latest aircraft designed by the Grumman Company who had produced the Wildcat. I telephoned the Appointments Officer at the Admiralty offices in Colombo and pleaded to go with my friends to the Corsair squadron, trying to make a case that we had flown together as a flight for so long and the value therefore of our combined experience. Nonsense he said (quite rightly of course) and anyway, as a naval officer I must go where I was told. He reminded me that I was due to be flown by transport aircraft to China Bay early the next morning. I must get on with it, he told me, because 1839 Squadron needed another pilot urgently and one experienced enough to convert to the Hellcat quickly. So that was that. Jack and I had just a few quiet jars together in the Mess that evening; there was too much on our minds for a party. Each of us would have to convert on to a new type of fighter aircraft over the next two days, he on Corsairs and I on Hellcats, and fly them well enough to deck-land on to our respective Aircraft Carriers. We had been told that we would have only two or three days at the most to gain the necessary experience before landing on.

The following day, in August 1944, I was flown in a naval communications Beechcraft to China Bay where I informally joined 1839 Squadron when I met the Commanding Officer, Lt Cdr Shotton RNR with one of the squadron pilots, Jack Haberfield. Fraser Shotton had trained with me on the same fighter course at Yeovilton in 1941. How very long ago that seemed. He had been a merchant navy officer before the war and being then aged about twenty-two, had been quickly promoted to Lieutenant and now he had just been given command of the squadron. I remembered him as a quiet man, a cheerful co-trainee and companion of that time and felt glad to have him as my commanding officer. Haberfield was a New Zealander, a Maori with a smiling and friendly face, and his slightly chubby appearance belied his physical strength. Shotton explained that the squadron had been embarked in HMS *Indomitable*, now in Trincomalee harbour, for the past month. We three were due to fly on board her in two day's time.

That afternoon, after a quick lunch, Haberfield took me down to the squadron dispersal area where three Hellcats were parked in the shade of palm trees and ready for flight. This was my first sight of a Hellcat. I had heard about the aircraft, of course, and knew that the American Navy pilots had flown this latest fighter with great success against the Japanese in the Pacific. The Hellcat, with its round fuselage leading back from a huge radial engine, was basically like a Wildcat to look at but very much bigger. In fact, it seemed to me then at first sight to be a monstrously large aircraft for a single-seater fighter. One good factor, I could see immediately, was the wide undercarriage with each oleo leg mounted under each wing. Its armament was six 0.5 Browning machine guns and it was provisioned with racks for four rockets and for two 500lb bombs. In fact, it was a very fast and formidable Fighter/Bomber. I spent half an hour reading the Pilot's Notes, sitting in the spacious and well laid out cockpit while Haberfield pointed out the position of the various controls and described the aircraft's flying characteristics. Then, no good thinking about it any longer, it was time to go. From the nearby Ready room, I collected my new khaki flying suit and tropical helmet with oxygen mask, and made myself ready mentally to fly the Hellcat.

I climbed up the port wing to the cockpit and settled down on the parachute seat while the maintenance crew strapped me in. A quick look round the instruments and controls to remind myself of their unfamiliar position, checked the movement of the flying controls and then signalled the crew, by now waiting on the ground, that I was ready to start up. The huge engine bellowed into life. I checked the magnetos on the run-up and was ready then to taxi out on to the runway. Given clearance from the control tower to take off, I opened up the throttle fully and felt the acceleration from the powerful radial engine; a much greater response than the little Wildcat could give. Comfortably airborne after a short take-off run, I began a climb to 12,000 feet where I intended to carry out some stalls and slow flying with wheels and flaps down.

The weather was good; the midday cu-nim clouds had not yet built up. Down below I could see Trincomalee harbour crowded with shipping and, either side of it, the coastline of sandy beaches for miles and, inland, the jungle covered hills. The Island of Ceylon was as beautiful from the air as it was from the ground. I found the Hellcat to be a gentle giant; admittedly she dropped fast like a brick when stalled, but with no vicious roll-over. I practised slow flying with maximum drag, as for a deck-landing approach and, to finish, some steep turns. Satisfied with my control and handling of the aircraft, I returned to the aerodrome to make a normal landing. Later in the afternoon I took off again and climbed up to 32,000 ft to see how she handled at height and found control at that level to be better than anything I had ever flown before. Then down to 12,000 ft again for some of my aerobatics which, dreadfully imprecise as usual, nevertheless enabled me to learn how she handled. After landing, I felt ready for a session of ADDLs i.e. dummy deck-landings on the runway, scheduled for the next morning.

That evening, I had a long chat with Jack Haberfield who, as an original member, was able to tell me about 1839 Squadron and what it had been doing since it had been formed in 1943 at Eglinton Air Station in Northern Ireland with ten new Hellcats. All the pilots, except Shotton and Lt Cdr Jeram RN, the Commanding Officer, had been trained in America and moved initially to Canada where they gained experience on flying the Hellcat. Apparently there was a procedure for delivering both the Hellcat and the Corsair straight to Canada from the production lines in America where they were built. It interested me that, by the time these newly trained pilots had joined 1839 squadron at Eglinton, they had amassed some 330 flying hours compared with the 146 flying hours when I joined my first operational squadron 890 in 1941. During their working-up period the squadron had experienced bad luck when three of their pilots had been killed, one through oxygen failure at height. Two more were killed just before I joined; one crashed with engine failure over the jungle and the other crashed into the sea while diving and firing at a splash target behind the ship.

The squadron had embarked in HMS *Begum* during February 1944, the aircraft having been hoisted aboard at Belfast dock, for passage to the Far East. They arrived and were put ashore at an aerodrome on the south-east coast of India. They had a frustrating time there because the Hellcats were continuously unserviceable through lack of spare parts and the pilots were unable to do much flying. Moreover, apparently the accommodation and food were foul and, to top up the ill-luck, the CO Jeram became ill.

Not until June did the whole incompetent mess start to become sorted out when the squadron was moved at last to the Racecourse aerodrome at Colombo and new Hellcats, with spare parts, were delivered to them. At about this time, the pilots carried out their first deck-landings on HMS *Unicorn*. It was not a successful performance as, although none of the pilots were badly hurt, there were three barrier crashes.

At the end of July, the squadron at last embarked all their personnel, stores and equipment on to their ship HMS *Indomitable*. The following day, at the landing on at sea, the first Hellcat flown by the CO crashed badly. He touched down all right apparently, but very much too fast, so that the arrester hook pulled out of the aircraft which then continued through both crash barriers and over the side into the sea. Jeram managed to get out and was picked up by the attendant Destroyer. He had experienced a long innings of operational flying since 1941 (he had been on the fighter course at Yeovilton ahead of me) and the Medical Officer decided that enough was enough after the crash and declared him to be operationally tired and to be rested. I was glad to learn that a medical officer had taken such an initiative. It was unusual because I doubted whether many naval doctors had any idea at all of the mental stresses caused by normal day to day service flying, particularly from Carriers. Neither did the Admiralty have any conception of flying stress in operational squadrons. In consequence, aircrew were treated as if they were normal naval officers and were transferred straight from one operational squadron to another without any break of any sort in between.

All this information had brought me up to date with the squadron and its background and I looked forward to meeting my fellow pilots the following day when, after some ADDLs on the runway, I was due to land on HMS *Indomitable*.

So many pilots were coming and going between the aerodrome and Aircraft Carriers, that a resident batsman was available at China Bay enabling dummy deck-landings to be practised with him on the runway. The chap was already out there, on the side at the end of the runway, waiting for me when I taxied out early next morning in the Hellcat which I now regarded as mine. I ought to say at this point that, although most naval pilots considered dummy deck-landings on the runway as essential, I personally didn't set quite so much value on them. They were useful to practise holding the aircraft at the right attitude and speed on the final approach, but the static runway bore little relationship with a moving Carrier. Hence I completed no more than a couple of approaches towards the batsman before landing and taxiing back to the dispersal where I told a rather surprised Shotton that I was ready to go.

The three of us, Shotton, Haberfield and me, were due to rendezvous with the ship and her escorting Destroyer at midday a few miles outside Trincomalee harbour. Shotton briefed me that I would land first, while he circled above the ship with Haberfield. After landing, my aircraft would be pushed back to the stern of the flight deck ready for me to take off and complete a second landing. He and Haberfield would then come in to land behind me.

As soon as we arrived over the ship, she turned into wind flying the affirmative for me to land on and I broke away from the little formation of three to enter the landing circuit. On the downwind leg, I felt comfortable in the Hellcat as I went through the pre-landing actions; indeed she flew like a Wildcat but in a rather more stable manner. I kept to a gentle turn on the final approach finding it not difficult to hold a constant low speed while the visibility over the stubby nose, showing the flight deck and part of the Island, was better than I had expected. The Hellcat thumped down firmly on her wide undercarriage, catching the second wire. As I was being pushed back, I could see that there was a full gallery of Goofers on the Island, most of whom I could assume would be my new squadron mates, interested to see how the new pilot in their squadron would perform. Needless for me to write, I suppose, that I could not resist showing-off on the next landing to come in on a very steep turn indeed to the deck and put her down with a satisfying thump to catch the third wire.

Excerpt from Squadron diary:

13th September.

Today we steamed out of harbour at noon, in company with our old friends *Howe* and *Victorious*. We have an escort of two cruisers, *Cumberland* and *Kenya* and seven "R" class destroyers. *Victorious* is now carrying 36 Corsairs, and 12 Barracudas of 822 Squadron, which has just joined her. We have on board 25 Hellcats and 24 Barracudas.

Lt Shotton has been appointed as our C.O. Lt. Cmdr. Gramson, Gooloon has become C.O. of 1844 and Lt. Cmdr. Harrington is Wing leader. It is very much to be hoped that Shotton will be able to kindle once again in both officers and men the interest which had been falling off to such a great extent during our period of being mucked around.

Squadron Duties have been re-allotted as follows:—

C.O. .... Lt. Shotton. R.N.R.

Senior Pilot and Stores Officer. Lt.N.G. Mitchell.
Maintenance. .... S/Lt. Jenkins
Intelligence. .... S/Lt. Adlam.
Passive Defence. .... Lt. Bowe.
Armament. .... S/Lt. Haberfield.
Divisional. .... S/Lt. Neal.
Radio. .... S/Lt. Hicks.
Sports. .... S/Lt. Mackie
Safety Equipment. .... S/Lt. Smith
Staff Officer. .... S/Lt. Fitzpatrick.
.... S/Lt. Mackenzie
.... S/Lt. Rankin

A.R.V. Specialist. .... S/Lt. Valentine

S/Lt. Farquhar. has joined 1844.

HMS *Indomitable* was the largest of our Aircraft Carriers, having an extra half hangar which made her appear higher in the water, otherwise she was much the same as *Illustrious*. But, oh what a difference in my accommodation. I was given a cabin happily located just off the quarterdeck itself which I was to share with Noel Mitchell, the Senior Pilot of the Squadron. Although no more experienced than the other pilots who had joined in November 1943, Noel was a natural leader who fully deserved his appointment as Senior Pilot, second to the CO. He was also a trained Photo/Recce pilot and leader of the P/R section. As I came to know him and his style of flying, I put him into the 'Warrior' class, those with a zest for action.

On board at that time were two squadrons of twelve Barracudas; these were to be replaced a couple of months later by 857 Squadron with twenty-one of the new American Avenger aircraft; a considerable improvement on the Barras. The two squadrons of ten Hellcats each, when I joined, would be increased later to fourteen aircraft each. Truth to tell, with a few exceptions, the pilots were inexperienced and certainly so in our Hellcat squadrons. But what a pleasant, cheerful and optimistic team of chaps they were; all keen to put the dismal weeks of waiting behind them and to get on with the war. Younger at age twenty-two than some of them, I felt like an old codger amongst them. Having ten aircraft, we operated two flights with the CO and Senior Pilot as leaders, and two aircraft for P/R work. I was given a section to lead with Dick Mackie as my number two. He was a New Zealander and a very good pilot with a responsible attitude and quiet personality. I have made him sound so dreary and he was nothing of the sort; he was full of life and fun. But I suspect that of the two of us, he would probably have made the better leader; but we got on very well together and became good friends.

The ship remained at sea for the next three days to carry out an intensive working up programme. Hellcats carried out splash firing at towed sea targets, rocket firing and bombing at a range on the shore and dog fights at high level. Barracudas completed night flying and did well, in my opinion anyway, having only one barrier crash. They practised lots of dummy bombing runs on the ship but, unhappily, one of them suffered the notorious Barracuda tendency of stalling on the pull out from the dive and crashed into the sea killing all the crew. All the exercises were carried out ranging as many aircraft of both types as possible for take-offs and catapult launches so that all the flight deck crews were also given plenty of practice. It was a valuable period for me to build up my flying hours on the Hellcat and to become accustomed to the squadron procedures.

Back to Trinco harbour to refuel the ship and then two days later we were off again, this time accompanied by the Carrier HMS *Victorious*, flying Corsairs and Barracudas. With us were seven Destroyers, two Cruisers and a Battlewagon, HMS *Howe*. At the briefing, we were told that our main target was a large cement works at a place called Indaroeg in northern Sumatra and this was to be followed by an attack on shipping in Emmahaven harbour. When the fleet approached to within five hundred miles off the enemy coast, our Hellcats commenced constant patrols of four aircraft to provide a protective umbrella against potential air attack.

No such attack materialised throughout the whole operation and it was a boring task. While we were stooging about above the fleet, the Corsairs from *Victorious* were strafing the Japanese airfield in the area and, with the Barracudas, attacking the shipping in the harbour. The Barras from both Carriers did well by completely knocking out the cement works with the loss of only one aircraft. My guess was that our two Hellcat squadrons had suffered such a long period in the doldrums, with unserviceable aircraft through lack of spares, that we were considered to be inexperienced and not quite up to scratch as yet. Moreover, our squadron had recently lost its experienced Commanding Officer. Hence the plum job of strafing the airfield had gone to the Corsair squadron. Did I write 'plum job'? The time would come very soon when such a job would become a much feared and almost routine daily task. The good thing was that, in spite of continuous daily deck operations on patrol, there had been no crashes on the flight deck so that by the time we returned to Trinco, at least if nothing else, we had not disgraced ourselves as a squadron.

It was a pleasure to be living on board again, which was so much better than the stifling heat, insects and mosquitoes ashore at aerodromes like Puttalam and China Bay. Nevertheless, the heat on board was still difficult to bear since Admiralty ships were not designed for the tropics with air conditioning or anything of that sort. Fresh water for drinking and for showers too was in short supply. I doubt if there was anyone on board who did not suffer from prickly heat, which could drive a man dotty with its irritation but, at least, in my opinion, it was not as bad as the mosquitoes ashore.

In all Carriers in the tropics, the worst area was the hangar where the maintenance crews worked, wearing only shorts and gym shoes. It was a hell's kitchen of a huge enclosed space with the heat and the bedlam of the constant noise from the intense repair work, which frequently had to continue through the night. I felt it was important, as did most pilots, to spend some time with the men working on our aircraft there, if only as a gesture of appreciation for keeping us safely airborne. I went down to visit the engine-room of *Indomitable* once and found the heat to be appalling and unbearable unless one was accustomed to it, but it seemed to be a more orderly and calm environment compared to the hangar.

Mid-September and we were moving out of Trinco harbour, again accompanied by the same fleet of ships. Our briefing this time would be an attack by Hellcats and Corsairs on the large airfield at Medan which was expected to be full of Japanese fighter aircraft and troop carriers. Then we were to continue on to attack shipping and any other targets at Belawan. The fleet arrived off Sumatra to find what I called the 'Elephant Monsoon' sitting over the top of the whole area; in other words thick cloud at low level and pouring, incessant rain with little wind. This was a situation which I dreaded and hated because we aircrews had to sit around in Ready rooms waiting for a decision from the powers that be whether they would send the strike off or not.

If the decision was taken to 'Go', it would mean that some sixty fighter aircraft from the two Carriers would take off and would all be milling around, just above the sea and below a very low cloud base and in bad visibility, trying to form up into the formation of a controlled and effective strike force. It was a scenario for disaster.

The 'powers that be' to make this decision, however, were a Rear Admiral and the two Captains of each Carrier, none of whom had ever flown at all and two Commanders Air neither of whom, to my knowledge, had yet been seen to fly the aircraft under their command. Our only hope, I thought as I sat waiting with Dick Mackie, was that they would consult and listen to Ronnie Hay and Tommy Harrington, our Wing leaders from each Carrier both of whom had considerable operational experience because, in truth, neither of our Hellcat squadron leaders had much experience. We sat there waiting for a long time, indicative that our very senior officers were thinking seriously of sending off the strike. I was a coward, I suppose, nearly wetting myself at the thought of trying to form up and reach the target in that awful weather. But then, if these ignorant men were to say 'Go' then without question off I would have to go. How many pilots of the sixty aircraft, less experienced than I, would we lose bashing into each other and lost in the low cloud? After putting us on stand-by in our cockpits, at one point, the Admiral eventually decided to abort the strike.

The range of targets for the fleet was largely dependent on fuel conservation by the Destroyers who might not be able to continue in the area for more than two days so, if the weather did not improve on the next day, we might have to go back to Trinco with nothing achieved. But the next day was perfect weather by which time our fleet was close enough to Sigli, in northern Sumatra, for the Barracudas to be flown off to attack the large railway centre there which was of great importance to the Japanese army.

Hellcats were to support the Barracudas and to make strafing attacks against anti-aircraft (A-A) fire from the ground and any other targets of opportunity. There were eight of us flying above and to the side of the Barras and, looking down on the land of north Sumatra, I thought how very beautiful it was but also how menacing now that it was under Japanese control. As escorts, we had a grandstand view of the successful bombing of the railway yards. There was very little flak and no Japanese fighter aircraft so nothing really into which we could sink our own teeth.

As the ship approached Trinco, all the aircraft flew ashore first to China Bay. But after a couple of days both of our Hellcat squadrons flew on to land at the Racecourse aerodrome at Colombo from where we were to carry out a new training schedule.

It was a very good place to be stationed with comfortable sleeping quarters, called Bandas, much better than the equivalent cadjan huts at Puttalam inundated, as they had been, with creepy-crawlies. At the Racecourse, there was also a posh Officers' Mess which had been, I believe, the Racing Club. A skeleton crew of our aircraft maintenance personnel were accommodated in the Grandstand. It was a bonus too in being stationed just outside Colombo, the capital of Ceylon, where there were plenty of good hotels, restaurants and a cinema.

From rubber planters who worked inland, we received invitations to their famous 'Sunday Curry' lunches. These were a major event each week for the planters themselves as well as for us because, apparently, they were limited to one such curry meal per week due, of all unexpected things, to a shortage of rice. About ten of us would arrive in two Jeeps at the planters' house on Sunday midday, drink large glasses of iced gin and lemonade until about 4 pm when boys would serve the most enormous curry. To top up a mountain of rice on our plates, we were offered the choice of sometimes as many as twenty dishes some very hot but some, such as coconut, designed to cool it down. We usually arrived back at the Racecourse at around midnight, absolutely bloated with food and saturated in gin and only just able to stagger into our cots. It was purgatory to fly the Hellcat, while groaning with a dreadful hangover, a few hours later. But I found the whole Sunday of relaxation and friendship with the Planters well worth the agony. I might add that hangovers, a more regular feature of my life living ashore than at sea, were alleviated by strong doses of neat oxygen as soon as I climbed into the cockpit.

But we had not been sent to the Racecourse aerodrome for fun. The special training we were to undergo was in the procedures of forming up into large groups of Hellcats and Corsairs to fly as a Wing in support of the Avenger bombers. The purpose was to train and accustom six squadrons or more of aircraft to form up and formate together, regardless of bad weather and over large distances, to a given target. These were basically the same exercises I had done with 890 Squadron at Hatston a year earlier, but there were no chuckles this time, it was all deadly serious. There was a much stronger sense of reality and urgency now about this form of Wing training since we were all aware that very soon the British Pacific and Far East Fleet would expect to join with the US Navy in their battles against the Japanese in the Pacific. It would be a challenge to match up with the recognised efficiency of the American Carriers and their aircrews.

Ronnie Hay, who had been my senior instructor at Yeovilton fighter school, was now Lt Col Hay RM, DSC and had been appointed as the Air Group Co-ordinator responsible for training and leading the squadrons in these Wing formations. He kept us at it so that it was a daily occurrence for the squadrons to take off from their aerodromes in the south of the Island to rendezvous and form up off the coast of Colombo. It was often midday by the time we had formed up, which made it necessary for the Wing to climb up and around the, by this time, towering cu-nim clouds to reach our intended height at usually above 20,000 ft. The same radial engine of both Corsair and Hellcat had a supercharger to force-feed air into the fuel intake, which had to be selected at about 15,000 ft to enable the aircraft to reach the higher levels up to 36,000 ft. It was a bit like changing gear in a car. This Wing flying was a hot, sweaty and difficult business and I was thankful not to be sufficiently senior to be leading a squadron; it was tricky enough leading a flight, as I had to do sometimes. The problem for the leaders was to adapt to whatever weather conditions might be met on the way to a target and to manoeuvre the great gaggle of aircraft accordingly. But with constant practise we were all getting better at it.

Three weeks later, our Squadron returned to *Indomitable* and on 15 October in the company of the same fleet as before, the ship was headed towards the Nicobar Islands off the north tip of Sumatra. We aircrews began to refer to these monthly assaults on Sumatra as 'the Club Run'. On arrival at the area this time, the Battlewagon and the three Cruisers began lobbing their shells on targets at Car Nicobar while Barracudas from our ship were detailed to bomb the Japanese shipping there.

Eight Hellcats from our Squadron, led by Fraser Shotton, were given the task of strafing the Japanese gun positions ahead of the Barracudas to give them as clear a run as possible. It worked quite well in the sense that our earlier arrival ahead of the Barras encouraged machine gun and cannon fire at us as well as flak, thus revealing the Japanese gun positions around the harbour. I was leading the second flight and, following Shotton, turned and dived with my flight from 4,000 ft down towards where the flak was coming from to start firing at about 200 ft as we came in fast. We were all damn lucky to get away without being hit because, as I and all of us were to learn, commencing the attack right over the target at that height was quite the wrong way to go about a strafing operation. The Japanese normally would be delighted to have an aircraft target at 4,000 ft coming down to 200 ft in their sights. We would learn the hard way to come straight at our targets from the lowest possible level, more like 30 ft rather than 200 ft, having gained our maximum speed from a dive well out of the enemy's sight. To be fair, detailed intelligence maps of north Sumatra did not seem to be available at the time, so we had to find the target, by flying over it, before being able to bash it.

However, I guess we succeeded in keeping the Japanese heads down to some extent but not sufficiently because one Barracuda was shot down. We would also learn in the weeks ahead that the Japanese would rarely back away from their guns despite the intense gun fire we could put to bear on them from our six Browning machine guns and sometimes rockets too. I saw the Barracuda hit and watched hoping the pilot might be able to turn away out to sea where our rescue Submarine would be waiting. But he appeared to have lost all engine power and I last saw him heading towards the jungle. No one baled out. Later, back on board, I learned that the pilot was one of my friends, Buzz Aldwell.

I returned to the fleet with my flight in normal close formation prior to entering the landing circuit, having gone ahead separately from Shotton. As we approached at some 4,000 ft, bursts of flak appeared around us, but fortunately not close enough to hit us. Looking down, I could see unbelievably that our own ship, the *Indomitable*, was the culprit firing at us. I called up 'Mother' on the R/T to complain in no uncertain terms that she was firing her guns at us; her own aircraft! They stopped before I could finish my abusive call and I led my flight down into the landing circuit now behind the other four Hellcats led by Shotton and, as I did so, I rehearsed in my mind just how rude I was going to be to the Lieutenant Commander RN Gunnery Officer of the ship when I landed.

But it was time to concentrate on the landing and I must time it to land closely behind the number four of Shotton's flight ahead of me in the circuit. At the end of the downwind leg now and I could see that the first two had landed on and the chap immediately ahead of me, probably Jock McKinnon, was nicely placed on his final approach. Everything seemed fine until, seconds later, I saw him hit the round-down so that his Hellcat splashed into the sea, ahead of me, upside down and astern of the Carrier on the port side. I was not far behind him and recovered mentally from the shock of seeing him go in below me, just in time to open up to full throttle to abort my own landing. The Carrier slowed down while our escorting Destroyer searched for the pilot down in the sea. Meantime, I recalled my flight to rejoin formation with me while we circled and waited for the affirmative signal to continue landings. The signal came ten minutes or so later, because there was no sign of the pilot, and the show must go on. I was extra careful with my landing and no doubt so were the other three behind me.

As I climbed out of the cockpit after landing, someone confirmed to me that it had been Jock who had gone in. He had been with 1839 Squadron from the beginning and was a very popular young man who was considered to be one of our best pilots. Another reminder to me never to be cocky and over-confident about landing on a deck.

However, I was in the right mood to confront the Gunnery Officer about his people firing at my flight and, as soon as I had finished the de-briefing, made my way to the ship's Gun Directory. I was as scathing to him as it is possible for a RNVR Sub Lieutenant to be to a Lieutenant Commander RN and suggested that he take his chaps out on to the flight deck to have a good look at a Hellcat. He explained that his people had thought my flight of four Hellcats was a pair of twin-engined Japanese aircraft called Betties. My parting shot from the doorway before I left was to observe that, as he had failed to hit aircraft flying straight and level and slowly at 4,000 ft, there was little hope of his chaps ever knocking down a fast attacking Jap. Anyway, after an eventful and not very happy day, I felt better for my rude remarks and able to relish a couple of large pink gins afterwards.

On the following day, the fleet moved close to the northernmost tip of Sumatra to attack Sabang but the weather was so bad that even our 'powers that be' realised that there was no possibility of carrying out the planned attack. Nevertheless, aircrews spent a restless day having to be at readiness to take off should the weather improve. Meantime, the fleet returned to the area of the Nicobars where, on the third day, strafing attacks were carried out by our squadron on the well-camouflaged shipping in and around the bays of Nancowry. The other Hellcats in our Wing were detailed for the usually more boring job of Combat Air Patrol over the Fleet but, just the luck of the game, they encountered a number of enemy fighter aircraft, Oscars in fact, and shot three of them down without loss. The Corsairs from *Victorious* shot another three down.

It had been quite a significantly successful operation. Firstly, because the fleet with its Destroyers had been able to remain in the combat area for several days, having completed refuelling at sea with some success, such success being vital in preparation for operations with the United States Navy in the Pacific. Secondly, our fighters had met the Japanese fighters for the first time and had proved themselves to be superior. Only three aircraft with their aircrew had been lost; two Barracudas while striking at shipping and a Corsair on landing.

The aircraft of all three squadrons of *Indomitable* flew ashore to China Bay when the ship returned to harbour at Trincomalee. It was now mid October in 1944. Squadron personnel were also disembarked to China Bay and given seven days' well-earned leave and, for those men who wanted to see something of the country, special transport and accommodation was laid on. Aircrews were given similar leave and with it a surprise treat from Lord Nuffield (the Morris car manufacturer) who had contributed from his personal fortune a gift of ten shillings for each day of leave given to operational aircrews of the RAF and FAA. A welcome gift indeed because 70 shillings in those days was a goodly sum. Dick Mackie and I decided to visit Neuralia, up in the hills where the air was cooler, a place well known for its grand hotel and golf club. We hoped to meet some female company but had no luck as the few Wrens and nurses on leave were already fully engaged. We contented ourselves very well with hotel comfort and golf.

On returning from our leave to the squadron at China Bay on 5 November, we found that quite a few changes had taken place. The number of our Hellcats had been increased to fourteen as had happened to the other squadron in our Wing. In addition, three new pilots had been appointed to our Squadron. All three were senior RNVR Lieutenants with operational experience. So bang went my leadership of a flight and I reverted to number three position in the flight as a section leader.

This demotion worried me not at all. In those days, while living in a frightening and dangerous environment, my one ambition was to live. To live; but not I hoped at the cost of failing to do my job properly in this war. An important consideration for me because, although never having flown with any distinction whatsoever, yet the truth was that after three years in an operational squadron at war, flying from Carriers, I had become nervy; the 'twitch' we called it. There had been times when I had felt faint and shaky, not quite in my body, while walking across the deck to my aircraft. I had experienced a feeling almost of panic that I might lose control of myself; just turn away and go to sit down alone somewhere, my cabin, any where away from the sight of that damned aircraft waiting for me. It was an effort to disregard these feelings but it had to be done and I found that, once strapped into the cockpit, with the engine started and lining up for take-off, everything would fall into its normal place. 'Too much booze last night,' I would tell myself. And that was probably the truth of it since, on most evenings, I drank myself into a sufficient state of relaxation to ensure a night's sleep.

I have digressed and should not have done so because all sorts of things were happening at the squadron, not only new pilots and aircraft but new ideas about our attack procedures, and the intention was that, while at China Bay for the next three weeks, we would practise these new manoeuvres. Contrary to the type of attacks by our Hellcat Wing over Sumatra during the last months, we would in future fly in fast and at very low levels using rockets and skip bombs as well as machine guns. 'Ramrods' they were called. All this had emanated mainly from Lt Cdr Dick Cork, DSO, DSC, RN who had been appointed as the Air Group Co-ordinator for the Corsair Wing. This brilliant fighter pilot and leader would already by now have introduced our Hellcat Wing to these new tactics had he not been killed a few weeks earlier, at China Bay aerodrome, by an entirely unnecessary and avoidable accident.

From the many reports I have read, it happened thus:

HMS *Illustrious* was approaching Trincomalee in the semi-dark before dawn with all her aircraft ranged ready to take-off for China Bay with Cork's Corsair at the head of the range. It must have been 'Elephant Monsoon' weather because all the reports tell that there was low cloud at about 400 ft with scattered heavy showers and, most significantly, no wind. They debated, the Captain and Wings, whether it was safe for the aircraft to take off. Meantime, it had been planned that a sprog young pilot was due to take off from the aerodrome at China Bay to do his first Corsair deck-landing on *Illustrious*. He was due to arrive when the range had taken off and the deck was clear.

The first failure of responsible command by the Captain and Wings, as I see it, was to agree that Lt Cdr Cork should take off 'to see if it was safe to do so.' His Corsair was at the head of the range, so there would only be two-thirds of the deck available for take-off and there was no wind. It should have been no surprise, therefore, that on the take-off his Corsair disappeared from sight below the bows of the Carrier and the wheels were within feet of hitting the sea. But, by skilled flying, he had got away with it. On seeing this, these two Commanding Officers immediately aborted the whole exercise until an improvement in the weather and wind conditions. It is obvious that they should have done this in the first place.

The second failure of command was not to have signalled the Control Tower at China Bay to postpone the take-off of the new young Corsair pilot. It must have been obvious, even much earlier that morning, that the weather conditions were entirely unsuitable for a new pilot to do his first Corsair landings on *Illustrious*.

In the event, when it was still not full light, the new Corsair pilot taxied on to the runway at China Bay just as Lt Cdr Cork came in to land. Cork landed on top of the Corsair on the runway and both pilots were killed. There was an investigation which centred around who was responsible for the failure of Air Traffic Control at the aerodrome. That appears to me to be almost irrelevant. Neither aircraft should have been allowed to take off in the first place. As I see it, this needless accident was part of running an Air Arm with senior Officers who either do not fly (Captain) or are not in flying practice (Wings).

Meanwhile, we had been pressing on with the new style of attacks and becoming accustomed to fast manoeuvres at very low level with flights of four or eight Hellcats. Actually, it was quite fun dicing along

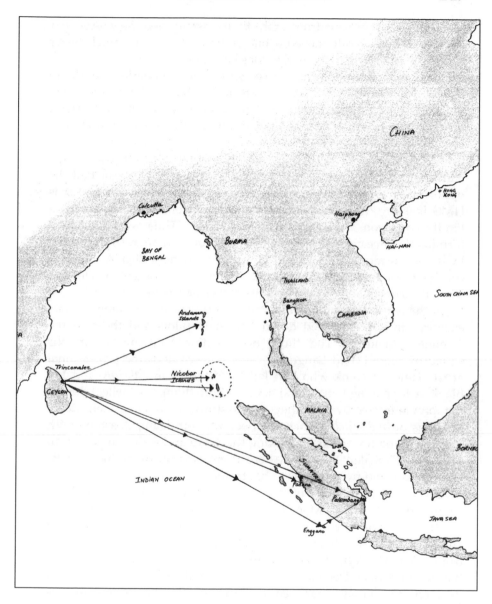

Map of South Asia

very fast just over the tops of trees or, in open spaces, below tree level. Our three new Senior Pilots had joined us in time to take part in these exercises. At the end of November, our Barracuda squadron was replaced by 857 Squadron with their twenty-one new Avenger aircraft. These aircraft carried a bigger bomb load very much faster and much further than the Barracudas could do.

In early December, all three squadrons embarked back to *Indomitable* and how glad we all were to be shot of China Bay. HMS *Illustrious* rejoined the fleet having spent some weeks in South Africa for repairs to be undertaken. I learned that my three particular chums, Jack, Winnie and Johnnie Lowder, who had earlier been transferred from *Atheling* to *Illustrious*, had enjoyed a good rest and that Winnie had married an attractive girl from Cape Town. But I never had the opportunity to see either Jack or Winnie again. A new arrival was HMS *Indefatigable* with a complement of a Hellcat PR squadron, a Firefly squadron and two Seafire squadrons. Thus we now had a formidable force capable of flying off two hundred aircraft, supported by a Battlewagon, Cruisers and Destroyers. A new Rear Admiral in command of this fleet of Aircraft Carriers was appointed. He was Vian, the same man who had been in charge at Salerno.

In the early days of December, the ship was at sea doing various exercises intended to 'bed down' our new pilots and those in the Avenger squadron. The three new senior Lieutenants for our squadron were David Langdon, a well-known and fine professional artist, Timo Schwenk who had led the Seafires in *Atheling* and Ian Black. After having had several hours ashore flying the Hellcat during the previous two weeks, they successfully completed their deck-landings on *Indomitable*. Then the fleet was off again, this time with our new gung-ho Admiral, cracking the whip and raring to go, for an attack on Pankalan Brandan where there was an oil refinery to be knocked out and two airfields to be strafed.

On arrival at the area off the western coast of Sumatra, my old enemy the 'Elephant Monsoon' was much in evidence and the weather was absolutely foul. The strike was aborted at 6 am but half an hour later, no doubt after a whip-cracking exhortation and decision from our brave Admiral, the squadrons took off into the murk from the three Carriers. Despite the very low cloud and poor visibility, all the aircraft eventually managed to form up without suffering any loss from collisions and set off for the targets.

The Gaggle, for it could be nothing else in that weather, hit the coast some thirty miles south of the refinery target which was entirely obscured by cloud and heavy rain. It didn't help matters that our maps didn't cover the area south of the target. After orbiting about in a clearer area to the north, an oil storage depot was found and bombed by the Avengers.

On the way back, the fighters formed up alongside the Avengers, since escorting them was out of the question in such appalling visibility. All the aircraft from *Indomitable* returned and landed safely but there were aircraft and aircrew losses in the other two Carriers. It was a combination of skilled flying plus damned good luck, in my

Excerpt from Squadron diary:

20th DECEMBER   D - DAY

... CAME THE DAWN — AND THE RAIN. THE AIRCRAFT WERE STARTED SOON AFTER SIX OCLOCK AND STOPPED ALMOST IMMEDIATELY WITH A VIEW TO POSTPONING THE DO. HOWEVER, TAKE-OFF WAS EFFECTED AT 6.30.

THE GAGGLE HIT COAST 30 MLS: SOUTH OF PANGKALANBRA...etc. WHICH WAS OBSCURED BY CLOUD AND RAIN. (OUR MAPS WENT ONLY DOWN TO 2 MILES SOUTH OF TARGET)

WELL, IS SEEMED SUCH A PITY TO WASTE GOOD BOMBS THAT, AFTER ABOUT 12 ORBITS, THE COOKIES WERE DROPPED ONTO AN OIL STORAGE DEPOT. ONE DRUM FIRED. ONE OR TWO BURSTS OF FLAK MADE A LATE APPEARANCE. NO ENEMY FIGHTERS SEEN. S/LT's HICKS AND TAYLOR SHARED A "SALLY" WHICH HAD NOT APPARENTLY OBSERVED THE AIR DISPLAY

THE AVENGERS WERE IN NO GREAT HURRY TO DEPART, BUT AFTER SEVERAL PROMPTINGS FROM THE FIGHTERS OVER THE R/T, ("COME ON, LETS GET TO HELL OUT OF HERE!" - GAMMY), AN ATTEMPT WAS MADE TO REFORM. THEY LEFT IN 4 GROUPS. THE RETURN WAS MADE IN FOUL WEATHER. FIGHTERS FORMATED ON BOMBERS BECAUSE ESCORTING WAS OUT OF THE QUESTION IN SUCH BAD VISIBILITY.

ALL A/c OF 857 SQUADRON AND 5 WING RETURNED SAFELY.

P.M.

8. HELLCAT WERE LED BY. LT CMDR HARRINGTON (LT. JENKINS, S/LT's SMITH, AND FIVE 1844 SQUDN PILOTS) TO STRAFE THE AERODROME SOUTH OF BUBANG. THE CONTROL TOWER WAS SHOT UP BUT NO A/c WERE SEEN. A NUMBER OF PEOPLE WERE KILLED- PRESUMABLY JAPS. IN THE HARBOUR 2 SHIPS WERE LEFT BURNING. (8 CORSAIRS FROM ILLUSTRIDUS STRAFED SUBANG)

—— AND READINESS AND PATROLS.

---

opinion, that there were not several more losses in those clouds. That afternoon, when the Fleet was further north and the weather not quite so bad, eight of us in Hellcats took off and attacked the Japanese-held airfield south of Sabang. Not a lot there and no trouble.

End of the day and a sigh of relief from me that such fruitless pursuits had not caused any losses amongst us in *Indomitable*; I did not know then how many losses there had been in the other ships. The good aspect of flying from Carriers, I thought, was the well stocked bar as a welcome, followed by a hot meal and a comfortable bunk. As I started to fall into a sleep, befuddled with whisky fumes, I spared a thought for our Admiral and how we aircrews must all try to do better for him, if he was to get his 'K' or whatever it was he so badly wanted.

Christmas was nearly upon us with the huge Fleet at anchor in Trincomalee harbour. A party of aircrew went ashore to hack down a tall tree, which was erected on the forrard lift and laden with gifts (procured from the NAAFI canteen ashore) for distribution on the day to the ship's company. A whole lot of mail arrived for nearly everybody and mine included letters from Mother, Maddie and Phoebe, my sister. Father never sent me a letter throughout the war. There was one from Lalline, who wrote to say her final farewell to me having married at last her army officer. I would miss her very much for she had been not just a 'girl-friend' in the conventional sense, but a true friend and good companion. I wrote back to wish her much happiness.

Victory in Europe was nearly complete and, from all these letters I gained the feeling that people at home had little idea of what we were doing out here on the far side of the world, and to put it bluntly, except for our families not much interest either. In fact, our magnificent men of the army in Burma were still fighting and now winning their horrific war against the Japs. The Royal Navy had put together the biggest and most powerful fleet in its history and, unable to rely on any home bases out here, was about to begin the most logistically difficult battle of its life. The Fleet Air Arm, which in 1940 had been a very small arm of obsolete aircraft, was now reluctantly and belatedly recognised by their Lordships of the Admiralty to be the striking power of the Royal Navy, as well as an essential defensive force. Indeed, the Air Arm, consisting almost entirely of RNVR aircrews, had superseded the Battleships and Cruisers whose range, accuracy and strength of firepower could never come remotely near now to matching that of the Fleet Air Arm.

Nevertheless, that beautiful ship the *King George V*, for example, still had value because, provided it had air cover from the FAA and anti-submarine cover from Destroyers, was a prestigious ship eminently suitable as an Admiral's Barge. That is an unfair comment because, in fact, the Battlewagons and Cruisers served a valuable function as radar and AA ships for protection of the Aircraft Carriers.

For the first time, the four Fleet Carriers of *Indomitable, Indefatigable, Illustrious* and *Victorious* would be operating together. Consequently, a new method of controlling over two hundred aircraft during the forming up and return landings needed to be established. Hence, immediately after Christmas all aircrews of the four Carriers congregated in the Wardroom of *Indomitable* to be briefed on a revised procedure which had been devised by our Wing leaders and squadron commanders.

Ronnie Hay, with all his wealth of experience as an enormously successful fighter pilot since the start of the war in 1939, had been the right man to lead the thinking. Moreover, he with others had learned much from our combined operations with the American Carrier, the USS *Saratoga*, earlier in the year. Ronnie Hay, unlike most of his peers in the RN who had survived those early years of the war, had never ceased to fly the latest aircraft available and, as Co-ordinator of the Wing, always flew the Corsair. Ronnie (I never dared call him that in those days) was a small handsome, confident man who rather enjoyed projecting his image as a laid-back rather blasé Colonel Blimp, whereas in truth he had a keen and intelligent mind. There is a delightful story of his enforced attendance at an Air Warfare course for senior officers of the three services. He was seen to be apparently reading the racing form book through most of the lectures. Because of this and in the expectation that he would make an ignorant mess of it, he was deliberately selected, at the end of the course, to give an exposition and analysis of what had been taught. It was known that he did so lucidly and brilliantly.

There was a period of two days in which to try out the new method of forming up after take-off and then the landings on the four Carriers. It was based on the placing of a pivot ship, some distance from the Carriers, from which the squadrons would establish separate rendezvous areas at which to form up before either proceeding to a target or, on return, entering the landing circuit. It was a practical scheme, devised by experienced pilots, and it worked.

On 1 January of the new year 1945, the three Carriers of *Indomitable, Indefatigable* and *Victorious* with their supporting fleet, set out for another strike on the oil refinery at Pankalan, which we had failed to hit previously because of bad weather. This time the plan was to fly off the Carriers from the western side of Sumatra and fly overland, about eighty miles over mountains, to surprise the Japanese from a different direction. We arrived at the flying-off position on the 4th of January to find perfect weather conditions. Most of our Hellcats would act as top and close escorts to the Avengers and Fireflies, about seventy aircraft in all, but I felt fortunate to be one of the eight to carry out an advance Ramrod on the Japanese fighter airfields at Medan and Tanjong. We were to take off about an hour before the main force and join up with and follow the lead of eight Corsairs from *Victorious*.

Excerpt from Squadron diary:

---

2 JAN. 1945   D-2

BRIEFING FOR STRIKE AGAINST PANKALAN BRANDON :—
    IF WEATHER PERMITS, OPERATION 'LENTIL' WILL BE CARRIED OUT ON
    THE 4 JAN. THURSDAY. WEATHER BEING UNSUITABLE THURS. FRI. AND
    SAT. WE SHALL RETURN.

OUR OWN FORCES

INDOMITABLE	VICTORIOUS	INDEFATIGABLE	4 CRUISERS	8 DEST
18 AVENGERS.	18 AVENGERS	18 FIREFLYS	SUFFOLK	
28 HELLCATS.	30 CORSAIRS	24 SEAFIRES (C.A.P)	ARGONAUT	
		5 HELLCAT (P.R.U.)	B. PRINCE.	
			CEYLON	

ENEMY FORCES

    5 DINAHS
    25 SALLY ⎫ MEDAN
    30 OSCAS ⎭
    5 JAKE ⎫
    10 SALLY/HELEN ⎬ TANJI
    25 NELL ⎭

    VERY LITTLE INFORMATION ABOUT
    FLAK AND DEFENSES ON AIRFIELDS.

MAJOR WILLIAMS BRIEFED US FOR EVASION AND ESCAPE.

A RAMROD OF 8 HELLCATS AND 8 CORSAIRS WILL GO IN BEFORE
BOMBERS TO STRAFE 4 AIRFIELDS SOUTH OF TARGET.

    Our function was to knock out Japanese fighters on the ground or in the air before they could attack our main force on its way to the oil refinery. At the briefing, it had seemed a more exciting prospect than escorting the bombers and I liked it.

    It was a pleasant change to form up after take-off with only seven other aircraft and then our flight of eight Hellcats took position at a reasonable open distance behind and below the Corsairs. There was a distance of about 120 miles to the first target at Medan. The arrangement was that, once at the target, the Corsairs would remain at top cover to deal with any Japanese fighters already airborne while we Hellcats, at ground level, would set about strafing aircraft and whatever other targets were on the airfield.

As soon as we had passed over the mountain range, flying at 12,000 ft, we separated from the Corsairs and put our noses down to pick up speed, intending to arrive at the target airfield going fast and low. I was leading the flight on the left and approaching the enemy airfield now coming into sight, I put us into a wide echelon port as previously briefed. The other flight on my starboard side led by Noel, the Senior Pilot, were also in similar wide formation. We were flying very low and wide enough to pick our individual targets as we came on to the airfield. And what a mass of fighter aircraft, grouped on either side of the runways, was laid out for us as targets. We had caught those horrible little bandy-legged barbaric Japs with their pants down.

I had only to jink slightly to the right to line my sights up on the first of four enemy fighters (Oscars) which, with a number of Japanese around them, were probably preparing to start engines ready to taxi out for take-off on patrol. I could see the pilots in their cockpits as I flew low and fast towards them. I had done this sort of thing quite a few times by now, but the intense and lethal firepower produced by my six Browning 0.5 machine guns could still shock me. At that speed there was not much more than seconds in which to fire and hit the targets. But it was enough. The first Oscar disintegrated then burst into flame as I flew over and past it and I had seen the bullets hitting the cockpit, with the pilot inside, and the men near the aircraft. So quick and apparently silent had been our attack that only then did the gun emplacements of the enemy come alive and begin to fire at us. The Hellcats on either side of me had found targets too, and keeping very low and fast, we flew on past and clear of the far end of the airfield.

I called on the R/T for my flight to break left and come round for a second attack, as the other flight had done but breaking to their right. And so we came in again on another run, hitting more targets, but keeping very low as the best means of evading the cannon and machine gun fire from the Japanese gunners who, by now, were recovering from their total surprise at our attack. None of us were hit and we climbed up to rejoin the Corsairs overhead and headed for the second Japanese airfield at Tanjong. But that airfield, when we got there, was empty of enemy aircraft and so the Corsairs flew around firing at gun emplacements and at anything that moved. Two enemy twin-engined Recce aircraft wandered unsuspectingly on to the scene and were promptly shot down. Nothing else seemed to be going on so Hellcats and Corsairs returned to land on their respective Carriers where I found a fairly large hole, probably from a cannon shell, in the rear of my Hellcat's fuselage. Fortunately nothing of significance had been hit and it had not affected flying the aircraft during the landing.

At the later de-briefing we learned that the main force of Avengers, on their way there and back to the Pankalan refinery, had been attacked by a swarm of Japanese fighters, five of which were shot down by the escorting Hellcats and Corsairs. Evidently these Japanese fighters had taken off from Tanjong airfield before our flights had arrived there making it obvious, in retrospect, that the Corsairs acting as our top cover would have been better employed in flying direct to Tanjong. But aircrews of the Avengers complained bitterly that their escorting Hellcats and Corsairs had deserted them to have dog-fights with the Japs. As for the strafing of Medan airfield by our eight Hellcats, it was recorded that we had destroyed nine aircraft on the ground and damaged probably beyond repair another eight. Our total losses for the whole operation were an Avenger, a Firefly and a Corsair.

The post-mortem on the second strike against the Pankalan oil refinery concluded that it had been a success, having put the whole refinery out of operation. But our Admiral Vian was scathing about the lack of discipline in the air by our aircrews. During the coming weeks, we aircrews would discover that he tended to be scathing about many of our efforts and we could only presume that it was his method of keeping us up to scratch. But it was a poor form of leadership. His method would have been better received had he showed himself more interested in obtaining an understanding of the factors involved in flying from Carriers. It would have been appreciated if, for example, he had flown in the back of a Firefly or Avenger during any one of the major Wing exercises, just to see what it was like. To be fair, however, I do know that he experienced a short flight later on when, for the purpose of a meeting, he was ferried across from one Carrier to deck-land on another in the back of a Firefly.

The last two strikes had been rehearsals for the next major operation against the largest refinery of all at Palembang on the west side of Sumatra. The oil output from this refinery, assessed at nearly 40% of the total Japanese requirement, was therefore of truly immense importance to Japan and it was known to be very strongly protected.

CHAPTER THIRTEEN

Palembang and the Pacific

Unknown to us as aircrew, the Commander in Chief of the British Pacific Fleet, Admiral Sir Bruce Fraser, with Government support, had been involved during 1944 in discussions with the American High Command on what part the Royal Navy would play in the Pacific war now that naval operations in Europe were coming towards an end. It was understood that the Americans were not at all keen for us to take part at all, reckoning, not without reason, that the Royal Navy had neither the logistic means nor the expertise to conduct a campaign in the Pacific. They reasoned that they could not afford to nursemaid us while we adapted to the different conditions of that huge area. However, apparently agreement had been reached and now, at the end of 1944, the Royal Navy was ready and preparing to proceed to the Pacific.

Before joining with the American Navy, however, Sir Bruce Fraser was determined that the Royal Navy should have achieved some major success in the Far East to prove our worth to the Americans. To this end, he had chosen the two big oil refineries at Pladjoe and Soengei Gerong, both near the town of Palembang on the west coast of southern Sumatra, as the target. The output of aviation fuel for the Japanese from these two refineries was known to be 38% of the total requirement for their war machine. In consequence these targets were massively defended by batteries of ANTI-AIRCRAFT fire and surrounded by four airfields of fighter aircraft flown by the pick of their instructors and pilots. Their Lordships at the Admiralty were opposed to the strike, maintaining that the losses would be huge with little likelihood of success. Most of them, still besotted with their Battleships were unable to believe that the Fleet Air Arm was a formidable enough force. Sir Bruce had stuck to his guns and had received approval for the British Fleet to make the attack while it was on its passage through to the Pacific.

The attacks our Aircraft Carriers had been making against the airfields, shipping and other targets in northern Sumatra during the past months had, in effect, been rehearsals for this major strike. Now, on 13 January 1945, the aircraft of the four Carriers, *Indomitable*, *Illustrious*, *Victorious* and *Indefatigable* were to take the major part in an extensive exercise to simulate an attack on the airfields and harbours of Ceylon, which would be defended by the Royal Air Force. From before dawn until dusk simulated attacks were carried out all day and nearly every one of the aircrews completed three sorties in the day. The sky above Ceylon seemed filled with aircraft diving and swooping about over the Island and perhaps it was fortunate that there were no collisions. It was an exhausting day and it was right that we were made to do it because, as we were to find, it was typical of many days to come in the Pacific. Nevertheless, two good and experienced Corsair pilots were killed making their final deck-landings of the day on HMS *Illustrious*. They were probably very tired and unable to summon up the full concentration required to deck-land that difficult and dangerous aircraft.

On 16 January, the British Pacific Fleet left Trincomalee harbour en route for Sidney in Australia but with the intention of carrying out the major strike against the refineries at Palembang on the way. The four Fleet Carriers with their total complement of over 200 aircraft were supported by the *King George V* Battlewagon, four Cruisers and nine Destroyers.

After refuelling at sea during the approach to Sumatra, the fleet arrived at the flying-off position, near Enggano Island off the west coast, ready to strike as planned on 23 January, but the monsoon weather was at its worst and remained so until the early morning of the 24th when the skies started to clear. Sixteen of our Hellcats from *Indomitable* were to be the middle cover for the Avengers during their flight to the target and back. It would be a distance of about 200 miles over sea, mountains and land to Palembang. Each of the forty-five Avengers was loaded with four 500lb bombs. The Fireflies, armed with rockets, were supposed to take position ahead of the Avengers but were rather late getting there owing to an accident on take-off. The Corsairs were top and rear cover.

The take-off and forming up of one hundred and fifty aircraft in limited space, because the skies were not yet entirely clear and relying on navigation lights because it was still dark, can most kindly be described as 'hectic.' Although it was early morning, I had sweated buckets by the time I had formed up, flying number three to Sammy

Langdon's flight. But I must admit that our many exercises and training at this sort of thing paid off so that, as the sky lightened, the main body of aircraft were in position and on course for the oil refinery at Pladjoe. However, the timing had gone haywire and we were late due to an accident to two Avengers on take-off and another having to make an emergency landing. The Fireflies had also been delayed due to unserviceability. The question did occur to me, not for the first time in my naval career, what necessity was there for a take-off before dawn anyway? What the hell difference would it have made if we had waited just half an hour longer? Were we to believe that the Japanese didn't man their radar stations until after breakfast? Never mind; as far as I was concerned at that time we were off at last.

Our Hellcats took up position over the Avengers, as we started the climb to reach 13,000 ft over the mountains ahead of us. We were flying slowly, keeping close to the bombers on the climb and at that speed we would not be much use to them as fighter protection. Sure enough, our Wing leader Tommy Harrington, increased speed weaving us from side to side over the Avengers. Once over the mountains, it was much easier as the Avengers were able to set a much faster pace losing height down towards the target area. There had been no sighting of Japanese fighters so far and already it was possible to see in the distance the river which I knew, from many briefings, to wind alongside the refinery.

Then suddenly came an excited call on the R/T. 'Bandits! Three o'clock up!'

There were specks like gnats in the sky growing larger at each second and becoming Tojo fighters as they dived fast towards the Avengers below us. Immediately came from our leader, 'Break right – Go!' Throttle wide open, guns set to fire, mouth dry, I turned hard and fired almost immediately ahead of one of the Tojos as it hurtled on its way past me towards the Avengers; I didn't see the actual hits but my bullets must have deflected him off his course. I turned the Hellcat half on its back and pulled it hard round to follow the Japanese down. He kept straight on down past the Avengers and, although by this time he was well ahead of me, I longed to follow because my Hellcat eventually would have caught him in the dive. But I remembered the strict orders that, this time, the fighter escort must not desert the Avengers.

Reluctantly I broke away from the chase and I remembered the basic rule to keep turning and look out behind and all around me. I found myself alone; my number two, Dick, and the rest of the flight were nowhere to be seen. But I was much nearer the refinery now and could see how huge it was and realise how vital a target it must be. An immense amount of flak was coming up at the Avengers who, by this time, had deployed for their attack. Moreover, as far as I could see the whole perimeter of the refinery was being protected by fat balloons tethered at about 3,000 ft. Nevertheless, the Avengers and the Fireflies too were pressing on with their attacks regardless of the balloon cables and the intense flak of all types coming up to meet them. Full marks to them all for sheer guts, I thought. But there was no point in my hanging around here now that they had made their attack and, much higher up, I could see the trails of the dog-fights that were still going on.

Sensibly, as it seemed at the time, I made straight for the rendezvous position, on the other side of the town of Palembang, to meet the Bombers and escort them on their return journey. I arrived to find most of the Avengers already there together with six of our other Hellcats. An awful lot of R/T chatter was going on making it difficult to know who was doing what and where but the obvious action for me was to join with the few Hellcats now escorting those Avengers who, by now, were beginning to make their way back to the Carriers. The return was uneventful, no attacks were made on us and gradually the rest of the escorting force joined up. The time was only about 9.30 am when our Carrier group was ready to start landing back on board HMS *Indomitable*.

I didn't find out the whole story until the big de-briefing afterwards. I learned that the separate 'Ramrod' of twenty-four Corsairs from *Illustrious* and *Victorious*, which had set off at full speed to hit the Japanese airfields in advance of our main strike, had in fact arrived too late. The Japanese fighters had all taken off already and had been waiting for us at 20,000 ft; hence all the dog-fighting in the area high over the refinery.

The Corsairs carried out strafing runs on the airfield near Palembang, too late really as the fighter aircraft had all gone, but they sustained five casualties from the heavy Japanese cross-fire. One of those killed was Bud Sutton, a Canadian who I knew particularly well from our early training days together at Gosport, Netheravon and Yeovilton. He was a fine, strong character of a man who had already earned a DSC. What a waste.

Looking back on that situation all these years later, the obvious and sensible course for the Corsair pilots to have taken would have been to acknowledge that they had 'missed the boat.' The Japanese aircraft had gone and, in reality, there was very little to be gained by strafing the bits and pieces of equipment on an airfield saturated with anti-aircraft gun emplacements. But common sense rarely prevails in wartime.

The Seafires from HMS *Indefatigable* had suffered a bad time. Because of their very limited range, they could not take part in the strike and had to act as Combat Air Patrol for protection of the Fleet. But they had so many crashes from deck-landings; being the usual Seafire disasters of broken backs, burst tyres, smashed undercarriages and hitting the barrier that the task of CAP had to be taken over by the other Carriers. As I listened to this, I wondered if their Lordships would ever learn that Seafires were entirely unsuited to Carrier operations or whether, in fairness to them, they had perhaps tried and failed to obtain more American aircraft?

Whereas the Avenger boys had done a superb job of bombing the refinery out of action, the Corsairs and Hellcats had failed again to escort them sufficiently well especially, apparently, between the refinery and the rendezvous, where they had been mauled by the Japanese fighters. I realised that, although I had done the right thing in breaking away from my potential 'kill' of the Tojo, I ought afterwards to have followed the path of the Avengers to give them some protection, instead of going straight to the rendezvous. The operation had been a success having certainly put the refinery out of action for months, but the bill to be paid was the loss of aircrews from two Avengers, six Corsairs and one Hellcat. The Hellcat pilot was Jack Haberfield; he who had welcomed me so kindly into the Squadron three months earlier and who was a most popular member of the squadron.

The fleet withdrew and steamed well to the west of Sumatra where the tankers were awaiting them at the rendezvous for the refuelling operation. Apparently the refuelling went rather badly through lack of experience at this sort of thing and the operation took two whole days. Moreover, the tankers were not carrying the amount of fuel required anyway so that there was only just enough for one more strike at the Palembang refineries, whereas three strikes had been planned originally. While the Carriers were bobbing along at about two knots, tied by hoses to the tankers, the aircrews were subjected in the windless heat to a number of de-briefings and discussions about the next strike. The aircrews were lambasted again for their unnecessary chatter on the R/T and general indiscipline in the air. Fair criticism, but the thought went through my mind that the RN seamen officers needed to get their own logistic and refuelling act together too.

On completion of the refuelling, the fleet approached the same flying-off position near Enggano Island on the early morning of 29 January. The weather was bad with heavy showers, low cloud and poor visibility, but with such limited fuel available for the fleet, it was understandable that a press-on spirit would have to prevail despite the bad weather, if the oil refinery at Soengei Gerong was to be attacked at all. And press on we did because flying off was only postponed for twenty minutes until 06.40 when, at that hour, visibility was still not at all good.

The plan of attack was much the same as before except that eight Corsairs would remain behind as CAP over the Fleet. Our Admiral evidently distrusted the Seafires to do the CAP job by themselves after their debacle of deck-landing crashes during the previous strike. I felt sorry for the pilots who had the ill-luck to be appointed to a Seafire squadron; it was not their fault that they were expected to fly an aircraft so unsuited to Carrier work. How thankful I felt to be in a Hellcat squadron. The other change was that the Avengers would take a different and longer route, clear of the heavy ANTI-AIRCRAFT fire, to the same rendezvous position. Our Hellcats were mid-cover for the bombers, as before.

Since early that morning at 6.10 am, I had been sitting strapped into the cockpit of my Hellcat, among thirty other aircraft ranged on the flight deck, expecting to be flown off at any moment. Then the postponement had been announced over the Tannoy, for which I was exceedingly grateful because the weather was foul and entirely unsuitable as an air space in which to form up some 120 aircraft from the four Carriers. And I was still there, half an hour later, in my by now familiar state of personal twitch about whether the Admiral intended to send us off regardless or would he, as I hoped, wait for better conditions. It was semi-dark with low clouds above but already I could see, looking towards Sumatra in the East, a glimmer of light in the far sky. In another half hour the sky could well be quite clear. Just as I was thinking that, the Tannoy burst forth with the order from Wings, 'Start engines.' What was it with these people, I thought angrily, that they were so determined for us to get airborne so unnecessarily early and regardless of the dangerous conditions? I had the ridiculous thought that our Admiral had become besotted in his boyhood from reading 'Biggles', the dashing hero and airman of the First World War, who invariably flew 'Dawn Patrols'.

With the order to start engines, the deck party and maintenance crews moved away to safety at the sides of the flight deck before the engines burst into life to make forty huge and lethal propellers thrash the air. At the same time I felt the vibration as the ship's engines increased to maximum revolutions and the ship heeled over to port as it started its turn to starboard into wind. Tommy Harrington's Hellcat, first to be off, was already facing straight down the flight deck and, as the deck officer brought his torch downwards, so it began to move down the deck. I was number ten in the range and was girding myself up mentally for the take-off into the slipstreams of the first nine. In itself this was no problem but, in a large range of aircraft, I always hated the necessity of the jink to starboard just as my aircraft was at the end of the deck barely airborne, almost on the stall and still with wheels down. But it was an essential manoeuvre to clear most of my own slipstream away from the path of the chap taking off behind me, as the pilot ahead had done for me.

With a full range of aircraft there was a much shorter length of deck, but my take-off had been no problem because, with *Indomitable* thumping along at full speed, there had been plenty of wind over her flight deck. Now, fully airborne and the wheels up, was the time to peer through the murky weather, semi-dark and low clouds to see whereabouts all the other aircraft might be. In particular, I needed to start a circuit to the left looking for my Hellcat leader who, in turn, would be aiming for the group rendezvous area at 1,500 ft. So long as everyone remembered the procedure and could see to follow the Hellcat immediately ahead, all should be well. And so it was for the Hellcats who formed up surprisingly quickly but the Corsairs and Fireflies seemed at one stage to be dodging about all over the sky. The visibility improved by the minute which was fortunate as it enabled the groups of aircraft to sort themselves out and to form up eventually into the agreed pattern. It was a pity our Admiral had not waited just another quarter hour before sending us off; the form up would have been so comparatively simple and hassle free. However, there had been no collisions thanks to remarkably good airmanship all round.

We set off for the target as before but, this time, there was cloud over the intervening mountains which made life more difficult for the group leaders, particularly for our top cover who above us were forced into cloud at one stage. As for me, I had settled down more calmly after the hiatus of the form-up. In my mind, having got that part over, I could now start to concentrate on our attack and to keep my wits about me ready for whatever might happen. Just as well because the Japanese had been better prepared, this time, so that a squadron of their fighters had been waiting for us at some 20,000 ft on the other side of the mountains and over the plains before reaching Palembang. The Corsairs above us went for the Japanese and dispersed them quickly, shooting several down, so that there was no need for us to break formation away from the Avengers. But the main Japanese fighter force was concentrated over the target area of the refinery.

Thus our Avengers were vulnerable to the Japanese fighters at the time when they were deploying for their bombing run on the refinery and it was difficult for us in our Hellcats to protect them. We had broken up, turning towards the Japanese as they came down and I fired for brief seconds as one came within my sights, but continued turning with my number two, Dick, staying with me on my port side. As we turned, a Tojo came fast behind us from his dive, fired but missed as I didn't feel anything, and up into a climbing turn to our left. It was a stupid manoeuvre; if he had kept turning tightly, we could not have touched him but he lost speed on the climb and Dick, lifting the nose of his Hellcat, gave him a good burst of fire which I could see hitting the tailplane and disintegrating it. I followed with more bullets into the by now helpless Tojo and watched it burst into flame and smoke. It was a shocking sight but, such was my fear of the Japanese and of their inhuman barbarity, that I felt no remorse at all.

I signalled Dick to follow and I headed for the far side of the refinery, which had become nearly impossible to see through the columns of black smoke resulting from the successful bombing by the Avengers. But then again, it was difficult to escort them away from the target because they were so widely dispersed all over the sky at that stage. Eventually, we caught up with two of them and I positioned us at a protective height about 1,000 ft above and to their side. Four Oscars circled above us at one point. We started to climb at full throttle towards them whereupon they moved away, to find easier prey in the form of unescorted Avengers. The rendezvous area was reached at last where we were able to join with others of our aircraft and to form up into proper formations with fighter escorts for the flight back to the Carriers. Even so, there was a shortage of fighters, many of whom had continued dog-fighting with the Japanese further back. At about 10 am most of the strike force reached the Fleet and could break up into landing patterns for each Carrier. In the last stages of the return flight, six of the mauled Avengers had to ditch, but the crews were recovered.

The Fleet started to withdraw from the combat zone but the Japanese, by this time, had spotted its position and sent seven bomber-type aircraft (Sallys) to attack it. The Seafires from *Indefatigable* were already up on patrol and, to more than make up for their earlier debacle, shot down five of the attackers. Two more Japanese were downed by three Hellcats from 1844 squadron. All this was very exciting but the result was spoilt by the battleship *King George V* shooting down one of the Seafires. Worse still, in the same form of 'friendly' fire and over excitement, two shells from one of the Cruisers hit the flight deck of *Illustrious* killing twelve people including the Walrus pilot.

From the de-briefing, we learned that once again the advance Ramrod of twenty-four Corsairs had arrived too late at the Japanese airfields around Palembang so that the Japanese fighter aircraft were already airborne and waiting at 20,000 ft for our Avengers. Here was a situation in which, instead of our Corsairs taking-off at dawn, they should have arrived over the enemy airfields at dawn. It would have meant taking off in the dark but, for that much smaller number of aircraft, it would have been not at all a difficult operation for them to have taken off and formed up from the Carrier in the dark.

Nevertheless, Palembang was a resounding success in achieving its object of cutting the Japanese supply of fuel by nearly 40% for several months. This must have had a very considerable effect in limiting the Japanese war effort in Burma and particularly against the American forces in the Pacific. Apparently the Americans were very impressed with our results and just that little bit surprised? The subsequent assessment of the records showed that sixty-eight Japanese aircraft had been destroyed, thirty-seven of them in aerial battle and the others on the ground. Our forces had lost a total of forty-one aircraft; sixteen in combat, eleven ditched and fourteen from deck-landing crashes. Thirty aircrew had been killed; nineteen in Avengers, a pilot in one Hellcat, eight pilots in Corsairs and two in Fireflies.

A final story about Palembang has to be told. It is about Ronnie Hay, the Lt Colonel of Marines acting as the Air Group Co-ordinator who, while giving out directions to everybody here and there over the R/T, was interrupted in his continuous patter of instructions, by an attack on his flight of four Corsairs by twelve Tojo fighters. He was silent for five whole minutes while he personally shot down three Japanese fighters. His flight shot two more and the rest fled. What a fearless old warrior he was!

The British Pacific Fleet arrived at Sydney on 10 February to receive a warm and generous welcome from the Australian people. The Aussies pulled out all the stops to entertain all of us as, for instance, we learned that they had raised over half a million pounds towards a fund for the purpose. Hitherto, the Americans had used Sydney as their launching base for the war in the Pacific and had been very welcome. But now it was the turn of the Royal Navy to enjoy Aussie hospitality. I was fortunate to be in Sydney because most of the squadron had flown off the ship to Nowra, a small town eighty miles from Sydney with a nearby airfield.

While in harbour at the first drinks party on board hosted by our Wardroom, I met Joan Moorhouse. Perhaps the best way to describe our ensuing relationship is that I 'went steady' with her for that short period in Sydney very much as one would go out with a regular girl friend back in England. Joan was about three years older than I; no raving beauty but an attractive girl, slim with brown hair and a nice sense of humour. We went to dances, to restaurants and to the pictures together and I was fortunate to have such cheerful female company. As for any sexual activity this was limited to a cuddle, a kiss and an occasional tweeze of her nice little bottom. There was no flying to worry about and it was a happy and relaxed period during which I celebrated my twenty-third birthday on the 17th of that month, and with it came my promotion to Lieutenant.

On another evening, I was invited to dinner with her mother and father at their house on the edge of the City and was daunted at first to find that her father was a General, an equivalent I think to a Rear Admiral. I need not have worried; he was an excellent host and showed genuine interest in the detail of Carrier operations. He listened as, at his request, I explained some of the difficulties of flying from Carriers especially when operating with large numbers of aircraft. I remember thinking at the time what a bonus it would be if only our boss, Vian, could take the same degree of interest in the views of one of his pilots.

Meantime, we chaps who did the flying gathered from various rumours that the role of our British Fleet had still not been agreed with the American Command. Apparently, agreement could not be reached about where we would fight nor under whose overall Command our fleet would serve. However, despite this uncertainty, on 28 February the Fleet put to sea heading, we were told, to a place called Manus being a part of the Admiralty Islands a long way up

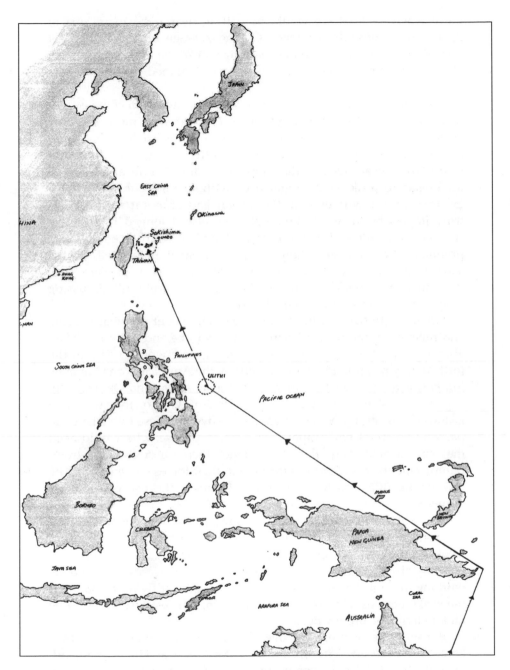

Map of the Pacific

north where at least we would be getting nearer the main area of operations against the Japanese. On the passage up there, the fleet carried out numerous exercises learning to use the American system of signals and procedures in readiness for combined operations with them.

We arrived at Manus on 7 March. What a dump; Trincomalee was paradise in comparison. It was a huge harbour with more shipping anchored in it than I had ever seen. Some of the Hellcats had been flown to an airstrip ashore but we did little flying while living on board. The heat aboard the ship was almost unbearably high, impossible to walk on the flight deck without thick-soled shoes, for example, and down below in the hangar and offices it was at times truly impossible to work. Like everyone else, I longed for the one shower I was allowed in the evening because fresh water was at a premium. We could go ashore for a swim but the sea itself, off the shoreline, was positively warm and not much relief or pleasure. The fleet languished there because the 'Powers above' were still discussing what part we were to play in the Pacific war.

On about 15 March I think, there was agreement on what the role and function of the British Pacific fleet was to be and, without delay, aircrews were briefed on it. In essence, our role would relate to the forthcoming major landing and assault by the Americans on Okinawa. But between Formosa, held in force by the Japanese, and Okinawa lay a group of islands known as the Sakashima Gunto, the two main Islands of this group being Ishigaki and Miyako. These two Islands in particular were of vital importance to the Japanese, who would need the six airfields on them to stage their aircraft and troop reinforcements from Formosa through to their forces on Okinawa. The task of the BPF was to deny to the Japanese the use of these six airfields.

As an objective, the task did not sound in any way glamorous but it would call for a massive effort from the British Fleet which would have to remain at sea for long periods to achieve it. The complement of some six thousand men in the four Aircraft Carriers would be working flat out day and night to keep the aircraft flying throughout the strike periods and, as we were to learn, the cost was going to be high in terms of aircrew lives.

But now the waiting was over and our fleet, designated as Task Force 57, had received its 'orders' from the American High Command. To put the situation in perspective in relation to the United States Navy out there, our Task Force, bearing in mind that it was the biggest fleet ever put together by the Royal Navy, was less than half the size of any one of the eleven Task Forces used in the Pacific by the US Navy. Think about that!

We left Manus and arrived on 22 March at the Atoll harbour of Ulithi to make final preparations for action and, astonished as I had been at the amount of American shipping in Manus, it was almost as nothing compared to the warships, tankers and supply vessels of the US Navy to be seen for miles in every direction here at Ulithi. The thought occurred to me that the Japanese, by initiating this war and in their manner of conducting it, had shown themselves to be not only barbaric, but also astonishingly stupid and lacking in military intelligence not to have realised what a massive force they were taking on, when they bombed the Americans at Pearl Harbour.

It is not only the immense wealth and resources available to the Americans, I thought, which makes them so strong but, looking at all that shipping, I could appreciate their astonishing organisational ability enabling them to make the very best of their huge resources in the fast production of war materials. It seemed to me that, above all else, they were supreme organisers which showed, not only in the speed of their mass production, but in the training of their armed forces. Johnnie Lowder, who had trained at Pensacola in America, had told me of their method of training with long and intensive hours of flying including constant checks every ten hours and at every stage by senior instructors. Ye gods, I had thought, how I would have loathed it and thank heavens for my flying training in England where the more relaxed approach of my instructors had suited me.

Most FAA aircrew, unless inexperienced new boys, realised that the US Navy operated their Aircraft Carriers at a higher standard than we did. Although the Royal Navy had been the first to experiment successfully in flying aircraft from ships way back in about 1918, the Americans had long since developed the idea and the technique of Carrier operations to a high degree while, in that meantime, our Lordships of the Admiralty had floundered around still playing at Battleships. For example, every man on the flight deck of an American Carrier had a specific job to do and had been given intensive specialist training to do just that job. Whereas, in our Carriers, the Commander would allocate a number of seamen, marines and engineers from the ship's company for flight deck work. These men then had to be shown their job and trained by the DLCO.

And of course the Americans had the enormous advantage that all their officers of high rank, even their Admirals, were experienced navy pilots who knew exactly what they were about and were capable each one of flying from an Aircraft Carrier. Thus, we had to learn from them the business of operating large numbers of aircraft from three or more Carriers in company. I imagine that sometimes it must have been difficult for the high ranking Admirals of the US Navy, being highly experienced naval airmen, to communicate with our own Admirals and Captains who had no first hand and direct experience of naval aviation. Nevertheless, the senior Admiral of our Fleet, Vice-Admiral Sir Bernard Rawlings, was highly regarded by his American counterparts, as indeed he was by us his aircrews. I doubt, however, whether our immediate boss Rear Admiral Vian was equally well respected.

As regards the Aircraft Carriers, ours were designed for the conditions around Europe and were unsuitable for the extreme hot weather of the Far East and Pacific, having insufficient provision of water for drinking and washing and no air conditioning. In consequence, life on board for everybody was generally uncomfortable. Yet, at that time, every man in each Carrier was living life at such intensity, with long hours of work, that there was really no time to think too much about the discomfort. The big plus factor of our British Carriers was the thick steel flight decks, compared with the wooden decks of the American ships. A United States Navy officer was heard to comment, 'If a Kamikaze hits a US Carrier, it's a six months' repair in harbour. In a Limey Carrier, it's a case of sweepers man your brooms.'

Before our Task Force set out on 24 March from Ulithi, there was a final conference of squadron commanders conducted by a Captain, as Chief of the Admiral's staff. It was described to me afterwards over drinks in the Wardroom thus. After the conference had been going for precisely one hour to the minute, in came Admiral Vian, the boss man.

He strode into the centre and said loudly to his Chief of Staff, 'All right that's enough, if we can't organise it in an hour, it's not worth doing.' Then turning to the squadron commanders; 'All I have to say is ... Get stuck in.' When I heard this story, I was profoundly unimpressed. Both the scene and the words seemed to be contrived with the intention of reflecting the bravura and warlike character of the Admiral himself, rather than to give supportive encouragement to his commanders. He was there to speak to men, many of whom with their aircrews, were very likely to be killed during the days ahead. It would have been better leadership if he had quietly emphasized the importance of the task ahead of them, expressed his confidence in them and wished them good luck.

At a similar meeting in the Wardroom some time later, attended by all aircrew wearing the normal daily tropical uniform of white shirts and shorts, Vian demanded to know why the aircrews were not wearing their wings. This, after three years as the Admiral in charge of Fleet Air Arm operations since Salerno, and he was the one person who did not know, or had never noticed before, that wings were never worn with that particular working uniform! This crashing blunder showed quite clearly how little contact this Admiral had with his aircrews.

We left Ulithi to join up first of all with the tanker force, which had preceded us. The Fleet needed maximum fuel before commencing the strike on the Sakashima Gunto Islands but refuelling seemed to take forever and at the end of a whole day I heard that it was never quite completed. The Americans, when we had the opportunity to watch them, would take less than two hours to couple up the hoses, complete the fuelling and then disengage from the tanker. It was surprising when I thought about it that our Admiral Vian, famous as a brilliant seaman, appeared unable to sort out the problems the seamen continued to have in refuelling his fleet.

The flying off position for our first strike on the airfields was 100 miles south of Miyako and from *Indomitable* we started with four flights of Hellcats led by Tommy Harrington taking off, as usual, at dawn. There was no opposition in the air over the airfield but the flak during our subsequent Ramrod of the airfield was lethal. But we were well led and we had no casualties. On our return to the Carrier, before we landed on, the next strike of Avengers and Hellcat escorts took off for their strike. As soon as we had landed, our aircraft were immediately refuelled and re-armed and, on completion, we returned to our cockpits and remained there on stand-by.

For the next flight just before noon, eight of us escorted the second strike of Avengers to bomb another airfield on the Island. After landing back on board, my flight of four led by Sammy could relax at 'readiness' for an hour or more which enabled us to grab some sandwiches from the Wardroom to eat while being briefed in the Ready room for the next strike. The final effort of the day was another ramrod attack on the third airfield of the Island. Back on board after a dusk landing gave time at last for a shower, lots of whisky and as good a meal as the hard worked stewards and cooks could provide from limited resources. More whisky and then it was time to hit the bunk.

It was a very long day, that first day, and we had been fortunate not to suffer any casualties although, as we learned from other Carriers in an exchange of signals, one Avenger had been lost and two Corsairs one of which was the CO of the Corsair squadron in *Victorious* who had been shot down by flak. I think that we in Hellcats were given a good start by Tommy who, on our first run, had taken us in fast and very, very low. Although there had been no attempt by the Japanese to use their airfields during that day, there had been one or two efforts by them to send reconnaissance aircraft to spot our fleet, but these had been shot down. It was reckoned that eight of their aircraft had been destroyed on the ground during ramrod attacks by Hellcats and Corsairs.

That first day set the pattern of the future strike days when I would hardly be out of my cockpit all day except for briefings, sandwiches and a quick smoke while at readiness. This same routine would continue for two days at a time. The two days of continuous attacks on the islands by the aircraft of all four Carriers would be followed nearly always by two days away from the islands, where and when refuelling from the tankers could be done and repairs made to aircraft. The replacement of aircrew casualties and aircraft was effected by using two back-up Escort Carriers enabling such replacements to fly on during the oiling period.

If I felt it hard to be sitting on an uncomfortable parachute in a cockpit most of the day for two days, either flying or at readiness, then so be it and 'ard luck, as they say. But in comparison, our maintenance crews had to work ceaselessly throughout all of the days and nights; particularly on those nights before the fleet returned to the islands when they would need to prepare and arm every aircraft ready for the strikes starting at first light next day. The fact is that there was little rest for anyone in the Carriers, whether they be officers, flight deck party, engineers, radar operators, seamen, cooks, stewards or whatever because the lives of them all would be dominated by the need to keep the aircraft flying. The two strike days were manic with constant action since all four Carriers would be turning into wind all day to fly off aircraft on strikes and landing them back on board non-stop from dawn to dusk. For many of the people, the two days away from the operational area for oiling were not much easier as there was so much to be done in preparation for the next series of strikes.

The second day of strikes continued in the same way from early morning but the Japanese were more prepared for us and the casualties among our four Carriers were higher. Moreover, we could see that much of the damage to their airfield runways had been repaired during the night. This was to happen constantly but, although our efforts might appear fruitless, the essential objective of denying the Japanese the use of these airfields was being achieved. The cost after the end of the second day amounted to the loss of seven of our aircraft and seven aircrew mostly from flak. Two of the Seafire pilots had been killed in deck-landing accidents and we had lost a Hellcat, but not the pilot, in a similar landing accident.

We suffered no casualties among the pilots of our Hellcats and Avengers in *Indomitable* but the airmanship and courage of one of our Hellcat pilots, Alec Wilsher, brought him back safely on board after a wheels-up landing. He had been wounded in the thigh, lost much blood but had given himself a morphine injection enabling him to overcome the pain sufficiently to just about fly the aircraft on board. He was expected to die but, with good care from our ship's Doctors, he recovered.

Excerpt from Squadron diary:

> 1839 Squadron made history when Alec Wilsher was hit badly in the thigh severing the nerve. He gave himself a shot of morphine & gallantly brought the Cab (and himself!) back. He lost a lot of blood. His hydraulics were shot up so he made a wheels-up landing – a beauty. He was in a critical state for some days but happily he's on the way to recovering by now.
>
> We kept on the same routine of 2 days in, 2 days out for oiling. Once we did 3 days in, and once we went to that delightful scenic place FORMOSA. This was marked by an increase of KAMA KASIS (which stands for the sods who deliver themselves on the flight deck – or try to) I think we shot 20 of them down. Indefat was hit by one but forced on, paying little regard.

As I have said, flying from Carriers had a particular advantage in that, provided you could get yourself back on board in one piece, all the facilities such as a Wardroom, whisky, meals, a comfortable cabin and a bunk were usually available and now I had received the reassurance of seeing how well our very good Sick Bay dealt with the arrival of a badly wounded pilot. The availability of these advantages on return from a strike could never be absolutely certain, of course, because the Carrier would always be an enemy's prime target, moreover, out here in the Pacific, there was the dominant threat of the Kamikaze attacks.

The Task Force was subjected to Kamikaze and other air attacks during this period of the strikes, but most of the attackers were hit down by our CAP patrols before they reached us; the Seafires having become particularly effective in this role. Unfortunately, two of them and one of our Hellcats were shot down by 'friendly' fire from the Fleet warships.

While I was away airborne over the Islands, the Fleet was attacked by twenty Japanese fighter-bombers. They were split up by our patrol of Hellcats led by our Wing Leader, Harrington, but one got through and machine-gunned the flight deck of *Indomitable* wounding seven men and killing one. *Victorious* was narrowly missed by a Kamikaze as was *Illustrious*. At a later date *Illustrious* and *Indefatigable* were hit by Kamikazes but, thanks to their steel flight decks, were able to operate again shortly afterwards.

For four weeks the routine of two days of strikes against the Island airfields and two days of replenishment continued. There were no great losses on any particular day; just a drainage of aircraft and aircrews lost mostly from flak and from deck-landing accidents. The pilots of both Hellcats and Corsairs were successful in air combat where very few were shot down. But the continuous task of either Combat Air Patrol over the islands and fleet or Ramrods of the airfields was an exhausting business. Usually it was arranged that a fighter pilot would alternate during the day starting off probably with strafing the airfields on the first flight, escorting the bombers on the second and CAP on the third. Sometimes, with a little bit of luck, only two strikes would be allocated for the day. Combat Patrol over the airfields, to make sure that no Japanese aircraft tried to stage through, would end with a strafing attack if any suitable targets were evident on the ground. But it was pointless to risk lives against the formidable and it has to be said courageous fire of the Japanese gunners, if the ground targets were not of any significance.

The prospect of air combat with the Japanese pilots was not a worry. We reckoned the Hellcat to be a far better aircraft than anything they flew and we had no doubt at all that every one of us was a superior pilot to the average Japanese. Our experience in the past four months had shown that to be so. Thus, to take off from the deck to carry out a CAP over the Fleet would be a comparative relaxation. But we dreaded each and every one of us the strafing or Ramrod runs on those enemy airfields. We came to know most of them and had worked out the best approach in attacking them; so much so that a pre-flight briefing from the Leader was often not necessary.

Having decided the approach, the flight leader takes all four down to low level in a fast dive from about 8,000 ft in loose finger formation, then a final turn in towards the airfield usually along the direction of the runway, all four aircraft spreading out with space between, then down, down as low as possible to ground level and flying at about 20 feet and full throttle at some 320 knots. Look for a target along the line of flight. Looks like a troop-carrier? Get your sights onto it, quick check either side that you are not running on to the same target as the others, now into the main gauntlet of Japanese machine-gun, cannon and shell fire from either side. So far the fire going over the top of you. Just keep going right down low and try to ignore it; concentrate on the chosen aircraft target ahead. Press the tit early now and give it as long a burst of fire as possible, only seconds of fire anyway but you are hitting it. Just hope it isn't a dummy target with Japanese guns already laid to cover it. Up over the top of it the danger moment, then keep down and out the other side and climb away to re-form with the Leader. Are we all four through and intact? Yes … this time. But some flak still coming up at us. What will the Leader decide to do as he looks back at the result? I know the problem; I have led a flight myself and know how everyone is hoping like hell that you as Leader will decide to call it a day. He evidently reckons we have done enough damage; he waggles his wings to sign that we are going home.

That described the third flight and strike of the day and the combination of tiredness and the relief at finishing was dangerous. There was the deck-landing still to be made and it would require concentration. The Carrier isn't really 'home' until you have landed safely back on board. So many of the deck-landing accidents, some of them fatal, occur at this late stage at the end of the day. My show-off days of steep turns on to the deck were over; all I wanted was to get down safely and I was much more respectful in my attitude to the signals of the batsman. Shortly after landing and de-briefing, it was dark and the ship turned away from the enemy island and ceased 'action stations' which had been in force since before dawn. Now the watertight doors throughout the ship were opened and I could go down to my cabin and look forward to a shower.

Since the arrival in the squadron of the three senior Lieutenants a while back, I no longer shared the particularly nice cabin near the quarterdeck and had been put into a cabin to share with an RN (engineer) Lieutenant. He really was rather a morose chap and we hardly spoke to each other. Our patterns of living on board were so very diverse; he spent his day and night watches in an engine room so hot that a human could not live in it without gradual adaptation over a long period, while I spent my day sitting in a cockpit, up top. I knew that he was disgusted because I went to my bunk every night befuddled with whisky. My mind otherwise would have been hyperactive reliving the strikes made during the day and thinking ahead to those for to-morrow. Fortunately the engineer (known as plumbers in the Navy) was often on watch when I came to bed but then, of course, he was disturbed whenever I had my early morning 'shake' for the dawn flight. Before the influx of new pilots, the Plumber had the cabin to himself so all in all his morose behaviour was probably understandable. But the situation didn't bother me much, I had decided nearly two years ago, after the death of Basil, that I did not want to form a close friendship ever again with a cabin-mate.

Admiral Rawlings was concerned, we were told, about the morale among men of the large ships in the Fleet, those in the Battleship and the Cruisers. The value of those big warships was in providing anti-aircraft fire against Kamikaze and other air attacks and in their extensive radar coverage. But their huge guns, designed for banging away at other Battleships, were unlikely to be of much use against airfield targets and so this part of the fleet had taken comparatively little direct part in the operation and had not come nearer than a hundred miles of the enemy islands. We heard therefore that a bombardment was proposed to be undertaken which, with all its fearsome noise and fury, would have the effect of cheering the men of the Battleships immensely and give them something to do. At the last minute, however, Admiral Rawlings cancelled the bombardment realising that it was unlikely to do much harm to the anti-aircraft guns surrounding the enemy airfields, yet would leave the Carriers without part of their protection.

It was on 9 April that Admiral Rawlings was asked by the American Admiral Spruance, who was in command of all naval forces in the Pacific, to carry out a strike on Formosa; he wanted us to bash a particular airfield and harbour there for some reason important in relation to the American assault on Okinawa. And so accordingly, on 11 April, the British Fleet was off Formosa ready to undertake the task. For aircrews this new sortie was a welcome change from the grind, which I personally dreaded, of strafing and bombing the airfields on the Islands of Ishigaki and Miyako; those airfields would probably be imprinted on our minds for ever, we had spent so much time on them. But the weather was bad over Formosa making it necessary to find alternative targets. It was almost a pleasure, when we did so, to be attacking shipping in a harbour where the return fire was not as intense in comparison to that of the airfields and, for the first time, I dropped or rather skipped a couple of bombs at a small elderly supply ship. They didn't seem to do it much harm, but I must have hit something because it appeared to be sinking slightly as we left. Anyway, Admiral Spruance expressed his particular approval afterwards of our efforts so we must have 'done good'.

From there we returned to join our tankers at the usual oiling rendezvous and, at that stage on 14 April, HMS *Illustrious* left the scene and departed for Sydney en route back to the UK. She and all her crew and aircrews had done well but now her overworked engines were giving trouble. I tried to contact my old friend of earlier days, Jack Parli, before they left but was unable to do so. However it was then I learned the sad news that Winnie Churchill had been killed in action a few days earlier. The action which caused his almost inevitable death was unbelievably foolish, I have to write, because he had attacked the Japanese airfield for a second run entirely on his own. A second attack at an airfield target by a whole flight was regarded as particularly dangerous, but entirely on his own was madness. What could he have been thinking of? Jack Parli, his close companion and greatest friend for the past five years, since they joined up in the Navy together, must have been devastated at the loss of him. But of course, Jack would have had to get on with it, and he did so to earn a DSC as Senior Pilot of his squadron.

HMS *Formidable* with her two Corsair squadrons and an Avenger squadron was there to replace HMS *Illustrious*. During that brief period of replenishment, Wing Leaders and Squadron Commanders from *Victorious* visited *Formidable* to brief their counterparts and their aircrews on the procedures we had learnt for attacking the airfields on the islands and on such safety measures as were sensible. To no avail apparently, as the CO of the Corsair squadron was killed on his first strike two days later when our attacks on the airfields were resumed.

There was little change in the situation. Each day our Avengers bombed the hangars and runways and every night the little yellow men came out of their holes in the ground to fill in the runway craters.

Each day our Corsairs and Hellcats strafed the airfields to hit petrol bowsers, aircraft hangars, gun emplacements, particularly any aircraft visible on the ground and to hit any Japanese personnel if we could possibly catch them running about in the open. And every day the Japanese poured back machine-gun, cannon and shellfire at our Avengers, Hellcats and Corsairs from their ever-increasing gun emplacements. Every day they knocked down one and sometimes two of us. But the continuous use of their six airfields was entirely denied to them during our presence.

Nevertheless, some of their bomber or fighter aircraft would fly out from Formosa to be met by our Combat Air Patrols either over the Islands or as they tried to attack the Fleet. Few of them got through; in air combat we rarely lost an aircraft. Sammy, in whose flight I usually flew but not on that occasion, met six 'Oscars' approaching the Fleet and with his team shot down four of them. One of the Hellcats, damaged in combat, crashed on landing back on *Indomitable*, killing the pilot. Days later, our flight were carrying out a strafing attack on Ishigaki when, on climbing away, I realised that Sammy was not with us. I had not seen him go but, circling the airfield, the crashed Hellcat could be seen. Sadly, I led the remaining three of us back to land on the ship.

There had been rumours that the fleet was due a longer period of rest and replenishment at Pedro Roads harbour in Leyte. And sure enough, we did indeed come into Leyte on 23 April to learn that the Fleet would be rested there for at least a week. What a blessed relief for the aircrews, but there was a mountain of repair and other work waiting to be done by the aircraft maintenance teams and the ship's company. Of course, aircrew had a party that first night on board including a truly loud sing-song; in my experience there was nearly always someone in the squadrons capable of bashing out a Fleet Air Arm song on the piano. But all that was as nothing compared to the sheer wonder and joy, as far as I was concerned, with which the next day ended.

First of all aircrew reported for a sort of briefing from Commander Air and Commander Ops, who was there to give us a larger view of the results of what had been happening during the past month; a sort of grim score card.

Since leaving Ulithi, the British Task Force had been continuously at sea for thirty-two days, the longest period since Nelson had blockaded the French at the beginning of the 19th century. Most of those days had been off the enemy coastline to strike at their airfields.

The fleet had lost forty-seven aircraft mostly from flak over the airfields but a large percentage also from crashes on deck-landing. Thirty aircrew had been killed and ten of them, as we knew only too well, had been our colleagues in *Indomitable*. It was reckoned that thirty-nine enemy aircraft had been shot down, mostly from air combat rather than A-A fire, and another forty destroyed on the ground. But the Japanese had been denied the use of their six airfields almost entirely which seemed to indicate that it had all been worth it?

Certainly it was worth it for our Admiral Vian who, despite his signals to the Fleet which had so often betrayed his ignorance of naval aviation warfare and some of which had even implied the cowardice of his aircrews, would in due course receive his desired Knighthood as a result of the success of those aircrews.

Commander Air then informed us that six pilots and two observers were to be sent back to the UK since they had exceeded their time on operations. I hoped, as I listened to this, that he must mean those who had been serving in fighter Squadrons before coming out to the Far East in 1944, in which case surely oh surely I prayed, I must be one of the six pilots?

Later that morning I was told to report to Commander Air in his cabin. He handed me a signal ordering me to return to the UK immediately. On arrival I was to take leave for seven days before reporting urgently to Lossiemouth for a course as Deck Landing Control Officer, that is, to be a batsman. How ironic, that after years of my gentle disparagement of Batting as a deck-landing aid I was now to become a DLCO!

In fact, at that particular moment, the job seemed entirely desirable since it would not involve me in any real flying; it was a kind of flying desk job. And this appointment was particularly fortunate too, because their Lordships of the Admiralty had not yet come to realise that flying as a squadron pilot, either ashore or from a Carrier, was rather more nerve wracking than normal service as a ship's officer. In consequence, they tended happily to appoint a pilot from one squadron and Carrier to another, for years without a break. After all, in my own case, I had been flying in an operational squadron now for four continuous years without a break, although admittedly without any distinction.

Moreover, as I thought about my new appointment, I realised how our batsman on *Indomitable* these past weeks had done a remarkably good and valuable job in helping very tired pilots down on to the deck safely, and this on top of his work in organising the flight deck from dawn to dusk every day. Indeed, he had justly won a DSC for his work often under fire. The more I thought about it, the happier I became with the appointment. After all I appeared to be right for the job because, looking at my log book, I realised that my last deck-landing had been my 102nd, a very unusual achievement in those days because one rarely flew from a Carrier except on operations and, moreover, I had done so without crashing an aircraft. It qualified me for the 'Perch Club' a fictitious club for those who had completed 100 deck-landings without a prang. Originally there was a zig-zag tie for members but in time it became available for all FAA pilots because, after the war, it became normal with improved aircraft and Carrier equipment, including in particular the angled deck, for a pilot to complete several hundred deck-landings, while accidents became very rare.

Nothing could detract from my relief and joy at the order to leave the Pacific and to go on my way home. My cabin-mate being on watch that afternoon in the engine room, I was able to take my time in packing up my clothes before obtaining my pay and air travel vouchers. As I was alone in the cabin, I was able to lie on my bunk and just let it sink into my mind that I really had survived, and tears of sheer relief flowed down my face. I had started out as a young tearaway fighter pilot, full of guts and go, but now I was no more than a rather tatty and tired old man of age twenty-three years, with the 'twitch'. I was very definitely not of the 'warrior' class … just an ordinary airman, in fact.

I learned later that, before the British Fleet left the Sakashima Gunto in May 1945 the final bill for the total time of seven weeks over those Islands was the loss of over two hundred aircraft, half of those from deck-landing crashes, and thirty-nine aircrew killed. I was lucky to be out of the final part of it.

I have to make my apology to the Seafire for, in the final stage of war in the Pacific, the aircraft did very well indeed as a Carrier-borne fighter. This was largely due to the initiative of a squadron commander who adapted an American long-range fuel tank to fit under the fuselage of the Seafire, thus improving the range and the consequent value of the aircraft considerably. But most pilots still found it to be a swine to deck-land.

CHAPTER FOURTEEN

Batsman and 1846 Squadron

After Leyte, I had been flown from Sydney by Transport Command of the RAF on a flight, via Colombo, to Lyneham in the UK. The whole long journey since leaving HMS *Indomitable* had been so fast, taking only four days, that it had a dream-like quality to it. I could scarcely believe the astonishing change in my life from the dreaded, hot and horribly dangerous world of the Sakashima Islands in the Pacific – to sitting quietly at home at Taplow in England, as I was now, chatting with Mother and Maddie by the fireside.

I learned in due course that the reason for all the speed and hassle of my journey was owing to a shortage of trained DLCOs for the number of Aircraft Carriers now in operation. Hence the rush, so very welcome to me, with which I had been shot back to the UK. The function of the batsman had now come to be regarded as so essential that a Carrier could hardly function properly as such without one. To my mind that view was just nonsense but it had brought me back fast to the UK and who was I to argue with it?

At Lyneham when we landed, I had been given a sheaf of food ration coupons and petrol coupons so that I planned to enjoy a simple leave, driving Mother and Maddie about in the old Austin which, although by now it had become a bit of an old banger, still functioned well enough for the purpose. I had in mind that, armed with all those coupons, we would just bumble around to country pubs and restaurants. Very recently, Father had taken himself back to the south of France, no longer occupied by the Germans, where he was busy settling back into his villa. My sister Phoebe and Johnnie Lowder, now married, were stationed at Ford in Sussex. Lalline, my long-term 'steady' was recently married and so I would have to keep my eye open for other female company.

It gave me a lot of pleasure, now that I no longer had a Fighter Squadron to rejoin, merely to walk about a town feeling like a normal, real person who has a whole long lifetime ahead of him. During previous leaves, I had not been able to rid myself of a feeling of doom and that I did not belong to the same world as people in the community at home who lived normal, safe lives. It was a joy this time to watch people going about their business, doing all the usual things of life and to feel that I belonged with them and no longer to feel jealous of them. Meanwhile, at that time, I was surprised to realise from talking with people in the pubs, how little thought they were giving to the war against the Japanese in the Far East. The war in Europe was all but over and the joy of that realisation seemed to have filled people's minds entirely.

I was due to report to Lossiemouth in the far north of Scotland on 10 May for the DLCO course which gave me little more than a week's leave at home. Hence, to find out more about my future, I paid a quick visit to the Admiralty where I learned that my next ship would be HMS *Begum*, another Escort Carrier, which was preparing even now at a UK port to leave shortly for the Far East. I said my goodbyes to Mother and Maddie, promising to see them again, if I could, before I joined my new ship. Then I set off to take the long and tedious journey by train to RNAS Lossiemouth at the top end of Scotland. I arrived there to find that the course had moved to the nearby small airfield of Milltown where I was thankful to be shown to a comfortable single cabin fairly near to the Officers' Mess. The next morning, after breakfast, I walked down to the office block from where the DLCO Course was being conducted.

There were only five other 'pupils', all Sub Lieutenants RNVR. Three of them had been drafted from Seafire squadrons and two from Barracuda squadrons and all of them had some experience flying from Carriers. The 'Head Boy' of the course was Lt Arthur Darley RN, my old adversary who had been the batsman in HMS *Illustrious* during my time in 890 squadron. I use the word 'adversary' because he was prone to become so cross when I ignored his signals but, to be fair, he was as good a batsman as anyone could be who so rarely flew and good in his organisation of the flight deck. During my time in the Pacific, I had come to appreciate the value of a good batsman waiting to help me land on when I was tired. And so I felt altogether more benign now towards Arthur and his DLCO course.

The Commanding Officer of the course and indeed of the whole business of 'Batsmanship' in the Fleet Air Arm was the same chap, now a Commander RN, who also had been in *Illustrious* at that time. As the course progressed, he would arrive from time to time to give a brief display of his now famous pirouettes and flamboyant gestures with the bats. But I contrived not to laugh. After all, despite his absurd self-important strutting and pirouetting, the school of batsmen which he had done much to create, had played a part at that particular time in the development of the Fleet Air Arm. Nevertheless, I still maintained that the role of the batsman, as a deck-landing aid, was never so vital and essential as it was made out to be. In any case, shortly after the war, an entirely new system of green, red and amber lights at the end of the flight deck, invented by Nick Goodhart, a flying plumber, would tell the pilot of his position on the approach.

There was a team of pilots, flying Swordfish and sometimes other aircraft such as Fireflies, who carried out circuits and landings all day on the runway at Milltown while we, as pupils, waved our two bats at them under tuition from Darley. After a few days of this, we pupils were all embarked into the back of four Swordfish which then flew us out to an Escort Carrier working in the usual area off the west coast of Scotland. Sitting helpless in the back of an aircraft, even the safe old Swordfish, while some other pilot deck-landed the thing, was an alarming experience. Thank heavens I had been considered as being too dim to be an Observer by the Selection Board all those years ago.

The next four days or so were spent taking turns to bat the Swordfish and an occasional Firefly on to the deck. In fact, of course, we were just going through the motions because the pilots appointed to carry out these landings could almost have done them with their eyes shut. They were known as 'the Clockwork Mice' since they did nothing else but go round and round the Carrier to touch down, after the tightest possible circuit, followed by an immediate take-off after touching down on the deck. These chaps would amass hundreds of so-called deck-landings compared with an average operational pilot who, as I have written before, rarely achieved as many as a hundred landings in those wartime days. But there was no comparison of a 'clockwork mouse' circuit and landing with that of an operational pilot, who would have to land on a deck, probably tired and stressed having completed perhaps one, two or even three strikes during the day. The large number of crashes and casualties on operations bore witness to the difficulty and danger of a real landing on the deck of an Aircraft Carrier.

I was able to finish my DLCO course early to enable me to take two days' leave at home before joining HMS *Begum*, my new ship, which was due to leave the harbour at Greenock within days. On arrival on board, after meeting the Commander, I found that I had been given very decent accommodation sharing a large cabin with an RNR seaman officer of similar rank. For the first time I was now a ship's officer and it was a strange feeling to be serving in a Carrier but without being a member of a Squadron.

That evening I met the Lt Cdr RN who was acting as Wings for the ship although he was an Observer and not a pilot. I learned from him that the ship had been used as a Ferry to take aircraft and aircraft spares out to the Far East and this would be her second such voyage for a similar purpose. It was not a very exciting prospect but, on the other hand I told myself, this would be the quiet life that I wanted.

Our first port of call was Belfast where there were some two dozen new Hellcats and their spares to be loaded on board and struck down securely in the Hangar. The flight deck itself would not be used for the purpose just in case, apparently, the ship might have to be used for its real purpose as an Aircraft Carrier. I had a formal interview with the Commander to ask if I could have a parade of those men selected for the Flight Deck party so that I could see how many of them, if any, had prior training or knowledge of Carrier work. I didn't want to waste any time in starting to train them and work with them in preparation for an aircraft, which might in the near future need to land on. He told me, however, that he was short of seamen and none could be set aside as yet for training in flight deck work. I met the Captain, who appeared to be as bored as I was with the ship, but at least I was given permission by him to act as a sort of second Watchkeeper on the Bridge under training. It was something of interest for me to do but, truthfully, I was bored stiff as we bumbled our way across the Bay of Biscay towards Suez, It was difficult to understand the ways of the Admiralty which, having sent for me hot foot from the Pacific to be a DLCO, had now appointed me to a ship which was not intended, apparently, to operate aircraft. The workings of the Admiralty were strange indeed.

About a week later, the ship entered harbour at Alexandria and there to my joy was a sight for bored eyes; no less than four Aircraft Carriers surrounded by their supporting Destroyers. Evidently these were the new Carriers on their way to the Pacific either to join or relieve those Carriers in the British Pacific Fleet I had so recently left. I busied myself up near the Compass platform to find out, via the Signals Petty Officer, all I could about these ships. I learned that they were the new Light-Fleet Carriers, HMSs *Colossus*, *Vengeance*, *Venerable* and *Glory* and, through binoculars, I could see Corsairs and Barracudas on their flight decks with men busy about them.

Somehow, I must get off this dreary Ferry Boat and get in amongst flying people again and here, in Alexandria harbour, these four Carriers presented the opportunity to do so.

It was customary when RN ships were in harbour, either at anchor or moored alongside, for officers to invite by signal their friends in other ships to come aboard for drinks and lunch or dinner. But I was unable to find out if anyone I knew was aboard any of the Light-Fleet Carriers with whom I could make contact. Certainly I was unlikely to know any of the new young Corsair or Barracuda pilots, although I might know the Squadron COs if only I had their names. I decided to take the bull by the horns or, more precisely the Commanders Air by their horns as I intended to send signals to all four Commanders Air of the four Carriers, starting with HMS *Colossus*, as follows; 'Permission to come aboard, please Sir. I am a DLCO with nothing to bat. From Lt Adlam RNVR.' Cheeky man that I was, but desperate because this was very incorrect procedure and I knew it. I ought to have sought permission from my Captain to apply for a transfer from his ship which would hardly have been a popular request and unlikely to be granted.

Within half an hour, before midday, I had a reply from Commander Lane in *Colossus* to come aboard and I lost not a minute in ordering a boat to take me across. I came up the gangway of *Colossus* to be greeted by the Officer of the watch who, advised of my visit, had detailed a sailor ready to take me down to the Wardroom to meet Commander Lane. All very promising so far, I thought. I glanced quickly round as I entered the wardroom but at first could see no one I knew. And then, over by the bar, was an enormous man who I remembered immediately as Tiny Devonald who had been the CO of a Corsair squadron in *Victorious* and I had met him briefly at the Racecourse Airfield in Colombo when all the BPF fighter squadrons had been working up there. He was talking to a small, black bearded Commander wearing wings who therefore must be Commander Lane and so I went up to introduce myself to him.

The Commander greeted me with a pleasant smile, offered me a drink, obviously approving my request for a pink gin and, without wasting time, questioned me in his quiet, clipped speech about my past experience. Tiny, who had also welcomed me, confirmed such knowledge he had of me when both of us had served in the BPF in the Far East. It was good to have his support because Tiny was a famous FAA fighter pilot who had won the DFC flying with the RAF in the Battle of Britain. Heaven knows how he had ever squeezed himself into a Spitfire; he was so large. But he was large in character too being well known for his devil-may-care attitude to life and to authority. He took me over to a group of young pilots, members of his 1846 Corsair Squadron, who were making cheerful chat together and with their Senior Pilot, Ken Evans.

After lunch with them all, Commander Lane sent for me. The senior DLCO of *Colossus* was with him, a Lt Cdr Buckley, and I was told that their second batsman had returned to the UK and that a replacement for him had been urgently requested. Lane told me that already he, with his Captain's approval, had sent a signal to the Admiralty appointments board requesting that I be transferred immediately to HMS *Colossus* as the second batsman. I was to return to *Begum*, pack my bags and to take up my appointment in *Colossus* that day. What a wonderful and astonishingly fast pier-head jump. I was totally delighted because, sure enough, on my return to HMS *Begum* a signal awaited me appointing me with immediate effect to *Colossus*. I didn't say goodbye to the Captain or anyone in *Begum* other than my cabin-mate; I just ordered a boat and left the ship with gladness in my heart.

For the first few days I was busy getting to know the men of the flight-deck party, many of them Marines, with whom I would be working and for the first time learning from John Buckley the detailed procedures of how a flight deck is operated. As a pilot, I had seen often enough what these men of the flight deck did but never before had I paid regard to just how they achieved their tasks. I enjoyed having work to do and new friends to make among the young aircrew and among the ship's officers. The immediate impression of HMS *Colossus* was that she was a happy ship.

Colossus was one of the new Light-Fleet Carriers of the latest design by the Admiralty but they had failed, unfortunately, to incorporate in her much of the essential learning about Carriers which ought to have been accumulated during the five years of war at sea. The size of these new Carriers, although narrower than Fleet Carriers with a flight deck only of some 680 feet long, was not a particular problem although not good. But the three main faults were, first, that they lacked the deck armour, so much envied by the Americans, and which even then was saving the British Fleet Carriers against Kamikaze attacks in the Pacific.

Secondly they were underpowered and could barely achieve 25 knots, so no lessons apparently had been learned from Salerno, as one example, where lack of wind speed over the deck had caused continuous Seafire crashes all day, every day. Moreover, low wind over the deck not only made landing difficult for pilots, but could limit the number of aircraft able to be ranged for take-off on any one strike.

And thirdly, accommodation for young aircrew officers was even worse than in a Fleet Carrier consisting of small narrow dormitories in which eight aircrew were expected to sleep, rest and change their clothes. During five years of actual war, the Admiralty apparently had learned absolutely nothing about basic Carrier design requirements.

However, there was some plus to the design in that these Light Carriers had a longer range and all defensive armament had been deleted enabling 40 aircraft to be carried despite their small size. On the other hand, the advantage of having 40 aircraft on board was lost if the Carrier, being underpowered, could only generate enough wind over the flight deck to range half that number. And I had learned that the Admiralty, instead of giving consideration towards the operational competence of these new Carriers, had made their conversion to merchant ships after the war the priority. In 1945, I was beginning to think of such matters but, at that time, I was still in such awe of those gold-braided Admirals and Captains that I would never have dared to voice my thoughts.

In the meantime the aircraft of both squadrons were ashore at Dekheila aerodrome, outside the city of Alexandria. The two Squadrons, 1846 squadron with 24 Corsairs and 827 Squadron with 16 Barracudas, were still at the stage of working up their young and inexperienced aircrews. I was due to go ashore to the airfield to start batting the aircraft, both Corsairs and Barracudas, on to the runway for ADDLs practice, i.e. dummy deck-landings. It was then that enthusiasm got the better of me because I decided that I must make the point, in which I had always strongly believed, that ideally a batsman should not purport to control a deck-landing unless he, himself, had deck-landed that type of aircraft. It might not be practical always, I realised, but it was right in principle.

If I was so convinced that it was right in principle, then I ought to follow it through which meant asking to fly the Corsair and then deck-landing it. Similarly, I must ask to fly the Barracuda. I would need to obtain agreement from Wings, i.e. Commander Lane, and also from the COs of each Squadron. To these people the idea of the batsman insisting on deck-landing aircraft which he had not previously flown, would be entirely novel, as it would be to the pilots. But I was sure that, once I had deck-landed these aircraft, I would have a much better knowledge of their performance and characteristics when on their final approach to the deck. I would be able to see much earlier if the pilot was getting into trouble and so to give him corrective signals. The other factor, I felt sure, would be the extra confidence in me it would give the pilots to know that I had deck-landed the machine and knew its foibles. In so many of my own landings as a Carrier pilot, I had tended to ignore the batsman's signals thinking, 'What does he know about it, he hasn't ever flown this type of aircraft.'

On the other hand, if I let the idea just lapse, I would probably cope adequately and be just as good an average batsman as any. There would be no need to gird up my courage to fly the Corsair, with its reputation as a difficult and dangerous aircraft to deck-land. Indeed, I knew all too well of the many Corsair crashes on landing, most of them fatal, which had happened with the British Pacific Fleet over the past year. If I insisted on flying it, I would have to overcome yet again the 'twitch', the awful fear of having to fly. I remembered how very many times during those last months in the Far East and Pacific, I had felt so shaky as I forced myself to walk towards and mount into the cockpit of my aircraft before a flight. The saving grace for me had been the recovery once I was in the cockpit, strapped in and preparing for take-off.

I am writing about this now, sixty years later, but at the time the 'twitch' was a taboo subject. Towards the end of the war, I believe that Doctors on board Carriers were given some advice on how to recognise the symptoms of twitch in pilots and how to help them. It really was vital to ground such pilots before they killed themselves and others in some fearful crash. The Seafire crash I had witnessed on HMS *Atheling* was a typical example of the pilot being in dread of having to deck-land his aircraft. Such pilots might recover their nerve if taken off flying for a few weeks. It seemed that I, with my ambitious intention to deck-land the Corsair, was a case in point because, after the past few weeks of rest from flying, I already felt more relaxed about the prospect of getting airborne again.

As well as the principle of a batsman being capable of deck-landing an aircraft, there were other factors at work which were pushing me towards seeking permission to fly the Corsair. The first was my pride and, whether I was imagining the situation or not, I felt that the squadron pilots, although very friendly, regarded me none the less as different and on a lower level of aviation. I realised now that this was just the same attitude as I myself had tended to take towards a Carrier's batsman. Although I was all too well aware that, as a fighter pilot, my performance over the past three years had been no more than mediocre, I considered that, as a Carrier pilot, I had proved myself to be as good as any and I was proud of my record. The truth is that, in spite of being rather scared of the Corsair, I was damned sure that I had the experience and skill to handle it and I wanted to show these young squadron pilots a thing or two on how to deck-land it.

As regards the Barracuda, despite its slightly menacing appearance and undoubted operational faults, I had seen earlier that, with its superb visibility for the pilot and good control at low speed, it would be a pleasant and comfortable machine to deck-land. I would be happy to fly it and land it on the deck as soon as an opportunity occurred.

Wings and the two Squadron Commanders were surprised at my persistence in asking for an opportunity to convert to the Corsair and Barracuda while at Dekheila airfield and to deck-land them in due course. Tiny had supported the idea straight away and I could see that Wings began to like it too although John Buckley, the senior batsman, was against it as being quite unnecessary. In the meantime, while these senior people were giving my proposal some thought, I went ashore to the aerodrome to start my job of batting the Corsairs and Barracudas for dummy deck-landings on the runway. It went rather well really; I formed a vision of how the approaches should be made correctly by starting with the Senior Pilot, Ken Evans. It was a sensible arrangement, which we had agreed between us, because Ken really was a very good pilot indeed and from his approaches I could establish in my mind a standard to set for the others. But I was surprised and impressed to find how good these young pilots were but then, of course, their training in America had included their final conversion to Corsairs. They had amassed some 350 flying hours by the time they joined this their first squadron.

The Senior Pilots of the two squadrons were busy organising the flying programmes each day for the training of their aircrews with no time or aircraft really to spare for me. I gave up on any prospect of flying the Barracuda in the near future and concentrated on Ken to let me have a Corsair to fly for an hour. Having checked up on my background, I think he was satisfied that I was reasonably unlikely to break the machine and finally he was able to make one available for me. And so one hot midday Mac, one of the pilots, accompanied me out to the tarmac where a lone Corsair stood fully fuelled and awaiting me for my first flight on the type. It really was a menacing looking beast of an aircraft with its cranked wings, very long length of nose ahead of the cockpit, huge propeller and engine. Of course, I had sat in the cockpit before to read the pilot notes carefully and now only needed Mac to describe the cockpit details and flying characteristics of the beast, which he did amiably and kindly but, did I detect just a hint of condescension? I was already regretting my keenness to fly this Corsair and it didn't help to know that Mac and everyone else in his squadron would be watching my take-off and awaiting my return.

This flight was particularly nerve-racking for me because I had flown nothing since my last flight in the Pacific. It would have been kinder if I could have flown, on this occasion, in an aircraft I knew well. But that was not possible, so now I must get on with it. The take-off down the runway was not difficult; the Corsair was easy to keep straight so, as soon as airborne, I selected wheels up, held it down to build up plenty of speed then whooshed up into quite a steep climbing turn to port. It was the sort of take-off that looks spectacular but is not in fact either difficult or particularly dangerous. Well, not dangerous normally, but it was pushing my luck rather to do it under the circumstances of not having flown for many weeks and on an unknown aircraft.

At 15,000 ft, I went through my usual routine, with a type of aircraft new to me, of steep turns and slow flying with wheels and flaps down. It had a sudden, frightening and vicious flick on to its back at the stall with no warning, which made it so dangerous to deck-land, so I was more careful after that. I found after several trials and errors that, in fact, the Corsair handled very well at speeds just above the stall, wheels and flaps down, provided there was plenty of power on always. With wheels and flaps up again, I half rolled onto my back, pulled through and up for a roll off the top of the loop. That, followed by a ropey slow roll was my lot and I returned to the aerodrome. Pity I was such a lousy aerobatic pilot, because it would have been nice to finish off with a couple of slow rolls over the aerodrome. But I felt almost back to the confidence of my earlier days and glad that I had insisted on flying the Corsair.

The next day, I completed three dummy deck-landings on the runway with John Buckley batting. This was one more dummy landing than I wanted but Ken, as Senior Pilot, had expected me to do five or six approaches and was rather cross when I refused.

Two days later, *Colossus* left harbour first of all to take back on board the eight Corsairs and four Barracudas which had been sent ashore to Dekheila and then to proceed on her way, through the Suez Canal, to Ceylon. Tiny, the CO of the Corsairs, was happy to stay on board to enjoy the cocktail party on board in the morning (Tiny could never refuse a party) and this gave me the opportunity to fly one of the Corsairs on to the deck that afternoon. And so it was arranged.

I was not permitted to join the squadron formation of Corsairs to land on the ship, no doubt because as an unknown quantity they thought I might spoil their smart circuit and landing procedure. I was to follow some ten minutes later and to arrive over the ship after all the others had landed and their Corsairs had been struck down below in the hangar. This would leave me with a clear deck with the barrier down for my landing. The intention was that, all being well, my Corsair would then be pushed back to the stern of the deck for me to carry out a take-off and a second landing. It seemed that Wings, having taken the risk of letting me prove myself, would give me a clear deck and plenty of time in which to do it.

The affirmative signal to land on was given and, as I looked down on the Carrier from the downwind leg, I experienced again that combined fear and excitement of a deck-landing. Making a steady gentle curving final approach, the Corsair at that low speed handled beautifully and I completed a good landing catching the third wire. As I was being pushed back, I could see a mass of squadron people on the Goofers' gallery of the Island who had watched my first good landing in the Corsair and now waited to see whether I could repeat it on the second landing.

It was a scenario full of potential disaster for a 'show-off' character like mine because, in spite of my very real fear of flying, I would never be able to resist an opportunity like this to put on an exhibition. Inevitably therefore, I came in on a very steep turn, ignoring Buckley's frantic signals with the bats to go round again, straightened up in line with the deck at the very last seconds, closed the throttle and thumped down to catch the second wire. Wow! Could ever a man be more pleased with himself than me as I taxied past the Goofers' gallery. To be fair; it really was important in the circumstances for me to put on a good show for the squadron pilots. But I had nearly overdone it and in due course I would have to make my peace with John Buckley, my senior batsman, who had every right to be angry with me for ignoring his signals. Thereafter, I felt that I had a more comfortable relationship with the squadron pilots who respected my ability to fly their Corsair and, in consequence, had confidence in me as their batsman.

Of all the Aircraft Carriers in which I had served, I reckoned that HMS *Colossus* was the happiest. At any rate, I enjoyed serving in her. It may have been partly because I no longer had a daily commitment to become airborne at that time, although later this would change, or perhaps because from the Commander downwards the ship's officers were such a relaxed crowd with quite a lot of RNVR amongst them. Not only the officers but the men with whom I worked, many marines among them, were cheerfully competent during all the long hours of flight deck operations; also I enjoyed playing deck hockey on the flight deck and football ashore with them.

Best of all perhaps were the young Corsair pilots (incidentally, I wonder why I constantly thought of them as 'young'; after all I was barely a year older than any of them.) They were so enthusiastic about their flying and their beloved Corsairs and they had been together for such a long time in their training that there was a great friendship among them all. In quiet moments, I thought with foreboding about their future, or the lack of it, ahead of them in the Pacific. The Barracuda crews were a fine team of slightly older chaps, particularly so were the Observers and their CO, a Lt Cdr in the RNVR, as were nearly all squadron commanders in the Fleet Air Arm by that time of the war.

Wings was a quietly-spoken man whom I liked and respected even though he never flew either of the squadron types of aircraft. He had been a Walrus pilot for a long period and it would in all fairness have been difficult for him to convert to the latest aircraft without a proper conversion course. He had supported me in my desire to fly the squadron aircraft and given me the best environment in which to do so. The ship's Commander was a young man for his rank, prepared to listen and to help if he could and he looked benignly upon our drunken cavortings in the Wardroom on party nights. Tiny Devonald, the CO of the Corsair squadron, had a great gift as a showman having a good voice and able to play his guitar like a professional. He would give recitals of amusing and rude songs of his own composition to the Wardroom and also to the troops gathered to hear him on the flight deck.

The Captain of *Colossus* was an ex-Destroyer Captain and, as such, well known in the Royal Navy for his dashing exploits earlier in the war. His background therefore was similar to the Rear Admiral Vian, famous or notorious whichever way you like to think of him, for his dealings with the Fleet Air Arm at Salerno, the Far East and the Pacific. Our Captain Stokes, however, realised that he needed to learn about Carrier operations, as it was a new experience for him, and so he listened to his senior aviation advisers before reaching decisions. His background as a Destroyer man was apparent at times when coming alongside or up to a buoy in harbour, he handled his large Carrier like a powerful motor-boat; coming in fast and expertly to a halt. The official harbour Pilot could be seen sometimes white with anxiety. The ship's company, proud of their Skipper, loved his manner of handling the ship. I believe that the Captain and his young Commander set the cheerful and rather dashing tone of the ship and much credit to them for making it a happy one.

Once I had flown with them, I became accepted by the aircrews and joined them ashore where we enjoyed sitting round the swimming pool and having drinks at the Sports Club in Alex and we received many invitations to lots of parties given by wealthy local people in their large houses. One particularly pretty girl I had tried to date but the competition with these cheerful young (there I go again) Corsair pilots was too much and she was seized from under me, so to speak, by Henry Anderson who, using his Irish charm, took her from me in the friendliest fashion. Also, my inability to swim well was a considerable disadvantage for me with the local girls as we sat round the Club pool in Alex, drinking our gin and iced lemonade. I could only watch when, every now and then, one of the others would dive in to perform a racing crawl.

Once back on board *Colossus*, however, it was back to flying for the pilots and time for me to find out if I was any good as a batsman, because there began a heavy programme of working up and flying before the ship went on to take her passage through the Suez Canal. John Buckley did most of the batting of the Barracudas, and very good he was too, while I tended to concentrate on the Corsairs. I have to write that the pilots seemed to like my style; I didn't fuss them too much, I let them alone largely to do their own thing and I concentrated on not too many but clearly positive signals during their final approach. Thus, I didn't fuss for instance when Ken, the Senior Pilot, came in always on frighteningly steep turns, as steep as mine had ever been. But then, the truth was that most of these pilots in 1846 squadron, with a long period of training behind them, were better than average and knew their Corsair aircraft well.

The Pilots and Observers of 827, the Barracuda squadron, were experienced operational aircrews with only just a few new boys among them. They too were a cheerful bunch and members of the two squadrons got on well together. During the hassle of those three days of exercises John Buckley and I formed a good friendship while we worked together to operate the flight deck. I had it all to learn and he taught me.

For the aircrews, the following days while the ship squeezed through the Suez Canal, was like a holiday as, many of them wearing just shorts, watched the scenery go by or played deck hockey. But their come-uppance was in the offing. A night exercise for the Barracuda squadron was being prepared for when the ship reached the Red Sea. On the afternoon before the night exercise the weather was intensely hot, humid and the visibility bad and limited by what appeared to be, not so much a normal cloud, but more like a reddish blanket around the ship with not a vestige of wind. It was strange and menacing weather, due it was thought to a recent sandstorm. How thankful I was not to be flying.

The intention was that twelve Barracudas would take part in the night exercise which was to bomb a fictitious target on the Egyptian side of the Sea. And meanwhile on that early evening the aircraft would have to be prepared and ranged ready for the take-off that night. At this stage the decision was made to catapult the aircraft, there being so little wind over the deck and bearing in mind that the maximum speed the ship could generate was no more than twenty-four knots. It was decided also to reduce the number of Barracudas taking part down to eight in view of the longer time factor of the catapult and consequent difficulty of joining up. As for me, apart from my one night landing two years ago in HMS *Illustrious* and watching sometimes from the Goofers' gallery other pilots landing at night, I had no real experience of night operations on a flight deck. And for that matter, I don't think now that anybody else in the ship had much experience of night operations either. Obviously not the Captain and probably not Wings with his Walrus background. The only pilot with previous night-flying experience from a Carrier was the CO of the Barracuda squadron and two of his Observers, Alastair Maclean and Nelson Abraham, two particular chums of mine, who were experienced.

I doubt if my senior DLCO colleague, John Buckley, had any previous night experience either but, as the man in charge of the deck, he took absolutely the right action by calling all his flight deck party together for a briefing and, with the engineers in charge of the catapult, rehearsed all the actions of moving the aircraft about on the deck at night and the signals with torches that would be necessary to bring the Barracudas forward on to the catapult. The catapult launches were due to start at 8.45 pm and an hour beforehand the thick night was upon us. I don't suppose any one of us had ever before experienced such a stygian blackness as that night; it was like a suffocating black blanket all round the ship and the lights on the flight deck hardly seemed able to penetrate it.

My job was to guide the Barracudas, with a pair of wand-like torches, as they taxied carefully forward up to precisely where engineers waited to fix the aircraft on to the catapult cradle. There, just ahead of the catapult, stood Buckley with a green torch in one hand and a red in the other. Holding up the red light until he received a signal from the Engineer officer that the aircraft was correctly fixed to the catapult, he would replace it with the green light and wave this round his head thus signalling to the pilot to open the throttle to maximum power. On the downward motion of the green light, the Barracuda with engine roaring would be hurled off the deck into the black night. As I brought each aircraft forward, there was just enough light to recognise the faces of the pilots, each one showing strain, while all round me came the noise of the ship at maximum revolutions, the noise of the aircraft engines, the shouts of men further down the deck giving directions and all this din and activity shrouded by that awful darkness.

As I did my job, I ached with worry for each pilot and his crew about to be launched off the deck in those conditions and I longed to shout 'Stop' to this unnecessary nonsense. There really was no reason why the exercise had to go ahead that night. But who of our senior officers had the knowledge and self-confidence to justify postponing it? ... None of them, apparently.

As the last of the eight Barracudas roared off into the night, I looked to see if any lights from the aircraft might be visible in the sky; but there was nothing in the utter blackness of the sky to be seen anywhere. The flight deck was quiet now except for the soft sound of the reduced wind over the deck and of the sea moving past the ship. The comparative silence in the pitch black around us was eerie as we tried and failed to hear aircraft engines in the sky above us. I thought about what it must be like up there and, in particular, about how damnably dangerous the catapult launch must have been for each pilot. Without even a vestige of an horizon, just total black night all round, the pilot would have needed to fix his eyes entirely on to the gyro-horizon in the cockpit as the aircraft left the deck. That gyro might well have been momentarily put off balance by the shock and acceleration of the catapult launch but nevertheless he would have had to rely on it absolutely. Once the pilot had climbed steadily up to some 200 feet, then it might be safe to start looking round the sky for the lights of the other aircraft in the formation.

John Buckley was being called up to the Bridge, presumably to talk with Wings about preparations for the landings. When he came down, he told me quietly that two of the Barracudas appeared to be missing. They had not joined up with the CO and his formation, neither had there been a single sound from their Radio/Telephones. Meantime the six remaining Barracudas were on their way back to the ship and we must be ready to land them on. It was another half hour before at last we heard aero engines above us. The aircraft had come down low to about 500 feet, flying in line astern, so that we could now see them by their lights. Buckley, on the batsman's platform at the stern of the deck, had put on his harness of batting lights consisting of a light at the end of each wand and a third light on his chest; thus he could indicate at night to the pilot whether his aircraft was positioned high or low on the approach. I stood behind him, ready to take over if necessary. We could just see the bow wave of our escorting Corvette about two hundred yards astern, but could see nothing of the small ship itself. But how comforting it was to know it was there.

The six Barracudas approached at long intervals of half a minute and Buckley batted them all down safely and without any of them having to go round again. It was the result of good combination between pilots and batsman. When the last Barracuda had landed, I went forward ahead of the barrier to supervise putting all six aircraft down into the hangar below. Meantime the crews moved slowly off to the Ready room for what would be a sad de-briefing of the night exercise. The CO of the Barracuda squadron, a man aged about twenty-seven, looked more like eighty as he walked across the deck with his face grey from the responsibility and intense concentration of leading his squadron in those awful conditions and with the realisation that two of his crews were missing. The conclusion from the de-brief was that each of the two lost aircraft had gone into the sea shortly after being launched from the catapult. In the pitch black of that particular night no one had seen them and, with the noise of the aircraft engines on the flight deck, no one had heard them splash into the sea. What a dreadful and pointless waste of the lives of six young men.

At the end of the Red Sea, the ship lobbed in at Aden for some reason (the dear old Royal Navy hadn't changed and never told us anything) but it was an interesting day ashore and some of us had a swim in the warm sea. I included myself among the aircrew now because I had been ordered to fly with 1846 Squadron who had lost a pilot through sickness. Consequently, while on our way across the Indian Ocean, I flew on two exercises with the squadron as number four in the same flight with the Senior Pilot, presumably so that he could keep an eye on me and see if I was good enough. Bless his heart, I never pointed out to him that I had much more squadron experience than he had. I was happy to recognise that he was a damn good Senior Pilot and leave it at that. We carried out simulated attacks, each flight from a different direction, on a target towed astern of the ship. The sort of thing I had done so many times before. But I wasn't going to say so. The fun of it was that, after landing my Corsair, I established a routine of running back along the flight deck to bat on those of the squadron not yet landed. It was my job still to do my share of the batting and, to be honest, I enjoyed the kudos of this unique double function of Squadron Pilot and Batsman.

Before the ship reached harbour at Trincomalee, both squadrons flew ashore to land at my old friend, Puttalam, from where in due course we were scheduled to carry out wing exercises in company with squadrons from *Vengeance*, *Venerable* and *Glory*, the other Light-Fleet Carriers. Meantime, HMS *Colossus* had sailed on round to Trincomalee harbour where she was due to be joined by the other three Carriers shortly after. Their squadrons would operate from three other aerodromes at China Bay, the Racecourse at Colombo and at Katakarunda.

All this build-up of aircraft in Ceylon and wing training of the squadrons was almost exactly as it had been for me a year ago when I was in the Hellcat squadron. It was all so much the same that I felt as though I was reliving a familiar dream, almost a nightmare. And the familiarity made me realise belatedly that I was heading for the same dreaded risks of strafing and bombing those damned Japs. Tiny Devonald, as CO of our Corsair squadron, would be the lynchpin of the overall training of the whole new Carrier Group because he had done it all before in the Pacific as a squadron commander. Meantime I had been promoted to lead one of the six flights of the squadron of twenty-four Corsairs; not forgetting also that I would have to do my share of the batting when the squadrons were on board *Colossus*.

One of the features in the design of the Corsair was the use of the specially strengthened undercarriage as dive-brakes. Tiny, based on his experience in the previous year against the Japanese, was convinced that better use should be made of the Corsair's dive-bombing capability. He reasoned that, if dive-bombing could be made more accurate, it would be a much safer form of attack and perhaps equally effective. In consequence, three flight leaders at a time flew with Tiny to learn his dive-bombing technique at the bombing range located on the coast near Puttalam. The essence was to start at 7,000 feet, select dive-brakes and fly almost over the top and slightly to the right of the target. Immediately the target appeared just behind the port wing, then roll over to port to dive apparently vertically down on to the target. In fact, this would give a dive angle of nearly 75 degrees, but it would seem vertical from the cockpit and at first I feared that my practice bombs would hit the propeller. Press the bomb release tit just before 4,000 ft and pull the aircraft up and away with the intention of avoiding the short-range fire of the Japanese gunners, which would be much more accurate below 4,000 ft.

The problems, which I knew from previous experience in Hellcats, were to aim the aircraft with any accuracy during the dive and then to judge the exact moment of the pull-out height. But Tiny reckoned that if we all practised hard and often enough, we would get it right. Well, we might have done perhaps if we could have had another couple of months at it but, in fact, the results showed that we rarely hit the target and our bombing heights were consistently wrong. We all improved with practice but not a lot. Instead, we reverted to the practice of low-level bombing and very low-level strafing attacks.

Replacement aircrews and Barracudas arrived at Puttalam for 827 Squadron and, since the new pilots needed deck-landing experience, there was an opportunity for me to join them in some dummy deck-landings on the aerodrome in a Barracuda, using the local 'resident' batsman. Wings co-operated again and allowed me to fly one of the Barras on board and to complete two landings. The actual deck-landing of the Barracuda, under the normal conditions of sea and wind, was as comfortable as I had expected it to be. Ugly duckling of an aircraft the Barracuda certainly was, but it was a pleasant aircraft to handle at slow speeds on the approach and I was glad of the chance to fly and deck-land it, although thankful not ever to have been appointed to a Barracuda squadron.

In mid July, all four Carriers of the Light Fleet group left Trincomalee harbour, en route for Sydney. The squadron aircraft flew out from their airfields in Ceylon to land on board their respective Carriers outside the harbour. It had been a busy last month in Ceylon, working up as an Air Group, learning to combine together in Wing formations and in simulated attacks on various bogus targets in preparation for operations in the Pacific. It was understood that we would join the Fleet Carriers who had moved further north of the Sakashima Gunto Islands, which I remembered only too well, and they were now operating off the Japanese coastline.

My previous ship, the *Indomitable*, was now in Sydney harbour having completed a repair to her engines and was awaiting our arrival perhaps to act as our lead ship, flying the Admiral's flag. If so, I hoped that at least we would have a new and different Admiral. It seemed that with the sole exception of myself everybody was excited and looking forward to the prospect ahead of them. However, I was careful of course to disguise my lack of enthusiasm and foreboding; it would hardly have been the right attitude to adopt among my fellow enthusiastic Corsair pilots, including Tiny who was raring to get going against the Japanese again. Our Carrier group was due to enter Sydney harbour but, before doing so, all the Corsair squadrons flew off to Nowra, the airfield some eighty miles south of Sydney, which had now developed into a major aerodrome for FAA aircraft. It was a dreary little town and we tried to liven it up by having a party for the Mayor and local residents which went down like a lead balloon.

There was a major change and a bit of a shock waiting for me when I landed back on *Colossus*. First of all to find that a new boy second batsman had arrived to take my place in the ship. An Admiralty signal was waiting for me which formally appointed me, as from 8 August, to 1846 squadron. Commander Lane, our Wings, was kind enough to express his regret that I had been replaced as batsman but said that there was a need for experienced fighter pilots. So goodbye to my combined and unusual role as a batsman/pilot, which I had enjoyed. I was once again committed to full-time flying duties.

CHAPTER FIFTEEN

Immediate Post-war: 1846 Squadron

The four Light Fleet Aircraft Carriers and their Destroyer escorts were now designated as the 11th Carrier Air Group and an Admiral Harcourt, with his Flag in HMS *Venerable*, was the new boss man. I had landed on *Colossus* to find myself once more a member of 1846 Squadron, instead of batsman for the ship, so I was involved immediately as a flight leader in the now intensive training exercises of the Air Group. These new squadrons in the Group would have to learn the procedures and skills for taking-off from the four Carriers and forming up their 160 aircraft into wing formations, just as we had learned the year before, when I was in the Hellcat squadron. Moreover, the ship's officers would have to learn the American signalling systems and refuelling procedures. All this was scheduled for the days ahead but, on 12 August, the Carrier Group was signalled to return into Sydney harbour. I had no idea of any reason for the early recall and neither did any of the other aircrews know what it was about.

Then on 15 August came the formal signal for the cessation of hostilities and the end of the war.

I learned for the first time about the Nuclear Bomb and its devastating effect on the two Japanese Cities of Hiroshima and Nagasaki and of the consequent total surrender by the Japanese. Presumably the Captain and other senior people in the ship to some extent were aware of what had been happening but, as a typical member of aircrew, I had known nothing about it. Initially I was quite bewildered and found it difficult to accept the fact of the war end or to appreciate the enormity of what it meant. There had been war throughout all of my adult life and, having taken my part in it, my mind was attuned to think only in the short term. Now it might be possible to think ahead. But just in those first days, it was difficult to do so. With realisation that the war was really ended, came a sense of stupendous relief that I would not, after all, have to repeat the type of 'ramrod' operations of only four months ago against the Japanese. Only now could I admit to myself how scared I had been at the prospect of having again to take part in operations against that barbaric and fanatical enemy. The probability at that time of an Allied assault on the mainland of Japan was even more frightening, since the casualties would inevitably have been enormous and the Fleet Air Arm would have been in the thick of it.

On that day in mid August 1945, all was joy as Sydney and the Royal Navy and all other shipping in Sydney harbour erupted in celebration. First was the signal to all ships of the Royal Navy to 'splice the mainbrace'; meaning rum all round to every man in the Fleet and a 'rum' bar was set up in the Wardroom for all officers to collect and drink their double tot. In an earlier ship, the *Atheling*, I had become very ill indeed from drinking navy grog (rum) when invited to the Petty Officers' Mess, which was the sort of unofficial and very unusual invitation that one could not refuse. As the result, I absolutely detested all forms of rum let alone the very strong navy grog and, even to this day, cannot bear the smell of the stuff. I drank a sip out of my glass for this very special occasion and managed to off-load the rest of it to someone else.

As it grew dark over Sydney harbour, so the celebrations began with Very lights and fireworks lighting the sky over the ships and the constant bangs of blank gunfire going off. There was plenty of whisky and booze going the rounds and two cans of beer each seemed to have found their way into the hands of the sailors. It seemed that the whole ship's company was on the flight deck to see the show but nobody became drunk or noisy, there was just a general air of happiness as the wonderful news of the war end was savoured and everyone could start to think of going home.

Alas, it wasn't going to be quite so simple as that and, in fact, did we but know it there would be many months yet before the *Colossus* and many of us in her would arrive back in the UK. The Government had made a promise, at the end of the war in Europe, to send servicemen back home and to return them to civilian life as soon as possible. However, there was the immediate priority for the Admirals, Harcourt in Sydney and Mountbatten in Ceylon, to reoccupy all the British Protectorates in the Far East of which the Japanese had taken possession since December 1941. Even more of a priority was to evacuate all the prisoners of war from those territories taken by the Japanese. The appalling ill-treatment they had received was known world-wide and it was essential that they should be rescued and looked after properly as soon as it could possibly be done.

Immediate preparations for the rescue and repatriation of the POWs were being made on the basis that Aircraft Carriers, with their huge hangar space, would be the best possible means of collecting and temporarily accommodating the many hundreds of men who had been prisoners of the Japanese. Most of the existing aircraft and their crews would have to be off-loaded from the Aircraft Carriers without delay to create sufficient space for that purpose. It followed that there was a need to determine quickly who amongst the aircrews would have to remain with their Squadrons in the Aircraft Carriers and which of them could be sent home. The Admiralty hoped to help resolve this question by immediately offering short-service commissions of four years to existing aircrews of the Fleet Air Arm. Those of us in the Fleet Air Arm, in the situation prevailing out in the Far East, would have to make decisions quickly about what we hoped for our future.

The 'Schoolie' in the ship, i.e. the ex-schoolmaster whose main job normally had been to forecast the weather, was armed with all the information about Government Grants and how to apply for them. His job now was to advise and help us decide what we wanted to do and how to go about applying for it and he held interviews with us all in turn all day, every day. I had been thinking about what I should do for hours and hours before my turn came to discuss the possibilities with him and I had a feeling that ideally I would like to be a solicitor; the law appealed to me for some reason although I knew practically nothing about it. The truth is that, having done little else but fly aircraft since I had left school five years earlier, I was so damned ignorant about the normal world and what went on in it that I needed good advice. I didn't feel that I could contact my Father; I had never received a single letter from him throughout the war and my last contact with him had been early in 1943. Anyway, his only advice I guessed would be for me to return to an engineering apprenticeship. There was no one else to whom I could turn other than this young Schoolmaster.

At the interview, I remember the Schoolie smiling rather condescendingly when I suggested my interest in becoming a Solicitor. He pointed out that my matriculation exam passes on leaving school had not been all that good and moreover, after a period of five years, it was going to be difficult for me to start learning again, particularly learning such a complex subject as the law. He told me that, after two years at University, I would be required to study for the very much harder examinations of the Law Society. The sum total of his advice was that I should apply for the short-term commission as aircrew.

I thought about it. Maybe the Schoolie was right. The self-confidence I now possessed stemmed from my flying experience and ability, but I had little confidence in my ability to do anything else. Admittedly there were some aspects of flying which I feared but, surely, peacetime flying would be comparatively easy? Or so I reasoned at the time. Moreover, pondering over the prospect of remaining in the Royal Navy, it dawned on me that the future of naval aviation and my own part in it, if I stayed on, could be much brighter than it had hitherto appeared to be. Experienced aircrew such as myself surely would gradually gain seniority up to the highest ranks among the Captains and Admirals. Thus at last, after having had to fight a war under the command of inexperienced leaders, ignorant of naval aviation, the Fleet Air Arm in a few years time would automatically come to be led by airmen who knew what they were doing; men who would be altogether better able to lead the new generation of Fleet Air Arm aircrews.

In looking back now as I write, I can't help likening the leadership of the aircrews by the Admirals during our war, to that of the British soldiers in the First World War led by their Generals. The soldiers had been described then as 'Lions led by Donkeys.' An equally apt description for the Fleet Air Arm aircrews surely would be, 'Eagles led by Penguins,' since so very few of the Admirals and Senior Officers who led them, whether they had wings on their uniforms or not, ever flew an aircraft.

Indeed, it might have been better if the Admiralty had never retrieved control of naval aviation in 1938, so that in Aircraft Carriers during the war, experienced Royal Air Force officers would have had the direction and control of air strategy and of all flying operations whilst the Captain would have remained responsible for the handling and safety of the ship. Such thinking was hurtful to me personally, because I took great pride in serving as an officer of the Royal Navy and in carrying out the duties of a naval officer, other than being merely the pilot of an aircraft.

Despite what I have written about the misfortune of naval aviation being under the control of Admiralty during the war, now is not the time for Admiralty, under pressure from the Treasury, to relinquish that control. Over fifty years after that war, by now half of the Admirals now serving must surely have had aircrew experience in the Fleet Air Arm. It would be absurd therefore, when now at last there are senior and experienced naval aviators in the Royal Navy, to hand control of naval aviation back to the Air Force.

And yet, as I write all these years later, significant changes may be taking place already and the Fleet Air Arm appears to be gradually returning under the control of the Royal Air Force. For example in September of 2004, I was invited to attend as a guest at a Dining-in night in the Wardroom of RNAS Yeovilton, the Fighter Station of the Fleet Air Arm, where I was astounded to find that half the members of the Wardroom were in the uniform of the Royal Air Force.

It didn't help the cause of the Royal Navy and its Fleet Air Arm when, for the Falklands War, the Admiralty reverted to its tradition of appointing because of his seniority, a seaman submariner, as the Rear Admiral in charge of the sea operations, when the whole enterprise of the war was so largely dependent on the best use of the two Aircraft Carriers and their Harrier aircraft. At the time, there were other Admirals of equivalent rank available, who were experienced naval airmen and, as such, would have known how properly and even more effectively to deploy the Harrier aircraft. They would have known, for example, never to waste the precious Harriers on the inevitably ineffective bombing of an airfield, but always to have them out ahead on combat patrol to protect the fleet and the troop carriers against the Mirage aircraft of the Argentinians. It is to my point that whilst, in his book, Rear Admiral Woodward writes lengthy and deserved credits about all the Captains of the various ships of his fleet, there is hardly a mention of the Squadron Commanders and pilots of the Harriers who flew daily with courage and with such effective impact on the enemy, and who did so all too frequently in dreadful weather conditions for flying.

I am sorry that I have digressed again from the main story, but I do get so cross looking back on some of the ill-considered actions and bad decisions of the Admirals and Admiralty, relating to naval aviation, during war.

Back then to 1945 when, believing that there were prospects of a good career as a naval officer and pilot in the Fleet Air Arm of the future, I made the most significant and foolish decision of my life. I decided to apply for the short-term Commission in the Royal Navy without any doubt in my mind that, in due course, I would be offered a permanent commission. It was an ill-considered decision which would cause me stress and worry throughout most of my future life as, by the end of those four years and by then married with two children, I reluctantly concluded that naval aviation was not the right career for me, particularly as a man with family responsibilities.

I rejected the permanent commission when it became subsequently available to me. By that time it was too late to obtain a university or other educational grant and in consequence, without any qualifications whatsoever, I struggled to find work. It was two years and many lowly jobs later, including lavatory cleaner, unskilled factory worker and worst of all door to door salesman, before I learned enough to get a foot on to the bottom rung of a career in industry. Even then, because of my lack of qualifications, there were many more years of ups and downs, with all sorts of different jobs before reaching the safe haven of job security with responsibility at Director level.

If I had not taken the short service commission, I know now from the eventual success in my working life, that I would have had no difficulty in passing the Law Society exams. And then, as a typical solicitor during the long fifty-five years of almost continuous boom in post-war Britain, I would have followed a gentle albeit rather boring upward path to comfortable wealth. No doubt to share my wealth, I would have been wedded by a nice girl with whom I would have enjoyed a life beset by no more than the normal problems of an economically comfortable family in peacetime. All that would have been pleasant enough and sometimes I looked wistfully across the divide of my age and experience towards my younger friends, now in their sixties, whose post-war schooling and time at University had made such a level lifestyle possible. But in retrospect, I am glad of the life I led as the result of that rash decision I made back in August 1945. Not only because it led me to my wife, Heather, but also because I worked with people of all types whom I would never otherwise have met and in environments which I would never otherwise have known.

And so in August 1945 my decision had been made and my application for a short service commission, together with several more from other aircrew in *Colossus*, were signalled to Admiralty. They were all accepted and approved within days. The Admiralty was evidently in a hurry to establish its nucleus of officers in the Fleet Air

Arm, particularly those serving in the Far East, where immediate and urgent peacetime missions had to be undertaken.

In the meantime, HMS *Colossus* was in a flurry of activity, taking on hundreds of camp beds and medical staff, as part of the preparations to collect and care for hundreds of our ex-Prisoners of the Japanese. The intention was to collect them from Formosa and other areas as soon as possible.

Those aircrew who had opted to leave the Navy and to get back into 'civvie street' were being sent ashore to await transport home to the UK. Nearly all of our Squadron pilots left and were replaced with some from the other Carriers in the Group leaving us with twelve pilots. The Barracuda Squadron was due to fly off eight aircraft and crew as soon as the ship left harbour. As regards all the twenty-four Corsair aircraft on board, we were horrified to learn that twelve of them, all of which had been lovingly maintained by the squadron for many months past, were to be ditched into the sea shortly after the ship left Sydney harbour. This was in accordance with the terms of the Lease Lend agreement with America which demanded, now that the war was ended, that HM Government must pay for the hundreds of aircraft provided under that agreement or ditch them.

Throughout September and until mid October, *Colossus* acted as a ferry ship collecting those poor battered, desperately thin and sickly ex-prisoners of the Japanese, mostly from Formosa, to take them to either Manila or Hong Kong. Good accommodation and hospital arrangements had been prepared for the POWs in both those places from where they would be shipped back to the UK as fast as was possible. *Colossus* could provide temporary accommodation for up to four hundred POWs but it was only suitable for the short ferry trips, although every effort was made by the ship's company to make them comfortable. All they seemed to want at that stage was to lie or sit quietly and be left, without talking much, to enjoy cigarettes, the good food and above all their freedom.

After completing two passages from Formosa to deliver our POWs to their hospital accommodation in Leyte, the ship arrived in Hong Kong on or about 17 October to offload into hospital another three hundred POWs. Officers and men of the ship's company were given various tasks ashore to help in the rehabilitation and reorganisation of the City pending the arrival of more professional administrators. To my joy, because by this time I badly needed something worthwhile to do, I was given the job of ensuring the security of the 'Go-Downs' on the harbour side of Kowloon.

I hadn't got a clue what this would entail and I didn't even know, as a start, that a 'Go-Down' was the local name given to a storage depot for goods and materials unloaded from ships. I was to be accompanied by a Petty Officer, a leading rate and twelve men, all dressed in gaiters and armed with rifles and cudgels and we were to go ashore for an unspecified period of time. Quarters had been found for the men in what had been a small hotel near the harbour and I was provided with a flat in Kowloon almost alongside their hotel. Despite my total ignorance of the task, it was a wonderfully interesting, new prospect and I was excited and pleased to have the job.

There was an existing manager for the 'Go-Downs' who had remained in charge under the Japanese during their occupation, as had the Overseer in charge of the Chinese labourers. My job, with my little platoon of sailors, was to protect the goods from theft. Sounded easy enough until I learned that the Chinese practically relied upon theft to make a living since they were paid such a pittance. In my little office, a long pliant cane was provided since the common practice apparently had been to mete out instant justice with it whenever a thief was caught. The first thief we caught was a very pretty young girl who, all too obviously, had wound a whole lot of silks around her body under her clothes. We were supposed to cane her and she evidently expected it. I couldn't cope with such a ridiculous situation and so, in the time-honoured manner and words of naval tradition, I said to my Petty Officer, 'Carry on then, Petty Officer.' And he, just a young chap like me, looking puce with embarrassment turned to the Leading Rate and said 'You do it.' 'Not bloody likely,' said he, an elderly rating in his thirties, 'my missus would never forgive me.' And so I gave up and told the girl she could go. At this, we were treated to such an incredulous and happy smile of thanks that we all felt vastly pleased with ourselves and our magnanimity, while hoping it wouldn't happen again.

The next thief caught by two of my chaps on patrol looked like a middle aged Chinese worker and, instead of the cane, I had him escorted to the Overseer. The man had begged and pleaded with me not to do that and I learned afterwards, to my shame, that the Overseer had banned him from seeking work again in the Go-Downs. No wonder, with a family to support, he had been so desperate. But the rate of attempted thefts dropped dramatically thereafter. Until then I had not understood the huge power held by the Overseer over his fellow Chinese workers. Early every morning they formed a long queue, young and old, outside the gates of the harbour and the

Overseer would walk along the queue selecting those who, as I realised eventually, offered him the largest share of their standard pittance payment for their day's work. I was told it was the form and not to interfere. All those in the queue brought with them a ludicrously small wooden bowl of rice which would be their food for the day.

The flat where I was accommodated had been occupied previously by a Japanese Army officer of high rank who had been taken away to a prison camp guarded by our Marines. It was, therefore, a smart and well-equipped flat which included a young Chinese girl as the 'amah'. The girl spoke very little English, in itself unusual for a girl in Hong Kong, but she made it very clear to me that she had also been the Japanese officer's mistress for which, presumably, there had been some addition to her weekly pay packet. If so, then the dear old Admiralty would now be paying it on my behalf. However, it was not quite such a perfect set-up as it might appear because this nice looking girl had imposed two unsightly blemishes on herself in the form of tight bindings round her chest covering her breasts and with similar bindings on her feet. Those tight bindings spoilt for me her otherwise attractive appearance and, since she spoke almost no English, I was never able to fully enjoy her company. Although she was also a super cook of Chinese food, I went out often in the evenings to meet friends in the restaurants, which were beginning to spring up in Hong Kong and Kowloon. Indeed, all around the City, trade of all sorts already was tentatively emerging. What a resilient people they were.

While in Kowloon, I had my first close up sight of the Japanese military. There was a platoon of about twenty of them who had been put to work repairing the road in the harbour area. Two Marines were guarding them but they hardly seemed necessary because these Japanese men, who were under the control of their Sergeant, carried out their work at an astonishingly fast pace; not walking but running from one place to another and seemingly intent only on getting their job done as fast as possible. All this was done under the eye of their sergeant who shouted continuously at them and of whom they were obviously very frightened. I had assumed that these grubby looking Japanese soldiers, whose ferocity in war and barbaric cruelty to those they conquered had created fear throughout the Far East, would make the most surly and dangerous of prisoners, full of menace. Apparently it was not the case. I learned later that the Japanese, in nearly all the areas they had occupied, offered no resistance once they received the order from their highest Military Authority to surrender.

Watching these Japanese soldiers at their work, I could visualize how they had accomplished such rapid repairs each night on those runways we had bombed daily on the Sakashima Islands. And seeing their unharmed physical condition, I compared them with our own people who, as their prisoners, had been found to be in such dreadful physical condition. I wondered if these Japanese soldiers even realised or appreciated the difference in their treatment.

In particular I remembered Jack Haberfield, that friendly New Zealander who back in 1944 had shown me the cockpit of the Hellcat and with whom I had flown in 1839 squadron, He had been shot down with eight other aircrew over Palembang. All nine, as was now known for certain, had suffered torture for three months before being taken out together on to a beach by their Japanese guards where they were beheaded, one by one, in front of the diminishing remainder. I wondered, as I watched and remembered Jack, could these Japanese people really be regarded as human? Well, fifty years later, they seem to have been accepted as such since they design and sell a huge percentage of the electronic goods and equipment used by the whole of the western world.

About three weeks later HMS *Colossus* left Hong Kong harbour and the general understanding amongst us was that we were on our way back to the UK via Cape Town. In the meantime, flying re-commenced because there were a number of new aircrew to be worked up in both the two squadrons consisting then of twelve Corsairs and eight Barracudas. I was now the Senior Pilot of 1846, not by any particular merit but because I was the only pilot of Lieutenant rank left behind although, since I had much more experience than anyone else other than the CO, my title of Senior Pilot seemed fair enough. The ship had a new batsman, a South African bearded chap, and I shared a part of the 'batting' with him when not flying.

As regards the flying, I found little pleasure in it. It seemed to me that I had been forever going through the motions of working-up a squadron and, although service flying especially from a Carrier was inevitably dangerous even in peacetime, I was extremely bored with it. Particularly now, with the war over, when there was no longer any intensity of purpose to it. I did so hope that there would be some new and different sort of flying job available for me when we returned to the UK. I was already beginning to regret my decision to take a short service commission and I needed a new type of job, if I was to revive my interest in the Royal Navy.

By this time, it was known that when we arrived at Cape Town the ship would have to proceed to the adjacent dockland town of Simonstown and there to remain in a dock for several weeks for engine repairs to be carried out. Meantime, the squadrons would fly ashore to Wingfield, the aerodrome for Cape Town. And so the next weeks were spent meeting a whole bevy of pretty, rich girls and having endless parties with them which usually took place in their large homes in and around Cape Town. Occasionally I would bumble around the sky in my Corsair doing my usual dreadfully bad aerobatics. The old guard of the original pilots in the Squadron had been replaced at this time by new pilots who had opted like me for the short service commission. We had a new CO, Donald Dick, an unusually good pilot and, as for me, I was to be superseded in the near future as Senior Pilot by an excellent type of chap. Not as much squadron experience as I had accumulated but, as he had more than a year's seniority than me as a Lieutenant, that would automatically make him the senior man under the RN rules. Anyway he was only with us for a short time, so it didn't matter.

While at Cape Town, I escaped marriage by the skin of my teeth. She really was a nice girl. Pam Foster, and I truly liked her and enjoyed her company. In that heady atmosphere of expensive parties, I believed that I was in love and rather liked the idea of settling down in South Africa with her as my wife. The reality was, I suspect, that I was more 'in love' with the idea of being in love and with the general scenario of the rich lifestyle out there. I got on well with her father and brother and it was implied that a job in her father's building company was in the offing when I left the Navy. Thank goodness for both her and for me, immature as I was, some instinct warned me that the affair was unreal and to back off slightly. Her father frequently lent me one of his large American cars for us to drive to the beaches or to parties. But it so happened that we never found an opportunity for full sex, cuddling and groping about in the car was about as far as we ever went.

It was a pity because perhaps Pam would have been happier and less intense, after I left Cape Town, if we had run the full sexual course. For one thing, I was not a good lover and she would most probably have been disappointed and have 'gorn orf' me fairly quickly. I do so hope that she was not really in love and that it was just an infatuation on her part. I discovered later that there were a number of marriages between South African girls and young British servicemen in those first months after the war. Very few were good marriages. The girls, many from wealthy families with plenty of servants, were unable to cope in England with the stringent food rationing, the cooking, the cleaning and the small, cold, rented accommodation which was all a junior officer could afford.

There was a grave shortage of young men in Cape Town, their own troops having not yet returned from the war at that time and so, to Pam and the other girls, the advent of our two Squadrons and aircrews at Wingfield might well have appeared as manna from the skies. Also there was an atmosphere of competition among many of her girl-friends who all wanted a piece of fighter pilot if they could get their hands on one. Moreover, to be honest, I have to write that I was slim and reasonably good-looking at that time and could cut a dash at the parties being the Senior Pilot of the fighter squadron and as a Lieutenant in uniform wearing wings and the medal ribbons just issued to us. For this first and only for a very brief moment in my life, I might have appeared as a figure of glamour? Who could blame Pam therefore for what followed?

The result of this bogus glamour was that, when I eventually left Cape Town in HMS *Colossus*, I was followed by letters written to me in loving terms by Pam and stacks of these letters in their mauve envelopes were waiting for me in every port thereafter. She must have written a full letter almost every day after I left and, I am so sorry, but I came to absolutely dread them. It was the worst possible thing a girl could do; it killed stone dead my feeling for her because to expect me to answer all those letters was altogether too demanding. I doubt if young women would ever do that sort of thing these days.

Pam's parents were divorced and her mother lived in England. Pam had written to her about this 'marvellous' young naval officer she wanted to marry and urged her to meet me when I returned to the UK. And so months later, when I was back in England on leave, I wrote to the mother and arranged the meeting. I was very nervous because somehow I had to convey to her, when we met, that I had no desire or intention of marriage to her daughter. This was a problem because, in the face of that deluge of loving letters, I hadn't had the guts yet to tell Pam kindly and firmly that I neither loved or wanted to marry her. Nevertheless, I wanted very much to make a good impression on her mother so that I would appear mature and a man of the world while explaining to her that I couldn't marry her daughter.

And so, idiot that I was, I booked a table for lunch at the Mirabelle, a hideously expensive restaurant in Curzon Street, London. I arrived early, very nervous and ordered a dry Martini. The restaurant was almost empty. I drank two more Martinis before the mother arrived. She was tall, well dressed in an austere and rather old-fashioned style and, as I rose to my feet, gave me her hand and a piercing look before she sat down in the chair held for her by the waiter. We talked of this and that and I ordered the meal and a bottle of wine after consulting her. She spoke about Pam's childhood and early life then, after asking me about the Navy, expressed her surprise that I had only a short service commission. But I assured her, garrulous by now with wine on top of the strong Martinis, that I was quite certain of a permanent commission in due course. 'Why?' she asked, to which I couldn't really find a sensible answer.

Before I could get round to the nitty-gritty matter of not wanting to marry her daughter, she said it was time for her to think about catching her train. So I hurriedly asked the waiter for the bill. It came. It was so staggeringly high that I had nowhere near enough money to pay it. So, cringing with shame, I had to ask her if I could borrow the balance. So she paid for her half. But before she left the table she said, 'You are quite the most un-impressive young man I have ever met. I shall send a telegram to Pam and her father immediately to say that for her to marry a young man like you, sodden with drink, would be madness and a total disaster. You will understand that I hope sincerely never to see you again and thank you for my half lunch.' And so saying, she swept out of the restaurant. Thus ended the most embarrassing meal in all my life.

But I digress – back now to November 1945 in Cape Town when the squadron was in a state of flux with most pilots and men leaving with new ones joining. The new pilots were reasonably experienced so that, apart from arranging some ADDLs for them on the runway, so that I could assess their deck-landing performance before rejoining the ship, we rarely flew. I could see little point in organised flying exercises at that stage.

About four weeks later the repairs to the ship were completed and, after a tearful farewell from Pam, I took off with the Squadron, following the new CO, Donald Dick, to land back on board *Colossus* again. It was a relief really to be at sea again and away from the cloying party life of Cape Town.

To our astonishment, the ship turned towards Ceylon instead of returning home to the UK. What on earth could be the purpose in going back there? As usual, no one appeared able to tell the ship's company and, if there was some purpose, it was retained as a secret by those in command. I had long since ceased to be impressed by Naval secrecy, reasonable sometimes in wartime perhaps but quite unnecessary in peacetime surely, and I had come to the conclusion that the Royal Navy really didn't know what it was doing half the time anyway and used the cloak of secrecy to disguise its inconsistency and uncertainty.

The voyage and visit to Ceylon appeared to me then as it does now, as a post-war and time wasting exercise without any apparent purpose to it. I doubted if there would be any work or flying of value to be done and it should have been an ideal opportunity for me to learn something other than flying. Had I been sensible, I would have started a correspondence course in some subject such as contract law, accountancy or plain book-keeping because, whether or not I remained in the Navy after the short four year commission, such learning would have given me something more than just this damn fool flying as a basis for my life.

A few days later the ship was approaching the coast of Ceylon and already the warm pungent smell of the Island was pervading the air around the flight deck as the Corsairs and Barracudas were ranged for take-off. We were to land at Katakarunda, a new airfield to me as a base although I had landed there before. I remembered it as being very similar to Puttalam although located some miles inland. Indeed, the runway, squadron offices and huts were almost identical and similarly surrounded by thick jungle. What was the squadron supposed to be doing here, I wondered?

Well, the obvious answer to that was pretty depressing for me because, since each of the twelve pilots except me had only joined the squadron fairly recently, it seemed that the squadron was here in Ceylon to 'work-up' into a capable fighting force again. I was the only remaining aircrew from the 1846 Squadron of six months ago when at the time I had doubled up also as one of the ship's batsmen. To fly low and fast over that jungle again, to carry out simulated bombing and strafing attacks on the same old ranges, would be 'Déjà vu' for me for the third time. I had done it all in 890 squadron flying Wildcats during the early months of 1944, again in 1839 squadron flying Hellcats for several months during the second half of 1944 and now here I was at it again in 1945 flying Corsairs with a new bunch of young chaps. In spite of the boredom of the current task, however, I was buoyed up by all my recent thoughts about the Fleet Air Arm and how it must inevitably develop in the future and maybe my rank along with it. I must be patient.

Actually, it wasn't all that bad because, until he left to join another squadron, the chap who had superseded me as Senior Pilot was there to do all the work and arrange the flying programmes which left me free for most of the time. I took the opportunity to have an oblique camera fitted to my Corsair and I practised using it for Recce work taking photos of various locations from different heights. I had a number two with me often, Geoff Higgs, a very pleasant companion in the air and on the ground, though quite a serious and solemn chap who, rather irritatingly, flew with greater skill than I did. Indeed he was to earn in later years a well-deserved AFC as a test and trials pilot. The other new pilots were also reasonably experienced having served, albeit briefly, in a squadron previously. I didn't think there was need to fly and train such pilots too seriously as the squadron would almost certainly be dissolved when we returned to the UK in a few weeks anyway. And yet, for some reason, pilots were transported up to India to collect new Corsairs for the squadron. This seemed quite dotty as we might as well have kept the Corsairs which, only three months previously, had been chucked into the sea.

This pointless existence at Katakarunda came to an end after Christmas and the call came at last to rejoin our ship. I arranged for a session of dummy deck-landings for all Corsair pilots on the airfield runway as some time had elapsed since any of us had landed on a Carrier and, wartime or not, to put a Corsair onto the deck demanded full concentration and practice. *Colossus* with her escort was waiting for us off the coast near Colombo and what a joy it was to see her in that dark blue sea, leaving a bright white wake behind as she turned into wind, increasing speed as she did so. After the doldrums of Katakarunda, I perked up and looked forward to the comfort and companionship of life on board again. But steady now, I must concentrate on making a decent safe landing. There was no point in showing off; after all there was no longer anyone I wanted to impress. All I wanted was to get myself home safely in the hope of a new type of flying job; anything other than working up and training a squadron please.

On a typically cold winter's day of low cloud and rain in March 1946, HMS *Colossus*, flying a huge long decommissioning Pennant, arrived in the Solent off the entrance to Portsmouth harbour. A range of our remaining eight serviceable Corsairs and eight Barracudas was prepared and ready on the flight deck to take-off and land at Lee-on-Solent. I was boot-faced and bad tempered at having to lead the Corsairs on the flight ashore but Wings was adamant that it was I who should do it. He seemed to think that there was some kudos for me in leading the last flight. Perhaps he thought it would be appropriate since I was the only remaining member of his original group of aviators. But I had wanted very much to be on board as the ship entered Portsmouth harbour to moor alongside the jetty where crowds of relatives and visitors would be waiting to welcome the ship home. It would be an occasion of much excitement and happiness which I didn't want to miss.

On walking across the flight deck to my Corsair, I saw that my fitter and rigger had fixed a long thin Pennant from the radio aerial, just behind the cockpit, which extended the whole length of the fuselage to the rear of the tailplane and already this long thin flag was waving gaily about in the wind. I wasn't too keen on the thing but felt that I had to disguise my bad temper to thank my two chaps for thinking of such a gay form of departure for me and for taking so much trouble over it. However, I had a good look at the attachment to make sure it was firmly fixed. Once I had started the engine and, by the time the wind had built up over the flight deck, the Pennant was stretched out tight along the top of the fuselage with the end of it flicking around the rudder. But I couldn't see this from the cockpit.

The weather was absolutely foul with cloud no more than a few hundred feet up and closing in with heavy rain. I had briefed the other pilots that I would not do a fly-past and that we would make straight for the aerodrome. Anyway, we all wanted to get down as quickly as possible and into the buses waiting to take us back to the jetty in time, we hoped, to see the ship come in. As soon as I got airborne off the deck, I felt something was wrong. I had to use left aileron to counteract a yaw to starboard and to keep the Corsair flying straight. I realised that the rudder must be jammed at an angle; the damned Pennant must have wrapped itself into the hinges of the rudder. On the radio, I told the two flights to break away from me and to carry on with their landings. I remembered to give them a course to steer since, although only three or four miles away, Lee aerodrome couldn't be seen. I was a bit panicky, not because I felt unable to cope with flying the aircraft but I had a ridiculously strong premonition that the jammed rudder, the very bad weather, the business of having to lead this 'last' flight and my ill-temper were all contrived by fate to indeed make this my truly final flight. After all the flying I had done in these past five years, what a damn silly way to go just because of a flag stuck up the arse of my aircraft!

I calmed down and flew around for a few minutes, to see how it flew at slow speed, before making my approach into Lee aerodrome. Keeping the Corsair on a gentle curving approach made it no problem really and so I clonked down on the runway for what, had I known it, would be my last flight in a Corsair. When I looked, a piece of the Pennant had indeed lodged in between the rudder hinge and I guess I was lucky it hadn't caught instead in the hinge of the elevator; that indeed would have been a disaster.

Before catching the bus waiting to take us to the jetty, I had what was left of the tattered Pennant unclipped from the mast and kept it for many years as a souvenir.

HMS *Colossus* had already moored alongside the jetty by the time we got there and so we pilots had missed all the noise and cheering of the arrival. But it was all very jolly; relatives, wives and girl friends were allowed on board with their members of the crew, while a cheerful drinks party was going on in the Wardroom. My old Mum and Maddie couldn't make the journey but I had phoned and they were waiting for me at home. Anyway, I doubt if my huge old Mother could have staggered up the ship's gangway.

Best of all was a signal from Admiralty appointing me to the RAF Central Flying School for a course as a Flying Instructor; just what I had hoped for. I was to have two weeks leave and then join the course, at Little Rissington in the Cotswolds, at the end of April.

On the way home, before changing trains in London, I visited Fortnum and Mason as usual to buy a huge and horribly expensive hamper of foods for my Mum, who dearly loved her grub and suffered under the very stringent rationing still in force. I had brought some lovely dress material from Ceylon for Maddie, who had started work when a girl as a trained seamstress in Paris. She didn't have a chance to make anything with it before Phoebe, my sister, visited and talked Maddie into selling her most of the material.

I did so enjoy spending money and, as my bank balance was extraordinarily healthy after another year abroad, I decided to spend nearly all of it, about £350, on a decent car. I had seen what I wanted at the nearby home of an RAF friend who also was on leave. It was an MG sports car, a type PB of 1936 vintage with bodywork the colour of Cambridge blue and mudguard wings of royal blue. It was gorgeous and I had to have it, so I used all the early part of my leave in negotiating to buy it for £365. There was no way of ever getting my huge old Mum into any part of the MG and so, for our visits to friends or outings to pubs and restaurants, I drove Mother's old Austin. I had enjoyed my leave very much but I was looking forward to the Flying Instructors course at Little Rissington and to an entirely new type of flying task.

However, while preparing to set off in the MG, I received a telephone call from the Appointments Branch of the Admiralty to tell me that my course at CFS was postponed until early in September. Instead, I was to report to Donibristle in a week's time to act as resident DLCO and general assistant to Commander Air. In other words, I thought, to act as general dogsbody for the Commander up there for a couple of months. The prospect for so short a period didn't bother me. I looked forward to the long drive up to Scotland in the MG but the pleasure of it, on the following week, was my undoing. I drove all the way to Scotland as fast as I could until, just before reaching Edinburgh, there was a nasty noise under the bonnet and I pulled up in clouds of steam. The aluminium cylinder head had cracked and I had to leave the car in dock for a whole month.

Hence, my time at Donibristle without a car had perforce to be spent quietly in the wardroom. And I quite enjoyed it. The Commander had shot off on leave shortly after I arrived leaving me to lord it from my little office near the runway, that being the nearest thing to a Control Tower of which the small aerodrome could boast. There was a Firefly squadron forming up and using the aerodrome prior to joining a Carrier and, as required, I would grandly saunter out to the end of the runway to do the 'batting' for their dummy deck-landings. How lucky they were, I thought, to have such a highly experienced chap to bat for them. They forgave me for being so pleased with myself and often I joined them on their visits to the 'Star' at Aberdour. But the memories of Jack Parli, Winnie Churchill and all the other members of 890 Squadron, of three years ago, were too nostalgic for me fully to enjoy that lovely little pub, although in fact it hadn't changed much since then.

So the time passed pleasantly enough at Donibristle. My MG was repaired but its performance was never as good again as it had been with the original cylinder head. I had learned my lesson though and, when September came, I drove at a sensible speed down to Little Rissington to commence the course at the RAF Central Flying School.

CHAPTER SIXTEEN

Return to Yeovilton

At Central Flying School we flew Harvards, a robust American training aircraft with all metal fuselage and wings, strong wide undercarriage and instructor's seat in the rear cockpit. The radial engine was powerful for a training aircraft and was well known for the extraordinary noise made by the propeller. It was the equivalent to the Miles Master on which I had trained as a pupil at Netheravon and which had been regarded at the time as a good trainer, but I have to admit that the Harvard was better. There were no real vices to it other than when stalled or spun, both of which are an essential part of learning to fly, it did so quite viciously. However, it responded immediately to corrective action; a factor which made it such a good training aircraft.

The aerodrome at Rissington was large, having two long runways and was perched on the top of one of the Cotswold hills. The Officers' Mess and accommodation were purpose-built to an established RAF pattern; really rather grand and certainly very comfortable. The essence of the place, of course, were the instructors who were all picked and experienced men and qualified as A1 instructors; their job during this long and arduous course would be to teach us how to teach others to fly. Central Flying School was famous, not only as the basis of flying standards in the RAF, but for giving similar instruction to many other Air Forces in the world. Even today as I write, CFS is a very nice little earner for the British Government from the flying tuition it gives to the Air Forces of Europe and the developing countries.

There were about twenty officers of equivalent rank on my Course, three from the Indian Air Force and four of us from the Royal Navy and the rest from the RAF. I should have mentioned earlier that, from the date of my short service commission, I was now RN with thick straight stripes of rank on my uniform sleeves. I became interested and absorbed in the flying; it was so different from any I had done before; it had to be precise and accurate always and to correlate with the instructional 'patter' relating to the manoeuvre one was demonstrating. Indeed 'patter' was an appropriate word because our instructors were adamant that we had to be almost word perfect in describing each manoeuvre as we demonstrated it. I would have liked to use my own words and manner of description but I learned at CFS not to deviate from the patter path. It had the value, I suppose, of ensuring that nothing of importance was left out of the instruction procedure.

The flying encompassed almost everything I had ever done before in the air but I was having to apply precision and polish to my airmanship and, for example, this improved my aerobatics. The same applied to my instrument flying and for the first time I learned to approach an airfield for a landing under GCA, Ground Control Approach. It is a procedure in which the Controller on the ground gives the pilot constant instructions as to height, rate of descent, airspeed and precise course to steer. On several occasions the exercise had to be done blind in actual bad weather conditions. All this gave me increased confidence for bad weather flying. Night flying too became not quite the nightmare of my earlier career.

But flying was only the half of it; at least two hours every day was spent in the classroom relearning in greater depth the ground subjects such as Principles of Flight, Navigation, Meteorology and basics of aero engineering and airframe design. University lecturers were used to teach us lecturing techniques and each of us, as pupils, had to give lectures and conduct discussions in the classroom. I was bad at all this ground work; I found it so difficult to learn after such a long period since leaving school. Indeed, I became quite worried at the possibility of failing the Course. Frequently in the evenings, therefore, I made some excuse to remain behind when the others went out to the local pubs, to give myself the opportunity to work surreptitiously on some of the ground subjects.

On one such evening, I went outside for a quiet stroll after dinner before starting work when I realised that it had started to snow. This was February 1947 and snow it did, continuously for days. The whole aerodrome, including runways and taxiways, was entirely covered in several feet of snow as were all the roads surrounding it. The aerodrome was not only inoperative for two weeks but inaccessible for that period. Thus I was stuck there snowbound whereas most of the other officers, pupils and instructors alike, had escaped down the hill either to pubs or to their married quarters. In fact, however, it was rather fun. Food and other necessary supplies were dropped from the skies by RAF transport aircraft, there was plenty of booze in the bar for the few remaining officers, two good snooker tables in the Mess and, best of all, the snow provided a wonderful opportunity for me to study those dreaded ground subjects.

Two weeks after the snow had gone our Instructors' Course was completed. There were only a couple of failures and the rest of us were qualified in either B1 or B2 category as Flying Instructors. This was a normally expected result although surprisingly, thanks to my snowbound studies, I was qualified at the higher level as a B1. An Admiralty signal appointed me from early April as an Instructor to join 700 Squadron at RNAS Yeovilton. I knew no more about it than that but, meantime, I was to go on leave over the next five days until April. My memories of Yeovilton, and of every one of the thirty-three young men who had shared with me the experience of Fighter School there in 1941, were still very strong although it also seemed such a long time ago. As far as I could find out, only seven of us on that Course had survived the war. Nevertheless, I was excited at the prospect of returning there and looking forward so much to whatever the new job would be that I could hardly disguise from Mother my impatience to set off from home.

I arrived at Yeovilton in the late afternoon and turned the MG into the well-remembered gates of the Officers' quarters. The two tennis courts in the centre were still there and, behind them, the long, low building of the Wardroom and Dining Hall. On either side were the long huts of cabin accommodation, about five huts on each side. It was almost yardarm time at 6 pm when I arrived but strangely at that time the car park in front of the Mess was fairly empty; it had been hallowed ground only for Commanders and Instructors in my previous time when, as a Midshipman, the car park for us was at the back. Parking in front probably was still reserved for much more exalted beings than myself, but I decided that I might as well start by putting myself about a bit and so I parked my lovely little car there anyway.

I was allocated a cabin nearby and, after unpacking and a quick wash, I made my way back to the Wardroom. There were a few more cars and four horses parked outside. Inside, the Wardroom appeared unchanged except that there were only a dozen or so people around the bar, instead of the mass of noisy, chattering young officers as I remembered it. Most of the people there were in civvies and some in riding kit but all were laughing and talking very cheerfully together.

As I walked towards the bar, the chatter stopped and immediately one of the group, a tall dark young man, came forward to greet me and introduced himself as Joe, the Captain's secretary. 'You must be Hank Adlam, the instructor for 700 Squadron,' he said, 'come and meet the others.' One of those in riding kit also greeted me; he was the Commander of the Station, Straw Morrel. What a wonderfully pleasant and laid-back group of people, I thought. Eventually, after a good dinner and more drinks and chat round the bar, I went to my cabin for bed.

The Squadron offices were located to the far left of the Control Tower where, by coincidence, I had attended as a pupil long ago. Here I met my Commanding Officer, Lt Cdr (E) Phil Illingworth RN, whom I liked immediately. He sat me down opposite him and we had a long talk over coffee and cigarettes about the squadron and its purpose and what my job would be. My function, he told me, was to retrain naval engineering officers, who had been given varying degrees of flying training in the past but who subsequently had been taken off flying. This had been in accordance with an Admiralty decision to cease the flying training of air engineer officers. Now, apparently, the Admiralty had reversed that decision. It had been decided, after all, that it was important for such officers to be able to fly the operational type aircraft for which, as engineers, they would be responsible.

My job, therefore, as the one instructor of 700 Squadron would be, firstly to assess the flying ability of each officer pupil, and then to give him sufficient flying instruction to convert on to service aircraft. Phil went on to tell me that there were expected to be about six officers on each course and the first batch was expected to arrive shortly. It was an entirely new course and it would be for me to decide how to run it, how many flying hours the pupils would need and how many aircraft of different types would be required. The other section of Phil's squadron was run by Nick Goodhart for the training of Maintenance Test Pilots. What a wonderful set-up and what a wonderful job I had been given. There were two large hangars for my allocation of aircraft which consisted of a Firefly, a Seafire, a Barracuda and a Harvard. After looking round these and meeting the Petty Officers in charge of maintenance, I asked Phil if I might now go away by myself for the rest of the day and think about the whole requirement. I arranged that, in the meantime, the Firefly and the Seafire be made ready for me to fly on the next day.

We met again at Phil's office first thing the next morning. I had prepared a hand-written paper setting out my carefully considered requirements. It was obvious that I would need at least two Harvards as a start since, at the beginning of the course, I would need to fly all day every day to assess each of my pupils and I could not afford for the one Harvard to be unserviceable. Moreover, a second Harvard would be needed for pupils who, having passed muster on a dual flight with me, might need a number of hours of practice solo flights before I pronounced them ready for conversion to service aircraft. As I understood it, some of these engineering Lieutenants had not flown for some long time and, in any case, some of them had not completed flying training before their training had been cut short by the Admiralty decree.

Secondly, I must have two of each type of service aircraft, not only to ensure the availability of a serviceable aircraft but because I did not want pilots sitting about in the crew room tooth-sucking in the absence of anything to fly. Also, I wanted to give them a good three-month course, aiming at sixty flying hours each on service aircraft. I aimed to bring them to a similar stage of competence as any pilot should be before joining an operational squadron; this would entail giving them a wide range of air experience on each of the service type aircraft. An ambitious programme indeed for a single instructor, which would involve me in many hours of flying. My excitement and enthusiasm at having this my own project to launch was matched by Phil's enthusiasm and without delay he set about procuring the aircraft I needed.

I doubt if there was an officer in the Royal Navy better than Phil Illingworth at charming his way past any procedural hindrances, such as lengthy form filling, that might stand in his way. He was not only good at everything he tackled; a good pilot, very successful motor-bike racer, scratch golfer, father of seven children and international yachtsman, but he was genuinely modest with all of it. He was unhurried in his approach to problems and seemingly never fussed by them. Hence I should not have been surprised when, two days later, he told me that the aircraft I wanted were on their way.

But I wanted more. Since I was to be the only instructor, I had envisaged the need to have the availability of my personal Radio/Telephone contact with any of the pupils in the air at anytime. Therefore I would need my own radio frequency so that I could talk and instruct without interfering with other air activities. I would need a van with an R/T set on my frequency for use, if it should prove necessary, at the end of the runway. Could Phil fix it for me, I asked? Yes, of course he could, and he did so. It had become rather like treating Phil as Father Christmas but finally I asked if one of each type of service aircraft could be put up on jacks, in the hangar with a power supply to the undercarriage and flaps. And this too would be done.

My opposite number on the squadron, Lt (E) Nick Goodhart; was supportive of my efforts and requirements. A test pilot himself, he was running a course for budding Maintenance Test Pilots and had an allocation of service aircraft similar in type to mine. Nick can only be described as an engineering 'whiz-kid' who later was to design the system of lights for deck-landing on Aircraft Carriers. This visual system of lights, which informed the pilot of his position on the approach, replaced the batsman on all future RN and USN Carriers. He was also a verbal whizz-kid; on an occasion when he selected the wheels up before the Barracuda was properly airborne and crashed it, he somehow convinced the Court Martial board that the Navy 'owed' him an aircraft based on the number of hours he had flown previously without breaking anything.

Later that morning, I got airborne in the Firefly and found it to be, as I had expected, a gentlemanly and pleasant thing to fly. Although slow for a so-called fighter-bomber, the Firefly had done well out in the Pacific using mainly rockets for strafing. I tried a few tentative aerobatics but it really was rather cumbersome for that sort of thing but I persevered as I would have to encourage my pupils to do aerobatics in it. I returned and completed a normal landing. Later I intended to carry out flapless landings so that I could advise my pupils in case their flaps ever failed.

The Captain's secretary had made an appointment that afternoon for me to meet the Captain of the Air Station, Captain Kaye Eddon, so I had to postpone my first flight in a Seafire until the following morning. I wondered what the appointment was about because I was not accustomed to meeting Captains except when they occasionally graced the Wardroom with their presence to say 'hello' to the junior officers. However, it turned out that Captain Eddon merely wanted to meet me as the chap second in command, so to speak, of the flying activities on his Air Station. He admitted that he knew nothing about aviation (which was refreshing!) but wanted to emphasize that I should take absolutely no risks in the training of the pupils as he was very anxious that there should be no accidents. We had a pleasant chat in which I acknowledged his anxiety but pointed out that, regardless of the care I fully intended to take, aircraft accidents in service aircraft under service conditions were so often unavoidable.

The following morning was time for me to fly the dreadful Seafire, for as such I had always regarded it, knowing so well the number of young pilots it had killed while being deck-landed. I didn't dread flying the thing; if other people could fly it then I most certainly could; I just didn't look forward with pleasure to the experience. I had been allocated a Seafire XV with a more powerful engine than the earlier models and assumed that it would have considerable engine and propeller torque which might give it a tendency to swerve badly on take-off. In preparation for the flight, I spent some time in the cockpit to learn the haphazard layout typical of a British designed fighter, so different from the orderly arrangement of an American cockpit. I didn't like the Seafire and I was prepared to damn it even before I had started the flight.

Well, I flew the damn thing and found that it was a beautiful machine to fly. An absolute thoroughbred of an aircraft requiring only the most delicate pressures on the controls for it to respond immediately and perfectly. I went through my usual procedure at height with an aircraft new to me and could find nothing to fear from its performance. I followed that up with some aerobatics to which the Seafire responded beautifully enough to flatter my dubious ability as an aerobatic pilot. Now back to the aerodrome for the landing and lets see, I thought, if I can find what it is that has caused so much difficulty and so many deaths in landing it on a flight deck. But on a runway with plenty of space, I found that the Seafire was the simplest of aircraft to land. All well and good, I thought, but I intended to do more landings in the week before my pupils arrived. As well as flapless landings, these would include dummy deck-landings at much slower speed with the long nose of the Seafire well up and with the intention to put the aircraft down firmly on a selected spot of the runway. These dummy deck-landings would be for my own satisfaction and not for the pupils to learn.

During the rest of that first week, I flew several times a day to carry out stalling and spinning in the Harvard, the Seafire and the Firefly but, as for the Barracuda, I decided not to allow the pupils to spin it or to use its dive brakes. I had always reckoned the wings and dive brakes of the Barracuda to be suspect and why push the pupils (or me) into a possibly dangerous situation in an aircraft which was already non-operational? I also carried out practice forced landings in all the aircraft, assuming engine failures at various heights, on the disused airfield at Henstridge near Yeovilton.

I found time to dummy deck-land the Seafire. The first attempt was abortive. Although apparently fully stalled when I thumped it down at very slow speed on the selected spot of the runway, the wretched thing still contrived to balloon upwards and would have put me into the barrier had there been one. After that I learned the trick of timing the closure of the throttle earlier, while holding the stall attitude, so that it came down a second or so later and stayed down on the spot. To complete my taming of the Shrewfire, I wanted very much to deck-land it and asked Phil if he could possibly fix it for me to do a couple of landings on, for example, whatever Carrier was currently in use for the Clockwork Mice. Sadly and I mean it, he was unable to do so.

I completed a lot of flying hours that week in preparation for the arrival of my pupils but it wasn't all work. By no means was it that, because the social life of the Mess was an essential part of the pleasant life at Yeovilton. There were nine good looking and attractive Wren officers and a glamorous RN Nursing Sister as female members of the Wardroom and I suppose about twenty-five other officers. Most of them were busy with the administration relating to the training of the aircraft fitters and riggers on the Air Station and just a few of us to do with aviation on the aerodrome. Nevertheless, they all got on well with each other with plenty of chat around the bar every lunchtime and evening and I was very happy to be a part of it. As there were no other Flying Instructors, I was pleased to consider myself, laughably, as the CFI (Chief Flying Instructor), a very grand title in the days when Yeovilton had been the fighter station of the FAA. This bogus title, plus my much-admired little MG, gave me an easy entrée into friendships with the Wren officers.

The members of my course, which came under the grandiose mouthful of 'The Flying Retraining of Air Engineers', all arrived more or less at the same time on the Sunday evening. There were six of them, all Lieutenants senior to me in terms of time in that rank but, as their instructor, of course, I was the boss and intended to make that quite clear, but in the pleasantest possible way. They appeared to be rather dubious about this, to them, yet another course and one in particular was already inclined to tooth-suck before we had even started. On the other hand, they brightened up on sensing the good atmosphere of the Mess and were impressed by the horses once again tied up outside. For some reason the horses outside the Mess seemed to set the style of the place. As I met each course member for a drink at the bar, I told him that I wanted his Flying Log book to be put in my cabin immediately after dinner and that I would meet him with all the others in their crew room on the airfield promptly at 8.30 am. There was much to be done and I didn't want any delays at the start, I told each one. After dinner, in my cabin, I made notes from their Log books on the flying experience of each one of them.

After an early breakfast, I was down at the squadron offices the next Monday morning ready to talk to the course members due at 8.30 am. They all arrived in good time and I started by outlining my programme of a sixty flying hours minimum for them over the next three months and of the standard I intended them to reach. I explained that during the next two days or more, if necessary, I would take each one of them dual in the Harvard to assess their capability. While I was airborne, there would be plenty for them to do in studying the Pilot's Notes for the Firefly, Seafire and Barracuda and making themselves one hundred per cent familiar with the cockpit layout and controls of each of those aircraft. For that purpose, I said, each type of aircraft had been raised on jacks in the hangar and power laid on so that, in the cockpits, they could familiarise themselves with the operation of the controls. At this point there was a shattering roar as a large motor-bike arrived just outside the offices with Phil on board. He came in and I introduced him as our Commanding Officer to the pupils whom he greeted with his usual enthusiasm.

After dealing out books of the Pilot's Notes on the Firefly to all six of them, we were ready to go and I selected the tooth-sucking chap as my first pupil for dual in the Harvard. He was Ace Bailey and he and I were to become firm friends. He had been grumpy and a bit of a moaner on arrival the evening before but he was probably reflecting the feeling of his group of senior Engineering Lieutenants. Despite their original enthusiasm, they had suffered disappointment and irritation when their flying training had been stopped many months ago and now was to be restarted. With such changes of mind by the Admiralty, their careers as Air Engineers must have appeared to be in a complete muddle. I think that they arrived without much expectation that my flying course would help them.

My intention on that first day was to take all six of them up for forty-five minutes each for my initial assessment which would enable me to set a preliminary programme of further flying. I wanted them to be waiting and ready to get into the front cockpit of the Harvard as soon as I had landed after each flight. On my knee, ready for my notes on each pupil, I had fixed the old wartime navigation pad which had been made for me years previously by Mac, my fitter in 890 squadron. I didn't know how or where Bailey had acquired his nickname 'Ace' but, in consequence of it, I was expecting my first flight to be with a character who would fancy his ability as a pilot to be much higher than the reality. I asked him to take off, climb to about 8,000 ft and then to carry out a number of basic manoeuvres all of which, rather to my surprise, he completed not just competently but very smoothly. It was evident to me that he was a naturally gifted aviator and I would be lucky if the others were anything like as good as this. He landed the Harvard well and taxied to where as arranged the next chap, Campbell, was waiting to get into the front cockpit.

Campbell, I knew from his log book, had not completed his advanced training over a year ago and it showed in his tentative handling of the aircraft. I urged him along for over an hour through the basic manoeuvres in the best manner of CFS instructional patter and, on returning to the aerodrome, he managed to land adequately well. How fortunate that at this early stage of my experience as an instructor, I was to have a pupil of Ian Campbell's rank and forthright character. As we taxied up to the aircraft park, Campbell asked me on the R/T whether we had formally finished the flight. 'Yes,' I said. 'In that case, Hank,' he said, 'I must tell you that if you don't curb your incessant talk in the air, you will certainly drive me mad and it is likely to be the same for the others.'

We didn't speak another word until after I had parked and stopped the engine, but I had been thinking deeply about his words. We stood quietly together by the aircraft before going into the de-briefing room. Then, 'Thank you,' I said, 'I needed that and you were right to tell me. Be assured that I won't ever make the same mistake again. I shall use few words in future and they will be my own words and with my own manner of demonstration. Please keep this between us; I have much to do for this course and it is essential that you all have confidence in me.' In making that promise, I did not intend to disregard all I had learned from CFS but to adapt it to my own style of instruction. Dear Ian Campbell, who became a good friend, had done me a service.

By missing my lunchtime pink gins and having a bowl of soup instead, I was able to adhere to my programme of completing an initial dual flight with each of the six pupils. Mulling over my notes that evening, I could see that I had one unusually good aviator (Ace), two other good ones and three not so good. But, at the end of the second week, they were all flying the Firefly and I was girding some of them up to fly the Seafire. By the end of the month, all the pupils were flying all three types of aircraft and carrying out the various exercises I set for them such as practice landings and take-offs, aerobatics (but not the Barracuda), short cross-country flying, dummy forced landings, some formation flying with me to start with and then together. They were to do some of these exercises at around 25,000 ft, to become accustomed to the use of oxygen and to feel how differently the aircraft flew at height. I did though make a point of not authorising flights above 20,000 ft unless there were two aircraft together for fear of oxygen failure for any one of them alone. Each week, I used the Harvards for instrument flying with the pupils 'blind' under the hood.

That was the pattern of the beginning of each of the five courses over the following eighteen months. During that period, I trained and converted thirty pupils to service aircraft and each of them completed on average seventy flying hours on the Course. There were no accidents except that Billie Braunton carried out an entirely successful forced landing in a field when the engine of his Seafire failed at about 10,000 ft. There were some 'hairy' landings and a few near accidents but the van at the end of the runway proved its worth and enabled me to give instruction through the R/T installed in it to any pupil having difficulty.

I sent pupils on numerous cross-country flights, sometimes on a Friday for a weekend if there was a Naval Air Station near their home. At Christmas time I sent Ace Bailey and Jag Mares off in the Firefly and the Barracuda to Eglinton Air Station in Northern Ireland where, armed with a list from Laurie the Wardroom Catering Officer, they filled the aircraft up with hams, cheeses, beef and turkeys all of which were plentiful in the local shops there, despite stringent rationing in the rest of the UK. Well why not? All my pupils needed to do such long flights as part of their training and they might as well usefully enjoy them. No excuse for me though when I used a Seafire to visit friends for a boozy evening at Culham and at Culdrose Naval Air Stations.

Phil Illingworth presided benignly over all these flying activities and, in view of the intensity of them, managed to procure another Seafire and Firefly for me. A huge bonus and unexpected pleasure during the hot summer of 1947 was the arrival of an old Seagull amphibious seaplane, normally used as a sea rescue aircraft, allocated to Yeovilton apparently merely because it was surplus to requirements elsewhere. But it was agreed in principle that it could be used as part of my course for conversion of pupils to service aircraft. Anyway that was my excuse for asking the pilot, Ken Kilroy, to give me some instruction on landing and taking off on water so that, in turn, I would be able to instruct my pupils, which I had no intention whatsoever of doing. I just wanted the opportunity to fly a Seaplane. And what fun it was. Ken and I would take three or four of the Wren officers on bathing parties, landing in the sea a mile or two off the south coast near Weymouth.

Also during that hot summer, with Phil's agreement, I arranged that the squadron would start flying at 8 am and finish at 12.30 pm enabling all pilots to proceed in the afternoon to a nearby open-air swimming pool for what I described as Dinghy Drill. It meant starting work very early for the maintenance crews but they too were happy to have the afternoon off.

The social life of the Officers' Mess was unusually pleasant. Even those who were married would remain for a drink or two and a chat before going home to their rented accommodation. There was always the nucleus of the unmarried Wrens as the basis of a party and, after dinner, there would often be an exodus of cars to two or three of the many country pubs which surrounded the Air Station. On Saturday and Sunday mornings many of the officers' wives would have drinks and lunch in the Wardroom and on many of these occasions Captain Eddon and his wife would join us.

It was a most unusual naval place and, if it might appear from reading this that it was more like a combined holiday hotel and flying club than a workplace, then I would not argue with that. But it was hard work too; I flew a very considerable number of hours each week and the briefing and de-briefing of my pupils took much of my time; not to mention the constant worry of whether I had trained them sufficiently well to avoid accidents and crashes. If the previous eighteen months since the end of the war had been somewhat tedious and boring, well, the return to Yeovilton was a definite high to make up for it. And it was to become even more of a high for me.

On an early evening in May of that year 1947, I was in the Wardroom. I was standing as usual at the bar where we were all talking animatedly, when I happened to look across the room towards the central fireplace where Dorothy, the Captain's second secretary, was talking to a Wren officer whom I hadn't seen before. She really was a most beautiful girl; slim with long honey-blond hair, but most striking to me was her face, so beautiful in structure and colour with a calm serenity about it and yet a happy face with laughing eyes. As I looked towards her, she caught my eyes on her and smiled at me; it was just a friendly smile. I have never forgotten it. Without showing any particular interest, I asked the others who she was and learned that she was Heather Leaman, just back from a course in Portsmouth and subsequent leave. She was second in command of the gunnery section of the Air Station.

I saw little more of Heather during the early part of that hot summer. In spite of that smile she was not a bit forthcoming with me and I, for my part, was busy with my own newly formed flying training course. And anyway, with the slightly glamour job as the only Flying Instructor plus the advantage of my sporty little MG car, I had no shortage of girl friends amongst all the other Wren officers. I understood that Heather too was busy as the Armament Store's Officer of the Air Station in charge of thirty men and two Warrant officers under her command. She was popular and had many friends around her and clearly did not need any attentions from me.

And yet, there must have been a strong mutual attraction between Heather and me, because gradually and almost inevitably it seemed, we were drawn to each other and began to go out together and alone without joining the customary parties. There was nothing spectacular about the development of the relationship, but by the autumn we were enjoying quiet evenings by ourselves at local pubs and sometimes taking with us a picnic supper. We were in no rush; confident in the love which we now shared, we began to spend happy weekends at hotels in Dorset, Somerset and even at Browns in London. We were both happy and busy with our respective jobs. Heather, as a Wren officer, had suffered some difficulty on her arrival at Yeovilton as the men resented having a female officer over them for the first time. But, by the time I arrived there, she had earned their affection and respect by her fairness and methodical rearrangement of their workload.

Inevitably, although naively we hadn't given the possibility any thought at all, the time came in the early May of 1948 when Heather told me she was pregnant. No panic; when she told me this as we walked across the playing fields to watch the cricket at the nets, I held her hand hard and said that it was the best of news in every way because now we would have to get married very soon indeed. 'So we shall then,' she said, pretending like me to be terribly casual about it all, but I could see that she was crying quietly as she said it. In retrospect, it seems to have been a very odd way to propose marriage to the beautiful young woman I loved and wanted so much. It was obvious immediately that this was what we had both wanted but, immature and insensitive man that I was, until then I just hadn't thought to voice the idea of marriage. But first there was the business of telling her parents, whom I had not yet met and of telling my Mother and Maddie, whom she had not met either. There was the need for Heather to inform her Commanding Officer of her resignation from the Wrens and for me to tell Captain Eddon of our proposed marriage. Although very cordial and congratulatory, Eddon thought it necessary under the circumstances to arrange for me to be transferred to Culdrose Air Station after the wedding. Meantime, we formally announced our engagement.

On 17 July 1948 we were married in the old church of Yeovilton village.

The wedding and the reception afterwards in the Wardroom were attended by masses of our friends, many of whom flew in from other Air Stations, and the occasion was an unforgettably happy one. As indeed it needed to be, because Heather and I unknowingly were about to embark upon a lifestyle full of ups and downs, like a yo-yo, for the next fifty-three years.

END

Appendix

SERVICE: DECEMBER 1940 – FEBRUARY 1949
Ships, squadrons and aircraft types served in during the period

Ships	Squadrons	Aircraft/function
While under training during 1941:		Magister
		Miles Master
		Hawker Hurricane
		Fairey Fulmar
		Blackburn Shark
USS *Charger*	890 Squadron	Wildcat
HMS *Battler*	890 Squadron	Wildcat
HMS *Illustrious*	890 Squadron	Hurricane
		Wildcat
HMS *Unicorn*	890 Squadron	Wildcat
HMS *Atheling*	890 Squadron	Wildcat
HMS *Indomitable*	1839 Squadron	Hellcat
HMS *Begum*		Batsman
HMS *Colossus*		Batsman and
		Squadron Pilot, Corsair
HMS *Colossus*	1846 Squadron	Corsair

(A total of 128 deck-landings – no prangs!)

Ships	Squadrons	Aircraft/function
Post-war, as a Flying Instructor:	700 Squadron	Harvard
		Oxford
		Seafire
		Seafury
		Firefly
		Barracuda
Post-war, as civilian instructor and commercial pilot:		Tiger Moth
		Auster
		Piper Cub
		Baron
		Musketeer
		Queenair
		Bonanza

Index